Animals, Ethics and Trade

~ are to be returned on or befo

Animals, Ethics and Trade
The Challenge of Animal Sentience

Edited by
Jacky Turner and Joyce D'Silva

London • Sterling, VA

First published by Earthscan in the UK and USA in 2006

ISBN-10: 1-84407-255-X   paperback
          1-84407-254-1   hardback
ISBN-13: 978-1-84407-255-2 paperback
          978-1-84407-254-5 hardback

Typesetting by Fish Books, Enfield, Middx.
Printed and bound in the UK by TJ International Ltd, Padstow, Cornwall
Cover design by Nick Shah

For a full list of publications please contact:

Earthscan
8–12 Camden High Street
London, NW1 0JH, UK
Tel: +44 (0)20 7387 8558
Fax: +44 (0)20 7387 8998
Email: earthinfo@earthscan.co.uk
Web: **www.earthscan.co.uk**

22883 Quicksilver Drive, Sterling, VA 20166-2012, USA

Earthscan is an imprint of James and James (Science Publishers) Ltd and publishes in association
with the International Institute for Environment and Development

A catalogue record for this book is available from the British Library

Library of Congress Cataloging-in-Publication Data has been applied for

The paper used for the text pages of this book is FSC certified.
FSC (The Forest Stewardship Council) is an international network
to promote responsible management of the world's forests.

FSC
Mixed Sources
Product group from well-managed
forests and other controlled sources

Cert no. SGS-COC-2482
www.fsc.org
© 1996 Forest Stewardship Council

Printed on totally chlorine-free paper

Contents

List of Contributors

Michael C. Appleby carried out research at the Poultry Research Centre and the University of Edinburgh for 20 years on behaviour, husbandry and welfare of farm animals. His publications include five books as author, co-author or editor, most recently *Poultry Behaviour and Welfare* (2004). From 2001 to 2005 he was head of the Farm Animals and Sustainable Agriculture section of The Humane Society of the United States in Washington, DC. He is now Trade Policy Manager with The World Society for the Protection of Animals, Eurogroup for Animal Welfare and UK's RSPCA. Contact: Dr Michael C. Appleby, World Society for the Protection of Animals, 89 Albert Embankment, London SE1 7TP, UK. Email: michaelappleby@wspa.org.uk.

Mahfouz Azzam is Professor and Head of the Department of Islamic Philosophy, Faculty of Dar Al'Ulum, Al-Minya University, Egypt, where he also heads the education development unit for the faculty. In addition to his university work, he has been an approved expert at the Arab world affairs centre of documentation and information of the Arab League since 1985, and is a member of the Supreme Council for Islamic Affairs and of the Egyptian Society of Philosophy. He is also active as a broadcaster on Egyptian and Arabic radio and television, and is involved in scientific programme and syllabus development in the Arab world. Professor Azzam can be contacted at: mahfouzazzam@hotmail.com.

A. C. David Bayvel is a veterinary graduate of the Universities of Glasgow and Edinburgh, a member of the Australian College of Veterinary Scientists and also holds a Masters Degree in Public Policy. His career has involved periods in private veterinary practice, the pharmaceutical industry and Government service. He has worked in the UK, Zambia, South Africa and Australia, and moved to New Zealand in 1982. He represents the Ministry of Agriculture and Forestry (MAF) on the New Zealand National Animal Ethics Advisory Committee (NAEAC), the National Animal Welfare Advisory Committee (NAWAC) and the Trans-Tasman Animal Welfare Committee (AWC). In New Zealand, he works closely with all groups with an interest in animal welfare policy and is currently actively involved with the Office International des Épizooties (OIÉ) in addressing animal welfare issues at an international level. David Bayvel can be contacted at: david.bayvel@maf.govt.nz.

Marc Bekoff is Professor of Biology at the University of Colorado, Boulder, and co-founder with Dr Jane Goodall of Ethologists for the Ethical Treatment of Animals: Citizens for Responsible Animal Behavior Studies. He is a prolific writer with more than 200 articles as well as two encyclopedias to his credit. The author or editor of numerous books, including the *Encyclopedia of Animal Rights and Animal Welfare*; *The Cognitive Animal* (co-edited with C. Allen and G. M. Burghardt); *The Ten Trusts: What We Must Do to Care for the Animals We Love* (co-written with Jane Goodall); and *The Encyclopedia of Animal Behavior*, his most recent books include *The Smile of a Dolphin*, *Minding Animals* and *Animal Passions and Beastly Virtues: Reflections on Redecorating Nature*. In 2005 he was presented with the Bank One Faculty Community Service Award for the work he has done with children, senior citizens and prisoners. His homepage is http://literati.net/Bekoff.

Stine B. Christiansen is a DVM from The Royal Veterinary and Agricultural University (KVL) in Copenhagen, Denmark (1993), and holds an MSc in applied animal behaviour and animal welfare from the University of Edinburgh, Scotland (1995). Currently she is doing a PhD at KVL on quality of life. Since 1998 she has been involved in research projects concerning animal ethics and has served as the scientific secretary of the Danish Animal Ethics Council.

Ros Clubb is an Oxford University-educated biologist. While studying for a PhD she investigated why some carnivore species appear to be particularly prone to the development of abnormal behaviour in captivity; research that encompassed mink reared on fur farms. Dr Clubb went on to co-author a report that reviewed the welfare of elephants held in European zoos. She is now a Programme Officer with the animal welfare and conservation charity Care for the Wild International (CFTWI). CFTWI funds practical projects around the world that make areas safe from poachers, rehabilitate sick or injured animals and provide sanctuary for those who cannot return to the wild. It also acts as a global voice for wildlife through research, education and advocacy. She can be contacted at Care for the Wild International, The Granary, Tickfold Farm, Kingsfold, West Sussex RH12 3SE, UK. Email: info@careforthewild.com.

Joyce D'Silva was Chief Executive of Compassion in World Farming Trust (CIWF Trust) between 1991 and 2005 and is currently Ambassador for the CIWF Trust, working to raise awareness of farm animal welfare globally. She has led campaigns and educational initiatives on major welfare issues such as the veal crate, the battery cage, the sow stall (gestation crate) and farm animal biotechnology. She was a leading advocate of the recognition of animal sentience in the EU, achieved in 1997. The author of numerous publications on farm animal welfare, she is the consulting editor of *Farm Animal Voice* and her recent publications include: *BST – A Distressing Product: An Analysis of the Health* *and Welfare Problems of Dairy Cows Injected with BST* (CIWF, 1998) and *The Meat Business: Devouring a Hungry Planet*, editors Geoff Tansey and Joyce D'Silva (Earthscan, 1999). Joyce D'Silva can be contacted at: CIWF Trust, 5a Charles Street, Petersfield, Hampshire GU32 3EH, UK. www.ciwf.org.uk. Email: joyce@ciwf.co.uk.

Björn Forkman is a lecturer and head of the group of Animal Behaviour and Welfare at The Royal Veterinary and Agricultural University in Copenhagen, Denmark. He took his PhD in ethology at Stockholm University in 1993 and has since worked at the Swedish Agricultural University, at Roslin Institute in Scotland and at Stockholm University. Most of his recent research has been on motivation and cognition in poultry, but he has also published articles on gerbils, pigs and dogs.

Jane Goodall, PhD, DBE, has studied the lives and behaviour of chimpanzees for 40 years, and from 1967 to 2003 she was Scientific Director of the Gombe Stream Research Centre, Tanzania. She is the Director of the Jane Goodall Institute (JGI) and initiated the Roots & Shoots environmental education programme that now operates worldwide. She is the author of over 70 scientific papers on chimpanzee behaviour and more than 20 books, including several for children, and she has received numerous honorary degrees and awards for her work in science, wildlife conservation and animal welfare. Her best known books include *In the Shadow of Man* (1971), which has been published in 48 languages; *The Chimpanzees of Gombe: Patterns of Behavior* (Harvard University Press, 1986); and *Through a Window: 30 years Observing the Gombe Chimpanzees* (1990), published by Weidenfeld and Nicolson in London and by Houghton Mifflin in Boston, which has been translated into more than 15 languages. Her autobiography, *Beyond Innocence: An Autobiography in Letters, the Later Years* (edited by Dale Peterson) was published in 2001 by Houghton Mifflin, New York. In 2002, Dr Goodall was appointed a United Nations Messenger of Peace. Further details of the work of the JGI and the Roots & Shoots programme are available at www.janegoodall.org.

Patrick Holden has been Director of the Soil Association since 1995 and has been an organic farmer since 1973. He was founder and first Chair of British Organic Farmers and served on the board of the UK Register of Organic Food Standards between 1987 and 1999. He is also a regular broadcaster, speaker and writer on organic food and farming issues, as well as engaging with government on food and farming policy. Further information can be found at www.soilassociation.org.

Keith Kenny is Senior Director, Quality Assurance, McDonald's Europe. He has been extensively involved in the development and implementation of McDonald's animal welfare programme through his prior role as Head of Supply Chain and Quality Assurance and his membership of the McDonald's European Animal Welfare Team. He pioneered the development of the pan-European McDonald's Agricultural Assurance Programme and the company's involvement in the research and development of commercially viable animal welfare farming systems. He holds a BSc (Hons) in Food Science from King's College London.

James K. Kirkwood is Chief Executive and Scientific Director of the Universities Federation for Animal Welfare (UFAW) and of the Humane Slaughter Association (HSA), Visiting Professor at the Royal Veterinary College, and Editor of *Animal Welfare*. For 12 years, prior to taking up his present post in 1996, he was Head of the Veterinary Science Group at the Institute of Zoology and the Senior Veterinary Officer at the Zoological Society of London. He is Chairman of the UK Government's Zoos Forum and Deputy Chairman of the Companion Animal Welfare Council. He can be contacted at: UFAW and HSA, The Old School, Brewhouse Hill, Wheathampstead, Herts AL4 8AN, UK. Email: kirkwood@ufaw.org.uk and kirkwood@hsa.org.uk. Websites: www.ufaw.org.uk and www.hsa.org.uk.

Tim Lang has been Professor of Food Policy at City University since November 2002 and was previously Director of the Centre for Food Policy at Thames Valley University. He has worked widely in the field of food and public health as an academic, in the voluntary sector and as a consultant to local, national and international bodies ranging from Parliamentary Committees in London and Brussels to the World Health Organization. He has researched widely in food policy, specializing in public and environmental health, trade and inequality. He is author and co-author of over 120 publications, including eight books and numerous reports for international bodies and articles for academic journals. He has been an adviser to statutory public groups and bodies, and to international agencies. He is on the Editorial Board of the *Journal of Epidemiology and Community Health*, *Global Change and Human Health*, *Food Technology Journal* and the *Food Magazine*. His latest books are *The Atlas of Food* (Earthscan, 2003), co-authored with Erik Millstone, and *Food Wars: The Global Health Battle for Minds, Mouths and Markets* (Earthscan, 2004). Tim Lang's homepage is: www.city.ac.uk/ihs/hmfp/foodpolicy/who/ lang_t.htm.

Peter J. Li is Assistant Professor of Political Science at the University of Houston-Downtown, US. His research interests include China's environmental politics under conditions of economic reform; culture and animal treatment; wildlife protection; and animal welfare legislation. He maintains an active research agenda on China's animal-related subjects and conducts frequent field studies on the Chinese mainland. He holds a PhD in international politics from Northern Arizona University, Flagstaff, Arizona, US. Peter Li can be contacted at: lipj@uhd.edu.

Andrew Linzey is a member of the Faculty of Theology in the University of Oxford and holds the world's first post in Ethics, Theology and Animal Welfare – the Bede Jarrett Senior Research Fellowship at Blackfriars Hall, Oxford. He is also Honorary Professor in Theology at the University of Birmingham and Special Professor at Saint Xavier University, Chicago. He has written or edited 20 books, including pioneering works on animals: *Animal Theology* (SCM Press, 1994), *After Noah* (Continuum, 1997), *Animal Gospel* (Westminster John Knox, 1998), *Animals on the Agenda* (SCM Press, 1999), *Animal Rites* (SCM Press, 1999) and *Animal Rights: A Historical Anthology* (Columbia University Press, 2005). Andrew Linzey can be contacted at: andrewlinzey@aol.com.

Paul Littlefair graduated in modern Chinese studies from Leeds University (1984) and spent three years studying in Shanghai and Nanjing. He worked on the British Council's East Asia desk in London before spending four years as a curriculum developer for a business training organization in Osaka, Japan. In 1998 he joined the international department of the Royal Society for the Prevention of Cruelty to Animals (RSPCA). He is currently senior programme manager overseeing strategies for over 20 countries in Europe and Asia where RSPCA International is active. He has special responsibility for promoting welfare in mainland China, Taiwan and Korea. Paul Littlefair can be contacted at: RSPCA International, Wilberforce Way, Southwater, Horsham, West Sussex RH13 9RS, UK. Email: plittlefair@rspca.org.uk.

Ben Mepham is Professor and Director of the Centre for Applied Bioethics in the School of Biosciences at Nottingham University. A graduate in physiology, he completed a PhD in biochemistry at the Institute of Animal Physiology, Cambridge, before moving to Nottingham in 1968. He is a member of the Food Ethics Council (of which he was the first Executive Director from 1998–2003), the European Society for Agricultural and Food Ethics, and from 2000 was a founder member of the UK Government's Biotechnology Commission (AEBC). His most recent book, *Bioethics: An Introduction for the Biosciences*, is published by Oxford University Press (2005).

Kate Rawles was a lecturer in environmental philosophy at Lancaster University for nine years before becoming a freelance in 2000. Dr Rawles received a three-year NESTA fellowship in 2002 to develop Outdoor Environmental Philosophy – short courses that combine critical thinking about environmental issues with the experience and emotional power of wild places, in order to inspire a commitment to more sustainable ways of living and working. She now works half of the time as a freelance outdoor philosopher and consultant, and half of the time as a senior lecturer in Outdoor Studies at St Martin's College, Ambleside. Kate Rawles can be contacted at: kate@outdoorphilosophy.co.uk.

Tom Regan is Emeritus Professor of Philosophy, North Carolina State University. During his more than 30 years on the faculty, he received numerous awards for excellence in teaching; published more than 20 books; won major awards for film direction; and received the William Quarles Holliday Medal, the highest honour North Carolina State University can bestow on one of its faculty. There is further information about Tom Regan at www.tomregan-animalrights.com.

Michael J. Reiss is Professor of Science Education at the Institute of Education, University of London, and Head of its School of Mathematics, Science and Technology. He is Chief Executive of Science Learning Centre London, Honorary Visiting Professor at the University of York, Docent at the University of Helsinki, Director of the Salters–Nuffield Advanced Biology Project, a member of the Farm Animal Welfare Council and Editor of the journal *Sex Education*. His research and consultancy interests are in science education, bioethics and sex education. For further information see www.reiss.tc.

Oliver Ryan is Principal Engineer, International Finance Corporation (IFC, the private sector arm of the World Bank), based in Washington, DC. He is a New Zealander with extensive experience in livestock production in Asia and has global responsibility for the technical and commercial appraisal, and supervision, of IFC's livestock and aquaculture projects worldwide. Further information can be obtained at www.ifc.org. Oliver Ryan can be contacted at: F8K–164 Agribusiness Department, International Finance Corporation, World Bank Group, 2121 Pennsylvania Avenue, Washington, DC 22043, US. Email: oryan@ifc.org.

Peter Sandøe originally trained as a philosopher at the University of Copenhagen and at Oxford University. Currently he is Professor of Bioethics at The Royal Veterinary and Agricultural University in Copenhagen and he is Director of the Centre for Bioethics and Risk Assessment, an interdisciplinary and inter-institutional research centre founded January 2000. Since 1992 he has served as Chairman of the Danish Ethical Council for Animals, an advisory board set up by the Danish Minister of Justice, and since 2000 he has served as President of the European Society for Agricultural and Food Ethics. Peter Sandøe can be contacted at: Royal Veterinary and Agricultural University, Rolighedshedsvej 25, DK-1958 Frederiksberg C, Denmark. www.bioethics. kvl.dk.

Vandana Shiva is a physicist, ecologist, campaigner and author of many books on the impact of globalized commercial agriculture on people and the environment. In India Dr Shiva has established Navdanya, a movement for biodiversity conservation and farmers' rights. She directs the Research Foundation for Science, Technology and Ecology, based in New Delhi. Her recent books include *Biopiracy: The Plunder of Nature and Knowledge* (South End Press, 1997);

Tomorrow's Biodiversity (with Yorik Blumenfeld, Thames and Hudson, 2000); *Stolen Harvest: The Hijacking of the Global Food Supply* (Zed Books, 2001 and published by South End Press in the US); and *Water Wars: Pollution, Profits and Privatization* (Pluto Press, 2002). Vandana Shiva can be contacted at: vshiva@vsnl.com.

Jacky Turner (joint editor) has a PhD from London University, is Former Director of Education and Research for CIWF Trust and now works as a freelance writer and consultant on animal welfare issues. She authored CIWF Trust's report 'Stop, look, listen – Recognising the sentience of farm animals' (2003, revised 2006, available at www.ciwf.org.uk). Jacky Turner can be contacted through CIWF Trust, email ciwftrust@ciwf.co.uk.

John Webster is Emeritus Professor of Animal Husbandry at the University of Bristol. He has served on the UK's Farm Animal Welfare Council (FAWC), developed the concept of the Five Freedoms, and is the founding father of the Bristol University Animal Behaviour and Welfare Science group that has gathered evidence and pioneered the arguments necessary to achieve improved welfare standards for veal calves, broiler chickens, laying hens and dairy cows. His recent work includes methods of animal welfare assessment in relation to farm assurance schemes. His latest book is *Animal Welfare: Limping Towards Eden* (Blackwell Publishing, 2005), which followed his book *Animal Welfare: A Cool Eye Towards Eden* (Blackwell Science, 1994). John Webster can be contacted at: john.webster@bristol.ac.uk.

Song Wei is an Attorney and is also Professor and Director of the Law Institute at the University of Science and Technology of China. Professor Song can be contacted by email at songwei@ustc.edu.cn. Tel: +86 551 3600246, Fax: +86 551 3606266.

David B. Wilkins qualified as a veterinarian at Cambridge University Veterinary School in 1963. After a spell in large animal practice, he went to Canada and worked on notifiable diseases – including tuberculosis, brucellosis and rabies – for the Canadian Government. A second spell in general practice in the UK followed and then in 1977 he joined the RSPCA as a veterinary adviser. In 1983 he became the RSPCA's Chief Veterinary Officer and spent part of his time assisting the newly formed Eurogroup for Animal Welfare, a pan-EU political lobbying organization based in Brussels, providing veterinary advice and information. He became Director of Eurogroup in 1992 and since 2003 he has been the Chief Veterinary Adviser to the World Society for the Protection of Animals (WSPA). He also is a member of the OIÉ's Working Group on Animal Welfare and coordinates the work of the International Coalition for Farm Animal Welfare (ICFAW). David Wilkins can be contacted at: wilkinsvet@lycos.co.uk.

Steven M. Wise is President of the Center for the Expansion of Fundamental Rights, Inc, in Coral Springs, Florida. He has taught Animal Rights Law at the Harvard, Vermont, and John Marshall Law Schools, and in the Masters Programme in Animals and Public Policy at the Tufts University School of Veterinary Medicine. He is the author of *Rattling the Cage – Toward Legal Rights for Animals* (Perseus Publishing, 2000), also published by Profile Books in the UK; *Drawing the Line – Science and the Case for Animal Rights* (Perseus Publishing, 2002), also published as *Unlocking the Cage* (Basic Books, 2002) in the UK; and *Though the Heavens May Fall* (De Capo Press, 2005). Steven Wise can be contacted at: WiseBoston@aol.com.

About This Book

In March 2005 a conference entitled *From Darwin to Dawkins: The Science and Implications of Animal Sentience* took place at the Queen Elizabeth II Conference Centre in London; it was attended by 600 people from 50 countries. The conference was organized by Compassion in World Farming (CIWF) Trust and brought together scientists, veterinarians, ethicists, students and representatives of governmental and inter-governmental organizations and of industry and of non-governmental organizations (NGOs) to discuss the growing scientific and ethical understanding of animals and how this understanding impacts on human activities that use animals and on how we treat them. This book is a collection of 24 of the invited contributions to the conference and focuses on the ethical and policy issues that arise from the study of animal sentience. Fourteen additional invited contributions to the conference are to be published in *Applied Animal Behaviour Science* (2006), edited by John Webster, and these focus mainly on the scientific study of the sentience of farmed, wild and captive animals and its practical applications. Details of all the invited contributions to the conference, the poster contributions and a free DVD/video (VHS or NTSC) of the conference are given in the Annex at the end of this book (p276).

About Compassion in World Farming (CIWF) Trust

CIWF Trust is an educational charity working internationally to promote global understanding of the sentience of animals and to advance the welfare of farm animals.

New and exciting research – much of it referred to in this book – appears to show that conscious decision-making, many aspects of cognition and a wide range of emotions are no longer regarded solely as the province of humanity, but can be seen – and studied – in the animal world. CIWF Trust brings this evolving story to the public via its dedicated website www.animalsentience.com.

CIWF Trust believes that current intensive factory farming practices impose suffering on animals by confining them, crowding them, mutilating their bodies and transporting them undue distances to slaughter. Normal social interactions between the animals are completely frustrated, causing mental distress.

Farm animals are not the only ones to suffer the adverse effects of intensive animal farming. The environment is polluted, precious water and grain resources are inefficiently utilized, small farmers are forced off the land and consumers are encouraged to eat cheap animal products, thus contributing to the global obesity epidemic and high rates of heart disease.

CIWF Trust works towards a more compassionate and sustainable planet by the adoption of agricultural systems that have a beneficial impact on human health, animal welfare and the environment.

CIWF Trust's wide range of educational and information resources can be accessed via its website www.ciwf.org.

Compassion in World Farming Trust
Charles House
5a Charles Street
Petersfield
Hampshire GU32 3EH
UK
Tel: +44-(0)1730 268 070
Email: ciwftrust@ciwf.co.uk

List of Acronyms and Abbreviations

AAF	Animals Asia Foundation
AATA	Animal Transport Association
AI	avian influenza
ASL	American Sign Language
AWI	Animal Welfare Institute
AZA	American Zoo and Aquarium Association
BHAEEC	Beijing Human and Animal Environmental Education Centre
BSE	bovine spongiform encephalopathy
BST	bovine somatotropin
CAG	IFC Agribusiness Department
CASS	China's Academy of Social Sciences
CCTV	China Central Television
CITES	Convention on International Trade in Endangered Species of Wild Fauna and Flora
CIWF Trust	Compassion in World Farming Trust
COMEST	World Commission on the Ethics of Scientific Knowledge and Technology
CRZN	Coastal Regulation Zone Notification
CSF	classical swine fever
CSR	corporate social responsibility
CWCA	China Wildlife Conservation Association
DNA	deoxyribonucleic acid
EC	European Commission
EEC	European Economic Community
EFSA	European Food Safety Authority
EU	European Union
FAI	Food Animal Initiative
FAO	Food and Agriculture Organization of the United Nations
FMD	foot and mouth disease
FMI	Food Marketing Institute
GATT	General Agreement on Tariffs and Trade
GM	genetically modified
HACCP	hazard analysis critical control point
IATA	International Air Transport Association

IAWC	International Animal Welfare Consultants (Ltd)
IBRD	International Bank for Reconstruction and Development
ICFAW	International Coalition for Farm Animal Welfare
ICICI	Industrial Credit and Investment Corporation of India
ICSU	International Council for Science
IDBI	Industrial Development Bank of India
IFAW	International Fund for Animal Welfare
IFC	International Finance Corporation
IFTF	International Fur Trade Federation
IMF	International Monetary Fund
JGI	The Jane Goodall Institute
MAAP	McDonald's Agricultural Assurance Programme
MEP	Member of the European Parliament
MIGA	Multilateral Investment Guarantee Agency
MPEDA	Marine Products Export Development Authority
MSR	mirror self-recognition (test)
NABARD	National Bank for Agriculture and Rural Development
NCCR	National Council of Chain Restaurants
NCD	non-communicable disease
NEERI	National Environmental Engineering Research Institute (of India)
NGO	non-governmental organization
OIÉ	Office International des Épizooties
PBUH	Peace Be Upon Him
rBST	recombinant bovine somatotropin
RSPCA	Royal Society for the Prevention of Cruelty to Animals
SAP	Structural Adjustment Programme
SARS	severe acute respiratory syndrome
SAW	sallalahu aleyhi wasallam, Arabic for 'Peace Be Upon Him'
SCAHAW	Scientific Committee on Animal Health and Animal Welfare
SCICI	Shipping Credit and Investment Corporation of India
SPS	sanitary and phytosanitary measures
TBT	technical barriers to trade
TNC	transnational corporation
UNDP	United Nations Development Programme
UNESCO	United Nations Educational, Scientific and Cultural Organization
USDA	United States Department of Agriculture
WBG	World Bank Group
WHO	World Health Organization
WSPA	World Society for the Protection of Animals
WTO	World Trade Organization
WVA	World Veterinary Association

Introduction

Joyce D'Silva

Compassion in World Farming (CIWF) Trust, UK

Philosophers and scientists have long argued as to whether animals are sentient beings. Can animals really feel pain – like us? Can they suffer – like us? Can they experience emotions similar to our own? Or are they just resources whose lives have meaning only in so far as they are useful to our own species? Is their apparent intelligence really only a simple response to an external stimulus?

Over the last 30 years, scientific opinion has moved sharply to agree that animals are indeed sentient beings. In truth, the animal scientists of today have begun to echo what Charles Darwin declared back in 1871: 'We have seen that the senses and intuitions, the various emotions and faculties, such as love, memory, attention and curiosity, imitation, reason etc, of which man boasts, may be found in an incipient, or even sometimes a well-developed condition, in the lower animals.'

If we agree that animals are sentient, then what does that mean for our own behaviour? This book brings together cutting edge international thinkers from the fields of philosophy, science, law and global policy who wrestle with this question. All agree that animal suffering should be minimized, but they disagree as to how far we should curtail our own human activities to enable animals to enjoy lives of well-being. If animals are sentient, then is it ethically permissible to cage them in zoos, laboratories and factory farms; to hunt them; to wear their fur; to trade them globally – even to eat them?

These are challenging questions and there is no doubt that this issue will be one of the key questions to be addressed by the global intellectual community and by international policy-makers and national governments during the 21st century.

The debate about animal sentience is not just a western phenomenon. As Peter Li points out in his chapter, the debate is already alive in China, where some philosophers are calling for a discussion on animal rights, whilst other protagonists are still claiming that, as animals can't feel pain and can't suffer, it does not *matter* what we do to them.

In the opposite corner to the traditionalists we find philosophers like Tom Regan, arguing cogently that, as an animal's life is as important to itself as my life is to me, then we are both 'subjects-of-a-life' and have an equal right to be treated with respect – or, as Steve Wise puts it, we may both have rights to bodily liberty and bodily integrity, which should be recognized in law.

Also in the opposite corner to the traditionalists – but nearer to the middle – we have the practical strategists like John Webster, someone who has played a key role in developing concepts of animal welfare, who proposes that we have a social contract with animals – yes, they work and die for us, but in return we recognize their capacity to suffer and do our best to keep them 'fit and happy' throughout their lives.

Pivotal to the debate are the global institutions and businesses. One might ask, why include them in this book? Part of their history and even their *raison d'être* is to treat animals purely as resources. The truth is that their influence on the lives of animals is so great that to omit them would be to tell a thinner tale.

Investment by global agencies such as the World Bank and the International Finance Corporation can deeply affect not just the livelihoods of farmers and the economies of nations, but the lives of the millions of animals farmed as a result of such investments, and possibly the wildlife living near the funded projects, who may be affected by forest clearance or polluting effluent.

The power of an organization like McDonald's to influence outcomes for animals is enormous. Their decision to use only free range eggs in the UK and some other European countries has directly influenced the supply chain. More hens have escaped life in a battery cage as a result. Their work in the US to improve the welfare of animals at slaughter has led to 'great improvements' according to Dr Temple Grandin (2006), one of the leading world experts in the field. Of course it's not enough to satisfy campaigners – why aren't *all* McDonald's hens free range, for example? Even Keith Kenny, speaking for McDonald's, admits 'there is still a lot more to be done'.

But agri-business and the food industry are realizing that the issue of animal welfare is here to stay and is increasing in intensity and global scope. In this book you can read of the apparently genuine efforts by David Bayvel (World Animal Health Organization), Oliver Ryan (International Finance Corporation) and Keith Kenny (McDonald's) to reconcile agri-business and global trade with the call for high animal welfare standards.

But are their efforts doomed to failure? Is the very nature of global agri-business and trade fundamentally flawed? Vandana Shiva and Kate Rawles would have us believe so, and make powerful arguments about the detrimental impact of intensive farming on the lives of the peasant farmers in developing countries and on the environment, including both wild and farmed animals. Patrick Holden makes a strong case for choosing the organic route, with its holistic emphasis on soil health and animal welfare. Yet even he admits the difficult choices that face this movement if it is to become a widely adopted farming method.

Is it too late to give a new direction to the sustainability agenda – a direction that includes animal welfare? The 'nutrition transition' – the change from simple grain, pulse and vegetable diets to high fat and sugar, meat, dairy and junk food diets – is sweeping the fast-developing countries, just as it swept through the western world during the 20th century. Tim Lang eloquently elucidates its dangers to our health in terms of the growth in non-communicable diseases (NCDs), such as heart disease and diabetes. Rawles points to the failure of the nutrition transition to fit into the global sustainability paradigm. She claims that true sustainability means considering human interdependence with all life.

All these viewpoints lead us back to our perception of who or what animals are. James Kirkwood takes us on a fascinating evolutionary journey, in which we discover our common ancestors in unlikely parts of the animal kingdom. Somewhere on that journey, sentience developed – just where may still be open to question.

Of course it's not just the contributors to this book – like Kirkwood, Andrew Linzey and Ben Mepham – who accept this evolutionary continuity. As Webster points out, it was Charles Darwin himself who recognized sentience as an essential feature of evolutionary fitness and believed it to be widespread in the animal world.

So how do we define sentience? Several of our authors grapple with this key question – and it is, of course, the crucial question, because if animals don't feel pain or fear or distress, if they cannot suffer, then the animal welfarists can pack their bags and we can proceed down the route so notoriously carved out by Descartes – the animals are simply machines reacting to stimuli; moral philosophers can be silent – there is nothing to worry about.

Although few still openly support this view, we – at least in the west – are cultural inheritors of it. To be fair to Descartes, his views had historical roots and have found support from sources as diverse but influential as leading proponents of Catholicism and leftist social radicals – both groups, for very different reasons, grounded in anthropocentrism. In practice, the anthropocentric worldview means always putting people's needs or wants first.

However, concern for animals and recognition of their capacity for suffering also has a long history, and one that grows more eloquent and respected day by day. Since Donald Griffin's work over 30 years ago, there has been a revolution in how scientists perceive animals. Philosophy too has been a major influence in the debate. Peter Singer, the author of the ground-breaking book *Animal Liberation*, and Tom Regan (whom you can read here) may base their arguments in different philosophical schools of thought, but they have both inspired a radical rethink of who animals are and what our relationship to them should be.

The consensus seems to be that sentient creatures are those who have feelings – both physical and emotional – and whose feelings matter to them. As world famous primatologist Jane Goodall points out, so much of what animals do is obviously more than an automatic response to stimuli. Although her field has been the detailed study of chimpanzees in their natural environment, she is quick to extend her conclusion that chimpanzees have 'personalities, minds and feelings' to other species too.

But it's useful to pause at chimpanzees. Their behaviour has been so well documented that the comparisons with human behaviour are unavoidable. Already, serious scientists are referring to chimp 'culture' in view of the different kinds of tool use found in geographically distinct groups of chimpanzees. With our DNA differing by only 1 per cent, it's not surprising that Jane Goodall regards them as 'ambassadors' for the animal kingdom.

Chimps, elephants, whales, pigs – the capacity for intelligence is undoubtedly widespread. Yet the contributors to this book seem to agree that it is the capacity for emotions that is the most important attribute of sentient beings. After all, it is how *we* feel that makes (or breaks) our day. If animals can express feelings of joy or grief, contentment, excitement, fear or anguish, then presumably it is how *they* feel that makes (or breaks) their day too.

Problems manifest when our own human species interacts with these animals. Do they *feel* better for our interference – or worse? A pet dog may be cosy and well-fed, even exercised regularly, but if he is alone all day, how does he – as a creature descended from a group-living species – actually feel?

As for the animals reared on our intensive factory farms – it is surely not beyond our own inherent empathy to realize that a hen caged for her productive life with four or five others has little potential for fulfilment or a state of contentment, that a pregnant sow confined on concrete between bars throughout her 16-week pregnancy is going to feel frustrated, agitated and probably depressed, that a dairy cow and calf separated soon after birth, as is the norm, are going to feel longing, maybe anguish, at their parting. Ros Clubb's disturbing account of the plight of animals bred for their fur demonstrates the extent to which the mindset of 'profit at any price' has spread.

Of course, Peter Sandøe, Stine Christiansen and Björn Forkman are right to point out the anomalies in how we measure an animal's welfare. Is a free range hen, who can move about in a natural environment, stretch her wings or even fly, better off than her caged sisters – even though she could be more susceptible to predators or to soil-borne parasites? Both Sandøe and Marc Bekoff favour a mixture of common sense informed by science as the guide to our treatment of animals. Science on its own is rarely sufficient to give us all the answers – values and even intuition have vital roles to play in guiding us. Jane Goodall challenges us to acknowledge how *we* really feel about animals when we make decisions about their lives.

Many of the authors are quite clear that, when in doubt about what an animal feels – or whether or how it feels – we should give the animal the benefit of the doubt. We should apply the precautionary principle.

Both theologian Andrew Linzey and attorney Steve Wise compare the moral case of children to that of animals. As Linzey points out, both are vulnerable; in our control; innocent; and cannot represent themselves, give consent or articulate their needs. He sees both groups as subjects of a special trust. Many of the authors articulate eloquently the case for recognizing the sentience of animals and enshrining that recognition in law.

CIWF ran a campaign in the 1990s to have animals recognized as sentient beings in the European Treaty – and were successful. A Protocol attached to the

Treaty in 1997 does indeed recognize animals as sentient beings. CIWF Trust is working to achieve a similar recognition by other governments and international institutions.

Meanwhile, the agri-businesses and global bodies such as the International Finance Corporation, World Bank and the World Organisation for Animal Health (OIÉ) are starting the process of acknowledging that there is a case to be made for good animal welfare. But it is obvious that combining good welfare with an outlook that views animals primarily as production units is a difficult task. No wonder Bayvel and Kenny talk of 'continuous improvement' rather than radical change.

The problem is that the global situation of animal farming is so complex and the cultural attitudes to animals so varied that it will not be easy to achieve a consensus for reform. As David Wilkins points out, even the substantial reforms achieved in the European Union over the last 20 years are under threat from world trade rules. And when Peter Li, Song Wei and Paul Littlefair describe the situation in China – one of the world's largest livestock producers – you can see that ensuring good welfare may be a tough battle in such a large and diverse country. But progress is undoubtedly taking place. In China, more and more people are expressing concern for welfare. In India, also rapidly industrializing, there is a long cultural tradition that recognizes animal sentience, in principle at least. Mahfouz Azzam makes it clear that – although concern for animal welfare is often not apparent at 'street level' in Islamic countries – Islamic teaching is rich in exhortations to care for other creatures. It would be totally inappropriate to consider such concern a prerogative of 'western' culture.

For those of us who are deeply concerned that all animals should have the opportunity to have lives worth living and to be spared suffering as far as possible, the future will certainly be a challenge. As several authors point out, we haven't yet solved human problems such as hunger and poverty; but there are strong links between these problems and the welfare of both wild and farm animals.

I personally believe that recognition of animal sentience and a radical change in how we treat animals in our society will be beneficial for us all.

Compassion may be a quality which is not unique to *Homo sapiens*, but it is certainly one we can all recognize in ourselves and in each other. Many of the authors in this book demonstrate that compassion is a 'broad-band' quality – it can encompass both our own human society in all its diversity, and also our sentient kin in the animal world.

If this book has an overarching message, it is surely this: if we are truly to acknowledge animal sentience (and to give the benefit of the doubt where we're not certain), then we need to actively work towards the day when all sentient beings can realize their potential in a world that supports both their individual well-being and the common good, and we need to have the vision and courage to enact and enforce strong laws supporting these ideals.

References

Darwin, C. R. (1871) *The Descent of Man and Selection in Relation to Sex*, J Murray, London

Grandin, T. (2006) 'Progress and challenges in animal handling and slaughter in the US', *Applied Animal Behaviour Science*, in press

PART 1

Animal Sentience: Evidence and Interpretations

1
The Sentience of Chimpanzees and Other Animals

Jane Goodall

Founder – The Jane Goodall Institute (JGI)

Chimpanzees' lives

Chimpanzees, in many ways, serve as ambassadors from the animal kingdom to the world of humans – as a bridge between 'man' and 'beast'. I began my study of the Gombe chimpanzees, living on the eastern shore of Lake Tanganyika, in Tanzania, in 1960. During the 46 years of continuous study since then, we have learned much of enormous significance, both for the understanding of chimpanzees and their complex society, and for the understanding of many aspects of our own behaviour and our relationship with the rest of the animal kingdom. Perhaps the most significant findings are those that show just how like us chimpanzees actually are.

First of all, there are the numerous physiological similarities between chimpanzees and us. The composition of chimpanzee and human blood is so similar that we could receive a blood transfusion from a chimpanzee. Their immune system is so like ours that they can catch or be infected with just about all known human contagious diseases. The structure of the DNA of chimpanzees and humans differs by only about 1 per cent and, now that the genome of the chimpanzee has been unravelled, it seems that the genetic similarity between us and them is even closer than was thought before. Most fascinating for me is the similarity in the structure, the anatomy, of the chimpanzee and human brain and nervous system. Thus it should not be surprising to find that these apes are capable of intellectual performances once thought unique to the human animal. It has been demonstrated in a variety of captive studies that they are capable of generalizing, abstraction and cross-modal transfer of information. They can understand and use abstract symbols in communicating. They can learn more than 300 of the signs used in American Sign Language (ASL) and can communicate with each other in this way as well as with their trainer. They are capable of self-recognition and can often understand the moods and needs of other individuals – in other words, they have a 'theory of mind'.

As the Gombe research continued, I gradually got to know more and more of the approximately 50 individuals who made up the community I was studying. I named them, and learned that each had a unique personality. I soon realized that they had extremely complex social lives.

Chimpanzees have a large repertoire of calls, postures and gestures with which they communicate information about what is going on within and around them. They kiss, embrace, hold hands, swagger and tickle – just like we do, and often in the same context. They not only use but also *make* tools – an ability once thought to differentiate humans from the rest of the animal kingdom. And they use rocks and sticks as missiles, often demonstrating very accurate aim. Chimpanzees are capable of compassion and altruism on the one hand, and of violence and a kind of primitive warfare on the other.

Particularly striking are the long-term affectionate and supportive relationships between family members that can last throughout life (chimpanzees can live more than 60 years). There is a long childhood dependency of five or six years, during which the infant suckles, rides on the mother's back and sleeps in her nest at night. And then, when a new baby is born, the older child remains emotionally dependent on the mother for at least another three years and possibly longer. Even after that, he or she repeatedly returns to spend time with the mother and the younger siblings. Learning plays an important role in the acquisition of social and environmental skills. We now know that in different parts of Africa, wherever chimpanzees have been studied, they use different objects as tools, in different contexts. Chimpanzees, like humans, can learn to make and use tools not only by trial and error, but also through observation, imitation and practice – one of the anthropologists' definitions of cultural behaviour.

Cooperation and altruism

The chimpanzees in the wild show sophisticated cooperation. This is particularly obvious during hunting and the sharing of the carcass after a kill. And our longitudinal study has yielded many striking examples of their capacity for caring and altruism. Let me share some of these stories. The first of these occurred when I was following a nine-year-old adolescent named Pom and her little three-year-old brother, Prof, along a forest trail. Suddenly Pom stopped and stared at a place along the trail ahead. Her hair bristled and she gave a tiny 'huu' of fear and ran up a tree. Prof continued along the trail. Perhaps he didn't hear the sound she made; perhaps he didn't know what it meant. As he got closer and closer to the place along the trail, his sister became more and more agitated. A huge grin of fear appeared on her face, every hair bristled and finally she rushed down the tree, gathered up her little brother and climbed back up the tree with him. There, coiled up at the side of the trail, was a big poisonous snake.

The second example concerns Madam Bee, an old female who became a victim of what was probably poliomyelitis. She lost the use of one arm and found it tiring to travel long distances between one food source and another. On several occasions when she arrived at a large fruit tree with her elder daughter, Little Bee, she lay on the ground while Little Bee climbed up to feed. Then, after feeding for ten minutes or so, Little Bee stuffed as much food as she could in her mouth, took some more in her hand, climbed down and laid the food in her hand beside her old mother. The two sat together feeding.

One example of true altruism at Gombe occurred when three-and-a-half-year-old Mel lost his mother. As mentioned, chimpanzee youngsters in the wild suckle until they are five or six years old – but they can survive on solids from about three years old. If Mel had had an older brother or sister, he would have been adopted, carried around and protected by that elder sibling. But Mel had no elder sibling and it seemed unlikely that he could survive. Then, to our amazement, a 12-year-old adolescent male, Spindle, adopted him. Spindle carried Mel on his back and let him cling to his belly if Mel was frightened or cold. He shared his food with Mel when the infant begged, and gathered him into his nest at night. When the adult males challenge one another for social dominance, performing wild displays, hurling rocks and branches, mothers quickly take their infants out of the way. Males have been known to throw or drag infants who get in the way. If Mel got too close to the adult males on such occasions, Spindle would run to rescue Mel, though he risked being buffeted himself, and sometimes was. Yet usually adolescent males are extremely cautious when in the vicinity of the big males when they are socially aroused, and keep well out of the way. It is without question that Spindle saved Mel's life.

In some zoos chimpanzees are kept on islands or exhibits surrounded by water-filled moats, since they do not swim. There are examples of chimpanzees risking their lives to try to save companions from drowning when they accidentally fall into the water. One adult male died when trying to rescue a drowning infant.

The implications for ethology

It was because of the striking physiological similarities between humans and chimpanzees that science seized upon chimpanzees as the ideal model for the study of certain human diseases – especially those that do not affect most laboratory animals. Yet at the same time, science was reluctant to admit to the equally striking ways in which chimpanzees resemble us intellectually, behaviourally and emotionally. Thus hundreds of chimpanzees were doomed to imprisonment in sterile lab cages just 5 feet square and 7 feet high. It was only after I had been a year in the field, when Louis Leakey got me into a PhD programme at Cambridge University (though I had no degree of any kind), that I first began to understand the bitter struggle between those who believe that animals can be exploited, used and abused in ways that might be of some benefit to the human species, and those who believe passionately that animals should be given certain rights that would protect them from such exploitation. At that time, in the early 1960s, many ethologists maintained that the behaviour of all animals – except the human animal – was little more than a series of genetically coded responses to sensory stimuli. To attribute human-like behaviour to non-human animals was to be guilty of anthropomorphism.

So, when I got to Cambridge I quickly found that I had done everything wrong. It would have been more scientific to identify the chimpanzees by numbers rather than names. And I could not talk about personality, mind or emotions in animals, since these things were unique to us – to the human animal. And even if they *were* present in animals, this could not be proved and so was best not talked about. Fortunately, throughout my childhood, I had had a wonderful teacher who had taught me that animals truly did have personalities, minds and feelings – and that was my dog, Rusty. So I was wary of accepting simplistic, reductionist explanations of complex behaviour. Luckily, at Cambridge I had a wise thesis supervisor, Robert Hinde, who taught me how to express my revolutionary ideas in a way that would save me from much hostile scientific criticism. (For example, I could not say 'Fifi was jealous' since I could not *prove* this, but I could say 'Fifi behaved in such a way that, had she been human, we would say she was jealous'!)

Since the Gombe study began in 1960, more and more biologists have gone into the field and started long-term studies on all manner of animal species: apes, monkeys, elephants, whales, dolphins, wolves, rodents, birds and so on. And these studies taken together have shown that animal behaviour is far more complex than originally admitted by science. We find that we are not alone in the universe; we are not the only beings capable of love and hate, joy and sorrow, fear and despair. We are not the only creatures with minds capable of solving problems. And certainly we are not the only animals to experience pain and suffering. In other words, there is no sharp line between the human animal and the rest of the animal kingdom. It is a blurred line, and becoming more so all the time. This has been clear to many eastern philosophies and religions, to the indigenous people around the world, and to thousands of ordinary people who have shared their lives, in meaningful ways, with dogs, cats, rabbits, horses and other animals brought into the home, living with the family.

Humans are indeed unique – for one thing we have an extraordinarily well developed intellect. I believe that the key factor in the development of this intellect was the emergence, at some point in human prehistory, of sophisticated spoken language. For this enables us to teach our children about objects and events not present, to learn from the distant past, to make plans for the distant future and to discuss an idea so that it can grow from the accumulated knowledge of a group of people. Our intellect has enabled us to develop truly astonishing technologies. We have been to the moon, we have invented modern electronic communications and computers that can play chess – the list is never ending. But being clever does not equate with being wise. Scientists feel the need to prove everything before they can admit to its truth. But sometimes this is not the best route. Common sense suggests that if, when an animal is wounded, it screams, tries to escape and shows other signs of distress, it is probably experiencing pain in much the same way as we would in a similar circumstance. When dog owners sense that their dogs are contented or sad, depressed or joyous, they are probably right. And even if there is only a possibility that animals are feeling as some of us believe that they feel, then they should surely be given the benefit of the doubt. We should not let the objectivity of the scientific method override human intuition, human compassion.

Farm animals

The blurring of the line between animals and humans raises for many people a range of ethical issues related to the ways in which we use and abuse animals for so many purposes all around the world. One such issue relates to the raising of animals for food in factory or intensive farms.

I was introduced to many farm animals when I was a child. In fact it would be true to say that I started my scientific career in a hen house! When I was four and a half years old I spent a holiday on a farm in the country. My family lived in London where the only animals around, other than our dog, were pigeons and sparrows. So seeing cows and pigs and horses out in the fields, and meeting them close up, was very exciting. One of my jobs was to collect the hens' eggs. There were no battery farms in those days and the hens were laying their eggs mostly in little wooden hen houses. Each day I put these eggs into my basket and after a while I began to wonder where, on the hen, was there a hole big enough for the egg to come out from? I examined the hens very closely but was unable to see such a hole. Apparently I then began asking everyone 'Where does the egg come out?', but without getting an answer that satisfied me. So when one afternoon I saw a hen going into one of the henhouses, and thinking, I suppose, that she was going to lay an egg, I crawled after her. Of course, this was a mistake. The hen, scared, flew off with squawks of fear.

Realizing that other hens would probably avoid that particular hen house, I climbed into an empty one, hid in the straw at the back and waited – and waited, and waited – until finally a hen came in. I can still remember seeing the slightly soft white egg plop onto the straw. Meanwhile my family had no idea where I was and, after searching all over, finally called the police. My mother, still searching, suddenly saw an excited little girl, covered in straw, rushing towards the house. Instead of getting mad at me for frightening everyone, she sat down to hear the story of how a hen lays an egg. When I look back on that incident, I realize that I showed all the hallmarks of a budding scientist. I was curious, I asked questions. The answers did not satisfy me so I decided I had to find out for myself. My first attempt failed, so I tried another method. And I learned that the most valuable attribute was patience.

Habituating an animal to human presence is tremendously important when you go out in the field. My first experience was when I was about eight years old, and on another wonderful holiday in the country. Close to where we were staying was a field of saddleback pigs. I remember climbing over the gate and moving slowly towards them – but they ran off. We were there for two weeks, and every day I went back to the field after lunch with an apple core. At first I put the offering on the ground as near to the pigs as I could get, and moved away a bit to watch. After a few days one pig approached and took the apple core, and eventually, to my great delight, he actually took the apple core from my hand. Then one day he let me scratch him behind his ear. This was the only time in my childhood I remember being really rude to an old lady. She shouted from the fence, 'Don't touch that pig, little girl, they're dirty and will give you a disease.' I shouted back very angrily, 'He's just as clean as you and me!'

When I first got to Gombe to study the chimps, somebody gave me two chickens that were meant to be eaten: a hen and a rooster. I cut the string that tied their legs together and they became good companions, eating many insects around the camp, including scorpions. I named them Hengist and Hildegard, and Hengist was a wonderful alarm clock. It was quite impossible to sleep through his predawn crowing. They were enchanting birds, each with a very distinctive personality.

It was a real shock when, in the 1970s, I read *Animal Liberation* by Peter Singer and learned about factory 'farms'. Places where hens and other poultry, cows and calves, and pigs were kept in crowded, stinking conditions; fed hormones to make them grow faster; and fed antibiotics as a prophylactic to keep them alive. I was horrified. And when I next looked at a piece of meat on my plate I realized that it symbolized fear, pain and death. And I never ate meat again.

It's encouraging to find that at least some farmers are beginning to return to the *old-fashioned* methods of animal husbandry. There are imaginative projects that attempt to improve conditions for some farm animals. One of these, funded by Barclays Bank, is at a large chicken farm in Ghana. The chickens at this farm are, indeed, kept in large numbers in a shed. But the building was designed with a wide ledge some 4 feet from the ground, so that while many of the broilers stay on the ground, others choose to fly up onto the ledge, from where they can look out of a window. It seems that this ledge, which goes right around the shed, has made a big improvement in the short lives of those chickens.

Intensive factory farming is not only unethical with regard to animal suffering, but also because of its adverse impact on the environment and human health. The use of farmland for grazing cattle or for growing grain to feed cattle is very wasteful, is causing the destruction of ever increasing areas of natural habitat and is placing unsustainable demands on water. Intensive animal farming practices also pose a significant risk to human health. It has been suggested that the use of growth hormones to increase milk production in dairy cattle could have adverse affects on consumers. The practice of giving animals antibiotics in their feed, to keep them alive in the highly stressed environment of the intensive farm, is causing many bacteria to become increasingly resistant to more and more antibiotics. There is a very real danger that we shall create terrifying 'super bugs' that will be unaffected by all known antibiotics.

Unfortunately, in spite of the very real ethical issues connected with intensive animal farming, many people prefer not to think about the animal suffering or the threat to human health. When I describe the suffering of animals in factory farms, or the horrors of the slaughter house, people often tell me that they love animals, and so cannot bear to be told about the horrible conditions farm animals must endure.

Education

One of the programmes of the Jane Goodall Institute that is helping to raise understanding of the true nature of animals and ways in which we humans exploit them and cause them to suffer is 'Roots & Shoots'. The name is symbolic: roots make a firm foundation, shoots seem small but to reach the sun they can break through a brick wall. And if we see the brick wall as all the problems, environmental and social, that we humans have inflicted on the planet, then Roots & Shoots brings a message of hope: hundreds and thousands of young people around the world can break through and make the world a better place for animals, people and the environment. The programme began in the early 1990s and there are now some 7500 active groups (a group can be a whole school) in more than 90 countries. We have programmes for children from preschool through to university. The most important message is that every individual makes a difference every day. We endeavour to teach children about the problems in the world around them, and encourage and empower them to take action to make change. Many groups work to improve the lives of stray dogs and cats, enrich the lives of zoo animals by making toys to relieve boredom, raise money to help endangered species, rescue hens from battery farms and learn about many issues of animal cruelty and conservation.

Empathy across species

There are two stories with which I should like to close this chapter. They both involve chimpanzees who were born in Africa and who were about two years old when their mothers were shot. Only by killing the mother is it possible to capture an infant chimpanzee. Both these young chimpanzees were sent, at different times, to the US.

The first, subsequently named Old Man (because newly orphaned chimpanzees look so listless and old), was sold to a biomedical research laboratory where he was used for cancer research. Old Man was fortunate – after some ten years of stressful life in the lab he was released onto a manmade island at a zoo in Florida. His companions were three females, one of whom had been rescued from medical research and two from the circus. After a while Old Man became father to an infant. About that time Marc Cusano was hired to care for the chimpanzees. He was told not to go near them as they were stronger than people, very dangerous and would try to kill him. At first he approached on a small paddle boat and threw food onto the island. As he learned more about the chimpanzees he became increasingly fascinated. He saw how they embraced and kissed each other, uttering loud excited calls as he approached with their food. He watched Old Man playing with the infant, carrying and protecting her, and sharing his food with her. It seemed to Marc that Old Man really loved the child. Marc wanted to develop a relationship with these amazing chimpanzee beings. So he went a little closer each day, and eventually dared hold out a banana. To his joy, Old Man took it from his hand. Then, one day, Marc stepped onto the island. One day he groomed Old Man. One day they actually played. They had become friends.

Then came the terrible occasion when Marc slipped as he walked across the island, and fell. The infant, startled, screamed in fear and instantly the mother rushed to protect her child and bit Marc on the neck as he lay face down on the ground. The other two females rushed to support their friend; one bit his leg, the other his wrist. Wondering how he could get away Marc raised his head – and saw Old Man charging towards him, hair bristling, lips bunched in a furious scowl. Coming, Marc supposed, to rescue his precious child. He told me that he expected to be killed. But Old Man physically pulled each female off, and kept them away as Marc dragged himself to safety. Without doubt, Old Man saved his life. How moving: a chimpanzee, who had been abused by humans, nevertheless reached out, across the supposed gulf between us and other animals, to help his human friend.

The second infant chimpanzee, who became known as JoJo, was sent to a zoo. There he lived for about ten years in a small, old fashioned zoo cage with a cement floor and iron bars. Then a new enclosure was built with a moat filled with water. Nineteen other chimpanzees were bought, carefully introduced to each other, and finally let out into the enclosure.

Soon after this, one of the new young males challenged the senior male – JoJo – with the swaggering displays, the bristling hair, the bunched lips and the hurling of rocks typical of a male chimpanzee. But JoJo didn't understand much about chimp behaviour – he hadn't had a chance to learn – and he was terrified. He ran to the water; he didn't even know about water. He was so scared he managed to climb over the railing built to prevent the chimps from drowning in the deep water beyond. Three times he came up gasping for air and then he disappeared under the water.

On the far side of the moat was a little group of people. Luckily for JoJo, there was a man there named Rick who visits the zoo one day a year with his wife and three little girls. He jumped in, even though a keeper told him he would be killed, that JoJo weighed 130 pounds and that male chimps are much stronger than humans. Swimming to where JoJo had disappeared, Rick finally found him, got the 130-pound dead weight over his shoulder, and managed to climb with him over the railing. He could feel JoJo moving as he pushed him up onto the bank of the exhibit. Then Rick turned to rejoin his slightly hysterical family. There was a woman there with a video camera. Her film reveals what happened next.

The people started screaming at Rick to come back because he was going to be killed. They could see three of the big males coming down with hair bristling to see what the commotion was about. And at the same time JoJo was sliding back into the water because the bank was too steep. This film shows Rick as he stood with one hand on the railing. He looked up at his wife and daughters, then towards where the three males were approaching, and then down at JoJo who was disappearing under the water again. For a moment Rick stood there motionless. And then he went back. And again he pushed JoJo up and, ignoring the people, ignoring the three big chimps, he stayed there pushing JoJo who was making feeble efforts to grab on to something. And just in time he got hold of a thick tuft of grass and with Rick pushing managed to get onto the level ground. Just in time Rick got back over that railing.

That evening, that little piece of video was flashed across North America and the then director of JGI-USA saw it. He called Rick: 'That was a very brave thing you did. You must have known it was dangerous. Everyone was telling you. What made you do it?' And Rick said, 'Well, you see, I happened to look into his eyes and it was like looking into the eyes of a man and the message was: won't anybody help me?'

And that's the message that I've seen in the eyes of so many abused, neglected animals whether they be chimpanzee orphans for sale in the African markets or chimpanzees looking out from their bleak sterile lab cages or under the frills of the circus. I've seen it in the eyes of chained elephants and dogs cast out on the streets, and in the eyes of animals imprisoned without hope in factory farms. If we see that look with our eyes and we *feel it in our hearts*, we have to jump in and try to help. And everywhere, today, there are people who have heeded that appeal, people who are speaking out on behalf of animals just as, 200 years ago, people spoke out on behalf of human slaves. And because our cause is right, we shall, eventually, succeed on behalf of the animals. In the meantime we must work even harder and never give up.

2

The Distribution of the Capacity for Sentience in the Animal Kingdom

James K. Kirkwood

Universities Federation for Animal Welfare and Humane Slaughter Association, UK

At the Amsterdam Summit in June 1997, agreement was reached by the European Heads of State to make provision in the Treaty of Rome (which established the European Community in 1957) '... to ensure improved protection and respect for the welfare of animals as sentient beings'.

'We live at a unique point in the history of science. The technology to discover and characterize how the subjective mind emerges out of the objective brain is within reach. The next years will prove decisive' (Koch, 2004).

Sentience: Solo to symphonic

My view about animal welfare is in line with the sentiment behind the agreement reached by the European Heads of State at their Amsterdam Summit in June 1997 (see above), though it is not, as I will discuss later, in line with what it actually says. For me, concern for an animal's welfare is concern for its feelings – concern for the quality of its life as it experiences it. (Here and throughout I use 'feelings' as shorthand for conscious/subjectively experienced feelings, likewise by 'feel' I mean consciously/subjectively feel.) Thus, it seems to me that welfare is: 'The balance, now or through life, of the quality of the complex mix of subjective feelings associated with brain states induced by various sensory inputs and by cognitive and emotion processes' (Kirkwood, 2004a). I think it is helpful, in this way, to reserve the use of the word 'welfare' to address feelings rather than using it to include health also. How an animal feels can be influenced by its state of health and by its environment, so these are of course often central to the subject of animal welfare, but it seems to me that there is much to be gained and nothing to be lost by keeping the meanings of the terms *health* and *welfare* distinct in this way.

To be sentient is to have the capacity to feel (in the sense defined above) something. Except in deep sleep or some pathological states, the lives of most of us humans are characterized by many kinds of feelings. Some of these, including sights, sounds, tastes, warmth and cold, and the various sensations arising from touch, are associated with our external sensors. Others are associated with internal sensors that provide our brains with information about the states of our bodies. The latter include general, non-localized or only vaguely localized feelings such as exhaustion, malaise or ecstasy, and localized feelings such as aches and pains. In addition, we experience a spectrum of feelings associated with the thoughts and emotions that may be prompted either by the inputs from these internal and external sensing devices, or (it seems) by the constant internal conversations – some conscious, some subconscious – of our brains. For example, fear (or, in others, delight) may be induced by a glimpse of a snake beside one's unshod foot, and feelings of sorrow or joy may be evoked by music or by remembering sad or happy events.

It is conceivable (though I struggle with the notion) that the kind of multi-faceted sentience that we experience – symphonic is a good word to describe it – may have sprung suddenly into existence from non-sentient ancestors. For example, some genetic change may have resulted in a crucial alteration in the organization, the patterns of communication, among brain modules, which resulted in the emergence of sentience. If this conferred a significant evolutionary advantage, then it might have spread rapidly through the descendent population of our ancestors. Such a scenario would be consistent with the views of those who believe that the current scientific evidence is that sentience is limited to humans only, or to humans and perhaps a very few other species (see, for example, Kennedy, 1993; Bermond, 1997; Macphail, 1998).

The other, and perhaps more likely pattern of events than this *non-sentient to symphonic sentience in one step* hypothesis, is that our kind of symphonic sentience evolved in stages from an earlier, simpler, 'solo' version. The first sentient organism may have been consciously aware of only one sense – one aspect of sight, for example (our conscious vision is formed from the coordinated activity of many distinct and separate brain modules that each handle specific tasks to do with, for example: colour, recognition of particular objects, position, distance and movement). This faculty for conscious awareness might then have been commandeered by evolution to enhance (if that is what it does) other aspects of vision, and then have been further applied to other senses such as hearing and taste, and then to cognitive and emotional processes also. I am not suggesting that this may actually have been the sequence in which various senses and neuronal processes came under the spotlight of consciousness – it might have happened in the reverse order – but only that there may have been a stepwise development in the range of phenomena that could be accessed within consciousness.

As stated above, to be sentient is to have a feeling of something. This implies that the phenomenon of sentience either exists or it doesn't: that an organism either is sentient or it isn't. How could this discrete presence or absence be consistent with the gradual process of evolution? There is no problem envisaging gradation in the intensity of a feeling – pain can vary from a barely discernible to a very severe sensation – but it is much harder to see how the very capacity to be aware of pain could be other than either present or absent. You either feel something, no matter how slightly, or you don't – it is hard to conceive a halfway stage here. This may well be an important issue – the explanation of which might prove revealing – but it is not one that can be pursued further in this paper. Brains work by passage of information among hierarchical assemblages of neurons. Perhaps sentience evolved with a slight change, by chance, in organization that resulted in a small assemblage of cells 'recognizing' patterns of activity of the previously insentient brain design.

Envisaged in this way, sentience may indeed depend upon a specific form of neuronal organization that either is present or not, but it may have started with changes that involved very few cells in the first instance. This leads on to the subject of this paper, which is the distribution of the capacity for sentience in the animal kingdom. It is appropriate to begin this with a brief review of the animal kingdom and of who or what is and is not currently included within it.

What is an animal?

The Amsterdam Summit agreement in June 1997 that provision should be made in the Treaty of Rome '... to ensure improved protection and respect for the welfare of animals as sentient beings' recognizes the crucial moral implication of sentience. Sentient beings have feelings and thus the capacity for pleasure and suffering. This agreement is an expression of society's stance that, in view of this capacity, it is morally important to consider the welfare of sentient beings in all our interactions with them.

However, the wording 'welfare *of animals as sentient beings*' implies that all animals are sentient and, in referring only to animals, implies that only animals are. It assumes that the distribution of sentience among all organisms maps exactly onto the distribution of animals among all organisms. (One senses from the wording here and in many other pieces of legislation that a strong grounding in phylogeny has not traditionally been seen as a key part of the legislators' toolkit.) These implicit assumptions could have been avoided by agreeing, instead, to ensure improved protection and respect 'for the welfare of sentient beings' or 'for the welfare of sentient animals'. These alternatives would have been preferable, in my opinion, since they make possession of sentience, rather than type of organism, the crucial issue. Are all animals sentient? Are only animals sentient?

The animal species are a relatively small subset (1–2 million) of the estimated 30 million living species. They are characterized by being multicellular, by not having cell walls and by being heterotrophic – that is, they eat other life forms or their organic products. Animals cannot synthesize organic matter from inorganic components. Most of the organisms large enough to be seen with the naked eye are members of the animal, the plant or the fungi kingdoms, but these are a small part of the whole diversity of life, which, it now seems, comprises dozens of types as different from one another as are plants, animals and fungi (Dawkins, 2004).

There is good evidence that life on earth was well underway 3.5 billion years ago. Our ancestors became multicellular around 900 million years ago, quite some time after we shared our last common ancestors with plants and fungi, about 1.2 and 1.1 billion years ago, respectively (Dawkins, 2004). We have a multitude of more distant relatives outside the animal kingdom that are animal-like in some respects, in that that they move around and feed on other organisms – and which were in fact classified as animals until very recently. However, the classification of animals has been undergoing radical revisions in recent years, partly as a result of emerging genetic evidence, and the taxonomists have moved some of the goal posts. Unicellular organisms such as amoebae, euglenids, flagellates and ciliates are no longer counted as animals. 'Animals' used to include three groups: Protozoa – single-celled animals; Parazoa – the sponges; and Metazoa – multicellular animals with differentiated bodies. The sponges, which have been promoted to the Metazoa, remain in, but the protozoans are out.

The kingdom Animalia (also called Metazoa) is divided into some 33 phyla (see Table 2.1). There is a remarkably diverse range of body designs and lifestyles within this kingdom and a very great range in complexity. One of the apparently simplest animals, the water-dwelling placozoan *Trichoplax adhaerens*, is a tiny flat irregularly shaped, three-cell-thick mat. It has only four types of cells, in contrast to the more than 250 types in humans. There are many ways in which complexity could be measured among animals, but on the basis of the genome, it would be reasonable to suggest that the vertebrates are at the complex end of the scale (Dawkins, 2004). In terms of complexity of brain design and function and of associated behavioural complexity, *Homo sapiens* may top the bill. The human brain has some 100 billion neurons and 100,000 billion synapses, so the potential number of ways it can be configured – the ways in which its neurons can be linked up – is staggeringly vast (Church-land, 1996).

Our own phylum, Chordata, containing about 45,000 species in more than 100 orders (see Table 2.2), is a relatively small one. By contrast, there are approaching a million species in the phylum Arthropoda. Our closest relatives outside our own phylum are the Ambulacrarians, which include the sea urchins and starfish. Our last common ancestor with these – which was probably small and worm shaped – lived about 570 million years ago (Table 2.3). A little further back in time, our most recent shared ancestor (also small and worm-like) with the protostomes, the large group of phyla which include the arthropods (e.g. insects, spiders, centipedes, crabs and lobsters); the nematodes and acanthacephalans (some of which are commonly responsible for parasitic diseases in mammals and birds); and the molluscs (such as snails, shellfish and octopus), lived about 590 million years ago (Dawkins, 2004).

Table 2.1 *The phyla of the animal kingdom*

Kingdom				Phyla	
Mesozoa				Porifera	Sponges
				Placozoa	*Trichoplax adhaerens*
Eumetazoa	Radiata			Cnidaria	Jellyfish, corals, anemones
				Ctenophora	Comb jellies
	Bilateria	Protostomia (>1,000,000 species)	Acoelomates	Platyhelminthes	Flatworms
				Nemertea	Ribbon worms
			Pseudocoelomates	Rotifera	
				Nematoda	Roundworms
				Acanthocephala and 7 others	Thorny-headed worms
			Eucoelomates	Mollusca	Snails, oysters, octopus
				Annelida	Earthworms
				Arthropoda and 8 others	Insects, arachnids, crustaceans...
		Deuterostomia (60,000 species)		Echinodermata	Sea urchins, starfish
				Chordata and 4 others	Squirts, lancelets, vertebrates

Table 2.2 *The orders of the phylum Chordata*

Phylum	Class	Order	
Chordata			
Tunicates	Ascidiacea		Sea squirts
Vertebrates	Agnatha		Lampreys, hagfishes
	Chondroichthyes		Sharks
	Osteichthyes	> 20 orders	Bony fish
	Amphibia	Anura	Frogs, toads
		Caudata	Salamanders, newts
		Gymnophiona	Caecilians
	Reptilia	Testudinia	Tortoises, turtles
		Crocodylia	Crocodiles
		Rhynocephalia	Tuatara
		Squamata	Snakes, lizards
	Aves	Anseriformes	Ducks, geese
		Galliformes	Fowl, pheasants
		Passeriformes	Songbirds
		and 25 other orders	
	Mammalia	Primates	Primates
		and 16 other orders of placentals	Other placental mammals
		and 7 orders of Marsupials	Marsupials
		Monotremata	Echidnas, platypus

The animal kingdom is very diverse. Do we have good grounds for assuming that all animals are sentient? Before returning to the difficult question of how we might decide which organisms are or are not sentient, I will briefly outline why I believe the matter to be of great importance.

Table 2.3 *Time since our last common ancestor with various other taxa*

	Time since last common ancestor (million years)
Chimpanzees	6
Macaques	25
Rats, mice, rabbits	75
Marsupials	140
Reptiles, including birds	310
Amphibians	340
Fish	440
Sharks	460
Sea squirts	565
Starfish, anemones	570
Protostomes	590
Jellyfish	
Placozoans	780
Sponges	800
Fungi	1100
Amoeba	
Plants	1200

Source: Dawkins, 2004

Why do we need to know which organisms are sentient?

The world currently faces a major challenge. There are over six billion of us humans and the population is still growing very rapidly. For animals of our body size we have biologically unprecedented rates of energy utilization (Kirkwood, 2001). On a small planet with a finite annual productivity of organic matter (food) limited largely by the sunlight falling on it, we are, whether we like it or not, in competition with many other species. It has been calculated that the total terrestrial net primary production each year is 120 billion tonnes of organic matter (equivalent to 400×10^{15} kcal/year) and that 24.2 billion tonnes (i.e. 20 per cent) of this is appropriated by humans (Imhoff et al, 2004). To a remarkable extent, we now influence the apportionment of essential resources amongst the 30 million other species, including the tens of thousands of species that are widely assumed to be sentient. We are thus faced with the challenge of meeting the requirements of the still very rapidly growing human population, whilst protecting, as far as possible, biodiversity and the welfare interests of other sentient species that we use or whose fates depend upon our actions.

Amongst other things, this requires that we make sound inferences and judgements about feelings in other animals: whether or not they have them, their quality – pleasant or unpleasant – and their intensity. In this way, when our interests conflict with theirs, as they will continue inevitably to do, we can attempt to balance these interests wisely and kindly, and to take proper steps to minimize risks to welfare (Kirkwood, 2004b).

One of the key pieces of wisdom we require for this concerns the judgement about where the boundaries lie between those organisms that are sentient and those that are not. There are two reasons why this is crucial. First, we often need to intervene in inter-species conflicts; for example, in preventing or treating diseases in vertebrates caused by nematodes or arthropods. And, in these cases, if we are to be humane, the approach we adopt has to take into account whether or not the protagonists are sentient. Secondly, protecting the welfare of sentient organisms from anthropogenic challenges is a massive task and the resources at our disposal are limited. If we cast the net too wide, efforts for welfare will be wasted on non-sentient organisms rather than being focused where they are needed.

We should note in passing here, that we (at least in western cultures) tend traditionally to side with the vertebrates when it comes to vertebrate/invertebrate conflicts. Thus we aim to make life better for sheep by trying to kill *Psoroptes*, the mange mites that cause sheep scab, and for cats and dogs by trying to kill fleas and other parasites, rather than striving to find ways to make life better for the mites and fleas. Likewise, legal protection for animal welfare is often limited, exclusively or almost exclusively, to vertebrates. When dealing with vertebrate/invertebrate conflicts this is not an unreasonable stance; however, it is very hard to make a watertight scientific case that the boundary between the sentient and insentient lies between the vertebrates and the invertebrates (Sherwin, 2001). In all our dealings with them, we have a special responsibility for sentient animals – a responsibility for their feelings. So, which species are sentient and should therefore be given welfare protection?

Which organisms are sentient?

This is a very difficult question. We humans each know that we personally are sentient and we can be certain (can't we?) that the first replicating molecules that began the tree of life 4 billion years ago were not. It follows that somewhere along the way sentience evolved, but we are not at all sure where. It may have been relatively recently and be present only in taxa closely related to us, or it may have evolved much longer ago and be more widespread. It may, like eyes, have arisen independently in various lineages. Scientific opinions have been diverse:

some have argued that sentience is probably limited to humans and some that there is no reason to exclude arthropods and other protostomes. Others have presented cases for placing the line at various intermediate positions in the 'tree of life' between these extremes (see the review by Kirkwood and Hubrecht, 2001). The matter is yet to be resolved. In a recent paper, Griffin and Speck (2004) reviewed 'evidence that increases the probability that many animals experience at least simple levels of consciousness', but observed that it remains possible that if and when an essential consciousness-generating mechanism is found, it might turn out to be something found only in human brains.

Before going on to discuss possible approaches to judging which species are sentient, it is worth reviewing why this presents such difficulties. Many take it as simply blindingly obvious that animals (or at least some of them) are sentient, but many others, throughout history, appear to have very readily accepted philosophical and religious teachings that, with the exception of humans, animals are not sentient (as reviewed by, among others, Rollin, 1989; Wise, 2000; Ryder, 2000). What is the problem? Very briefly, the difficulty is as follows.

It is easy to see why evolution equipped animals with the following:

- locomotory systems that enable them to seek food rather than waiting for it and to enable them to avoid predators;
- sensory systems to permit detection of good things from afar and to give early warning of dangers;
- additional and increasingly sophisticated capacities (e.g. for learning and memory), designs and strategies that increase the chances of feeding and breeding and to reduce the chances of starvation, disease or being preyed upon.

We should expect, therefore, even simple organisms to act as if they had feelings and intentions ('it's too warm here so I'll swim with my cilia towards that cooler spot'). But we should be cautious in assuming that all such behaviour is proof of sentience. We have an inherent tendency to interpret the behaviour of other animals as being based on feelings and intentions of the sort that seem to underlie much of our own behaviour (e.g. Povinelli and Vonk, 2003). It is thanks to our 'projection' of this capacity that *The Simpsons* exist – because we understand and empathize with what these drawings are 'thinking' and 'feeling'. It is not hard to explain why organisms evolved to behave *as if* they were sentient, but it is much more difficult to understand why evolution saw fit to make any animals *actually* sentient. In what way does it help?

It is very difficult to know when, during evolution, our ancestors evolved from 'blind' insentient mechanisms to mechanisms with the first glimmers of sentience – the first feelings of something: light, heat, salt, touch or whatever else it might have been. One might expect that this was such a dramatic and valuable new capacity that it would be associated with some obvious and marked discontinuity between the sentient and their insentient relatives. However, looking across the range of extant species, no clear stepwise change is readily apparent. Perhaps the reason for this is that the solutions to survival problems are likely to 'look' the same in both sentient and non-sentient organisms.

But if this is the case, if it is not obvious which organisms are and are not sentient from their natural behaviour, how might we be able to tell then apart at all?

How can we tell?

It would be very helpful in addressing this question to know the answers to two others: What evolutionary advantage does sentience confer? And what neural mechanisms does it depend upon? The answer to the first, perhaps surprisingly, remains elusive. I do not propose to review the extensive literature on this subject here. Christof Koch and Francis Crick (Koch, 2004), in line with a number of previous authorities, have proposed that consciousness may have evolved as a flexible way of tackling complex and novel situations, the solutions to which would otherwise have required a very large number of fixed subroutines. They hypothesize that: 'The function of consciousness is to summarize the current state of the world' (and of the organism itself in it) 'in a compact representation and make this "executive summary" accessible to the planning stages of the brain .... The content of this summary is the content of consciousness.' This has a very plausible ring to it (and is in line with the prevalent thinking on the subject, see Griffin and Speck, 2004), but it does not help much in distinguishing between the sentient and insentient at this stage.

Regarding the second question – concerning the neural basis of sentience – remarkable progress has been made in exploring the functioning of the mammalian brain in recent years and how it may generate feelings (see reviews by Ledoux, 1998; Rolls, 1999; Damasio, 1999, 2003; Glynn, 1999; Edelman and Tonini, 2000; Koch, 2004). However, whilst it has been clearly established that some parts of the brain are essential for aspects of conscious awareness in humans, knowledge of the structure and functioning of the simplest neuronal assemblage necessary to support consciousness is not yet at the stage at which it can provide a basis for critical evaluation of the occurrence of similar assemblages in other species.

There are two approaches to determining, or rather to providing, a firm basis for inferring sentience: behavioural and neurological. Some examples are outlined below.

Behavioural approaches

To be sentient is to have the capacity to be aware of something – to have something in mind. One approach to detecting sentience is to find ways to get animals to report or reveal what they have in mind (since revealing what you have in mind confirms that you have one). Koch (2004) has proposed, for example, that sophisticated actions that require retention of information over seconds (between receipt of the information and the start of the response) might be quite a robust practical test for consciousness in animals.

One approach to asking animals what they have in mind is that used by Inman and Shettleworth (1999) and by Hampton (2001) to enquire of pigeons and macaques, respectively, whether or not they 'know' when they remember an image they had recently been shown (the macaques 'said' they could). Of course, this particular approach aims to test for consciousness of memory, and would not tell us about consciousness of other phenomena such as feelings of fear or pain.

Another compelling demonstration of an animal directly reporting what it is conscious of comes from investigations of blindsight. Humans with blindsight, a condition in which there is loss of sight in part of the visual field, continue to be able to deal appropriately with visual information in this part of the field (Weiskrantz, 1997). Effectively their minds are blind but their bodies can see to some extent, using visual processing systems that are not consciously accessible. These people can, if asked, correctly point to a source of light, for example, whilst being able to see nothing. Cowey and Stoerig (1995) discovered that, after learning the test methods, macaques with blindsight could likewise respond appropriately to visual stimuli whilst reporting, by pressing a pad, that they did not see the stimulus. Some of the other ingenious approaches to devising ways to enable animals to reveal whether or not they have the capacity for consciousness have been reviewed recently by Griffin and Speck (2004).

Neurological approaches

If, in future, the minimum neural correlates of consciousness in humans are determined and the aspects of their structure and function relating to consciousness come to be comprehended, then it may be possible, equipped with this knowledge, to identify similar mechanisms in other species. It will not be enough merely to determine the neural correlates of consciousness in humans and then to see which species do or do not have corresponding brain regions, because the structure of central nervous systems varies greatly within the animal kingdom. Even within the vertebrates there is great diversity. Concluding their heroic volumes on the comparative anatomy of the central nervous systems of vertebrates, Nieuwenhuys et al (1998) comment: 'Looking back on this whole endeavour, spanning as it does more than two decades of work, we are struck by a combination of frustration and wonder... It would be satisfying to conclude with some clever and subtle principle that made sense of all that has gone before, to reveal the secret of brain structure and its organization. Instead we are left with a sense of awe at the myriad complexity of it all.'

The complexity is indeed awesome. However, unless we have an understanding of the design of circuitry required for consciousness, we will not be able to ascertain which species do or do not have it. It may be quite a while before knowledge has advanced to the point at which this approach can be applied, but remarkable progress has been made in pursuit of the neuronal correlates of consciousness in recent years.

It seems highly likely that there is variation among sentient animals in the range of sensory, emotional or cognitive states that can fall within the spotlight of their sentience. We may have the impression that we are consciously aware of most of our external senses, but it has been shown that we can acquire and respond to information received through these routes subconsciously also. For example, there is evidence that we respond to some pheromone chemical signals that we have no awareness of, to images presented too fleetingly to register consciously and, in the case of blindsight patients, to visual stimuli despite blindness (Weiskrantz, 1997). There is evidence that there are two routes by which visual stimuli are processed: a dorsal 'vision-for-action' stream to which there is no conscious access and a ventral 'vision-for-perception' stream that is necessary for conscious vision (Milner and Goodale, 1995). As Koch (2004) points out: although 'common sense suggests that awareness and thought are inseparable and that introspection reveals the content of the mind', we do not, in fact, have access to most of our thought processes. For example, we are not and cannot become aware of the processes of finding words and putting them together in the correct sequence when we speak or of how we coordinate all the movements necessary to catch a ball. Much of what we do is unconscious.

So, if much of the brain is involved with unconscious processes, which parts are involved in the generation of consciousness? The approach pursued by Crick and Kock in their quest to understand the basis of consciousness is to focus on determining the neural correlates of visual consciousness – to determine the essential components (Koch, 2004). What, very briefly, are thought to be the key elements at the present time? Parvisi and Damasio (2001) propose that 'core consciousness (the simplest form of consciousness) occurs when the brain's representation devices generate an imaged, non-verbal account of how the organism's state is affected by the organism's interaction with . . . ' any facet of its environment. They suggest that representations in various brainstem nuclei of the current state of the organism form key input to more rostral brain structures (the cortex) for the generation of more composite representations of its state in relation to the outside world. The brainstem is a key part of the substrate of consciousness in another way also, because it plays an essential role in controlling the overall arousal level of the cortex. Severe damage to the brainstem precludes consciousness. However, a functional brainstem is not enough for consciousness in humans. Koch (2004), reviewing available evidence, suggests that the con- scious perception of objects may be associated with electrical activity circulating between particular neuronal populations in the inferior temporal cortex or the medial temporal lobe and the prefrontal cortex. And, likewise, activity between the medial temporal cortex and the frontal eye fields could be the essential neural correlates for seeing motion. He concludes that unless activity in the visual cortex (in the occipital lobe) directly projects to the front part of the cortex, activities in the visual cortex cannot directly enter awareness. Current theories tend to endorse the idea that conscious awareness probably depends upon the activity of recurrent circuits between structures within the brainstem and the somatosensory and cingulate cortices (Damasio, 1999), between the cortex and the thalamus (Churchland, 1996; Edelman and Tonini, 2000) and within the cortex. Edelman (2004) has recently proposed that the point in evolution at which the necessary reciprocal thalamo-cortical connectivity appeared was around the time of the emergence of mammals and birds from reptiles (note, however, that the last common ancestor of birds and mammals was in the early days of reptile evolution, about 310 million years ago, so unless this property emerged twice, it must have had a precursor dating back at least to early reptiles).

It is, however, very early days to speculate about when sentience may have evolved. As emphasized above, until we have a have a much better under-standing of the design of circuitry required for consciousness (and/or of what behavioural survival advantages it confers that may be detected), we will not be able to ascertain which species do or do not have it and when it may have arisen. How do we deal with this uncertainty in the meantime?

Living with uncertainty and hopes for the future

We cannot avoid, until such time as there is much greater certainty about which species are sentient, having to make judgements based on the balance of two principles, between which there can be some tension. The first is that since the matter is a morally important one, we should, as far as possible, give animals the benefit of the doubt and treat them as if they are sentient – as if they have the capacity for feelings and thus for suffering. The second is that efforts and resources for animal welfare should be prioritized and focused where they are needed, i.e. for sentient animals. The fact is that, despite the absence of a solid scientific basis for determining sentience, lines have to be drawn. In making such decisions, it is important to be clear about what is proven fact and what is subjective judgement (Sandøe et al, 2004), and of the costs and benefits.

Sentience is the fundamentally, morally important basis upon which concern for animal welfare rests. The animal kingdom is very large and we cannot avoid interacting or competing with many members of it for essential resources (e.g. food or space). We need to make sound judgements about which species are and are not sentient. It is to be hoped that scientific advances in behavioural approaches to determining sentience and/or in determination of the neuronal correlates of consciousness in humans and the presence or absence of functionally equivalent systems in other species will be made in the future.

References

Bermond, B. (1997) 'The myth of animal suffering', in Dol, M., Kasanmoentalib, S., Limbach, S., Rivas, E. and van den Bos, R. (eds) *Animal Consciousness and Animal Ethics*, Van Gorcum, Assen, The Netherlands, pp125–143

Churchland, P. (1996) *The Engine of Reason, the Seat of the Soul*, MIT Press, Cambridge, Massachusetts

Cowey, A. and Stoerig, P. (1995) 'Blindsight in monkeys', *Nature*, vol 373, pp247–249

Damasio, A. (1999) *The Feeling of What Happens: Body Emotion and the Making of Consciousness*, William Heinemann, London

Damasio, A. (2003) *Looking for Spinoza: Joy, Sorrow and the Feeling Brain*, William Heinemann, London

Dawkins, R. (2004) *The Ancestor's Tale: A Pilgrimage to the Dawn of Life*, Weidenfeld and Nicolson, London

Edelman, G. M. (2004) *Wider Than the Sky: The Phenomenal Gift of Consciousness*, Allen Lane, The Penguin Press, London

Edelman, G. M. and Tonini, G. (2000) *Consciousness: How Matter Becomes Imagination*, Allen Lane, The Penguin Press, London

Glynn, I. (1999) *An Anatomy of Thought*, Weidenfield and Nicolson, London

Griffin, D. R. and Speck, G. B. (2004) 'New evidence of animal consciousness', *Animal Cognition*, vol 7, pp5–18

Hampton, R. R. (2001) 'Rhesus monkeys know when they remember', *Proceedings of the National Academy of Sciences*, vol 98, pp5359–5362

Imhoff, M. L., Bounoua, L., Ricketts, T., Loucks, C., Harriss, R. and Lawrence, W. T. (2004) 'Global patterns in human consumption of net primary production', *Nature*, vol 429, pp870–873

Inman, A. and Shettleworth, S. J. (1999) 'Detecting metamemory in non-verbal subjects: A test with pigeons', *Journal of Experimental Psychology and Animal Behaviour*, vol 25, pp389–395

Kennedy, J. S. (1993) *The New Anthropomorphism*, Cambridge University Press, Cambridge

Kirkwood, J. K. (2001) 'Helminth diseases and wildlife conservation', in Chowdhury, N. and Aguirre, A. A. (eds) *Helminths of Wildlife*, Science Publishers, Enfield, USA and Plymouth, UK, pp77–88

Kirkwood, J. K. (2004a) 'The importance of animal welfare', in Perry, G. C. (ed) *The Welfare of the Laying Hen*, Proceedings of the World Poultry Science Association Symposium on the Welfare of the Laying Hen, Bristol, July 2003, CAB International, Oxford, pp1–7

Kirkwood, J. K. (2004b) 'Introduction and overview' of Science in the Service of Animal Welfare: The UFAW Symposium, Edinburgh, 2–4 April 2003, *Animal Welfare*, vol 13 supplement, ppS1–S2

Kirkwood, J. K. and Hubrecht, R. (2001) 'Consciousness, cognition and animal welfare', *Animal Welfare*, vol 10 supplement, ppS5–S17

Koch, C. (2004) *The Quest for Consciousness: A Neurobiological Approach*, Roberts, Englewood, Colorado

Ledoux, J. (1998) *The Emotional Brain*, Weidenfield and Nicolson, London

Macphail, E. M. (1998) *The Evolution of Consciousness*, Oxford University Press, Oxford

Milner, D. A. and Goodale, M. A. (1995) *The Visual Brain in Action*, Oxford University Press, Oxford

Nieuwenhuys, R., ten Donkelar, H. J. and Nicholson, C. (1998) *The Central Nervous System of Vertebrates*, Springer-Verlag, Berlin

Parvisi, J. and Damasio, A. (2001) 'Consciousness and the brainstem', *Cognition*, vol 79, pp135–139

Povinelli, D. J. and Vonk, J. (2003) 'Chimpanzee minds: Suspiciously human?', *Trends in Cognitive Sciences*, vol 7, pp157–160

Rollin, B. E. (1989) *The Unheeded Cry: Animal Consciousness, Animal Pain and Science*, Oxford University Press, Oxford

Rolls, E. T. (1999) *The Brain and Emotion*, Oxford University Press, Oxford

Ryder, R. D. (2000) *Animal Revolution: Changing Attitudes Towards Speciesism*, Berg, Oxford

Sandøe, P., Forkmann, B. and Christiansen, S. B. (2004) 'Scientific uncertainty – how should it be handled in relation to scientific advice regarding animal welfare issues?', *Animal Welfare*, vol 13 supplement, ppS121–S126

Sherwin, C. M. (2001) 'Can invertebrates suffer? Or, how robust is argument-by-anology?', *Animal Welfare*, vol 10 supplement, ppS103–S118

Wise, S. M. (2000) *Rattling the Cage: Towards Legal Rights for Animals*, Perseus Books, Cambridge, Massachusetts

Weiskrantz, L. (1997) *Consciousness Lost and Found*, Oxford University Press, Oxford

3

Animal Emotions and Animal Sentience and Why They Matter: Blending 'Science Sense' with Common Sense, Compassion and Heart

Marc Bekoff

University of Colorado, US

There is more to life than basic scientific knowledge.

(D. Papineau, 2005)

There's a certain tragic isolation in believing that humans stand apart in every way from the creatures that surround them, that the rest of creation was shaped exclusively for our use.

(New York Times, 2005)

Let's try to work together

Discussions of animal emotions and animal sentience are wonderful for raising difficult and frustrating questions. This chapter is intended to be a non-traditional essay and I hope it generates kind discussion and that what I talk about is not dismissed on the grounds that I'm simply losing my mind. I assure you I'm not. Well, at least I think I'm not. I simply want to put forth some ideas that some might find controversial. Throwing caution to the wind is a good thing to do from time to time. It makes us dig deeply into our minds and hearts to see who we are and what we think about matters at hand. And sometimes we don't like where we end up, which can be outside of our comfort zones.

Let's for the moment put differences aside and see what we can do. Let's engage people who use and abuse animals and try to convince them to change their ways. Let's be proactive and let's educate them. Conflict is inevitable but, as Martin Luther King stressed, reconciliation is the necessary complement of conflict.

A summary of 'big' issues and difficult and frustrating questions

In this chapter I raise a number of issues that are important to consider in discussions of animal emotions and animal sentience. I argue for a paradigm shift in how we study animal emotions and animal sentience and what we do with the information we already have, 'scientific' and otherwise. It's about time that the sceptics and naysayers had to 'prove' their claims that animals don't experience emotions or don't really feel pain, but just act 'as if' they do. And until such claims are proven, let's assume that numerous animals *do* experience rich emotions and do suffer all sorts of pain. Just because something supposedly worked in the past doesn't mean that it works now or that it ever did. Animal emotions and animal sentience matter very much, not only because what animals feel must be used first and foremost for influencing how we interact with and use such animals, but also because broad studies of animal emotions and animal sentience raise numerous 'big' questions about the nature of science itself. We can also learn much about ourselves when we ponder the nature of animal passions and beastly virtues. Some of the issues that I consider here include:

1   Are we *really* the only animals who experience a wide variety of feelings? In my view the real question is *why* emotions have evolved not *if* they have evolved in some animals. So, for example, it's a waste of time to ask if dogs or chimpanzees experience emotions such as joy, grief, anger and jealousy. Animals' emotions function as a 'social glue' and as 'social catalysts'. It is highly likely that many animals exclaim 'Wow!' or 'My goodness, what is happening?' as they go through their days, enjoying some activities and also experiencing enduring pain and suffering at the hands of humans. *What animals feel is more important than what they know when we consider what sorts of treatment are permissible. When in doubt, err on the side of the animals.*

2   What are some of the difficult questions in studies of animal emotions and animal sentience that go 'beyond' science, or what we think science is and what we think science can do? Is science the only show in town? Are there different ways of knowing, and what might they be? How can we blend them all together?

3   Is what we call 'science' really better than other ways of knowing (e.g. common sense or intuition) for explaining, understanding, and appreciating the nature of animal emotions and animal sentience and for predicting behaviour? This is an empirical question for which there really are no comparative data, despite claims that science and objectivity are better. Until

the data are in we must be careful in claiming that one sort of explanation is *always* better than others. It's poor scholarship to take a univocal approach in the absence of supportive data. Let's also not forget that many explanations about evolution are stories with more or less authenticity or 'truth'.

4   Is science really value-free? What background values underpin how science is done and data are interpreted? Are scientists unfeeling automatons who don't have a point of view that influences their research? *Asking questions about science is not to be anti-science.*

5   Are anecdotes really useless? Is anthropomorphism really all that bad? Is subjectivity heresy? Should we have to apologize for naming the animals we study?

6   Do *individual* animals have inherent value independent of the instrumental value that we impose on them?

7   What do we *really know* about animal emotions and animal sentience? Who has it – what do we think the taxonomic distribution of animal sentience is and why? Does this really matter for influencing how we treat other animals?

8   Do we know more than we think we know?

9   Does what we *really know* about animal emotions and animal sentience translate into action on behalf of animal beings?

10   What does each of us *really believe and feel* about animal emotions and animal sentience?

11   Does what we *really believe and feel* about animal emotions and animal sentience translate into action on behalf of animal beings?

12   For those of us whose work involves using animals, what do we feel about animal emotions and animal sentience when we're alone, away from colleagues, and pondering how we make our livings? Are we proud of what we do to and for other animals and do we want others, including our children, to follow our path? Should we continue what we're doing?

13   What do we tell others, including our children, about how we make our livings? What words do we use and how do we explain the emotions and passions of animals whom we use and abuse for our and not their ends.

14   Who gets paid by whom, and why do so many slaughter house workers apparently not like their jobs and seek counselling? Harming animals intentionally surely can't be 'fun' or good for one's psychological well-being. These are among the practical matters that need to be considered.

15   How do we remain hopeful? There are some 'good things' happening, such as the conference on animal sentience organized by Compassion in World Farming Trust, out of which this book arose. And the recent victory of the McLibel Two, Helen Steel and David Morris, against McDonald's, gives us hope. I believe we must remain hopeful, but time isn't on our side. We're engaged in a rapidly growing social movement and we must educate people and have them consider difficult questions that are easier to put aside.

16   Where do we go from here? How do we educate and open minds and hearts? How might we work together to make the world a better place for all beings? We all know that the situation at hand *must* change, so how are we going to accomplish our goals?

17   To these ends, I endorse the statement agreed by delegates at the conference out of which this book arose: 'This conference calls on the UN, the WTO, the World Organisation for Animal Health (OIÉ) and their member governments to join us in recognizing that sentient animals are capable of suffering, and that we all have a duty to preserve the habitat of wild animals and to end cruel farming systems and other trades and practices which inflict suffering on animals.'

18   But should sentience be the key factor, and if so, why? Isn't just the fact that they are alive sufficient for us to leave animals alone? There are always difficult and frustrating questions to ponder and they won't go away if we play ostrich and bury our heads in the sand.

19   We must change minds and hearts, and time is of the essence. Far too many animals are harmed each and every second of each and every day worldwide on our behalf 'in the name of science' or in the name of 'this' or 'that'. We really are an intrusive species that brings far too much pain and suffering to other animals when we use and abuse them and when we 'redecorate nature'.

20   If one loves animals how can she or he eat them, especially, but not only, factory-farmed animals?

21   Why do we do what we do? Decisions about animal use and abuse are *individual* choices and none of us should claim that we do things 'because others make us do it'. Harming and killing other beings – human animals, other animals and yes, even other forms of life such as trees, plants and those living in bodies of water – is a personal choice. It's all too easy for a person to say something like 'I didn't want to harm that animal, but I had to do it because someone made me do it'. If we all own up to our personal choices, I really believe that the world will become a more peaceful place. And what a poor example the line of reasoning 'Oh, someone else made me do it!' sets for children. Each of us is responsible for our actions and the convenience of blaming others – including and especially large impersonal entities – should be discouraged. Individual responsibility is critical. It's a good idea for all of us to leave our comfort zones and to grow – to expand our horizons as we work to replace cruelty with compassion and dig deeply into our hearts. An important question to ask is 'Would we do what we did again?' and if so, why. We need a paradigm shift in how we study animal emotions and animal sentience.

22   We can and we do make a difference. Animal emotions and animal sentience matter very much. What should our guidelines be? Perhaps there are some types of studies that simply cannot be done.

23   I believe that good or right-minded people can do and/or allow horrible things to be done to animals because they really haven't travelled deep into their hearts or because they just don't know. So we need to educate them, and that is something we *can* do. The bottom line is that we must change minds and hearts and time is of the essence. If we can change minds and hearts and especially current practices in which animals are used and abused, we are making progress and there is hope.

24   Often, what is called 'good welfare' simply isn't 'good enough'. Animals deserve more and we can *always* do better.

Eyes tell it all: Dare to look at them if you can (I can't)

Let's begin with the eyes, the magnificently complex organs that provide a window to the world. Across many species an individual's eyes reflect what they are feeling, wide open in glee and sunken in despair. Jane Goodall writes about the young chimpanzee Flint's sunken eyes as he grieved the loss of his mother, Flo, and Konrad Lorenz also noted how the eyes of a grieving goose sink back into its head. Jody McConnery wrote of traumatized orphan gorillas: 'The light in their eyes simply goes out, and they die.' And Aldo Leopold wrote of the 'green fire' in the eyes of a dying wolf whom he'd just shot. I often wonder about animals whose eyes we can't look into.

Doug Smith, who leads the Yellowstone wolf reintroduction project, also recently wrote about the eyes of a wolf named Five, and how much he learned from looking into them: 'The last time I looked into Five's eyes ... she was walking away from an elk her pack had killed... As we flew overhead, she looked up at us, as she always did. But the look she gave me had changed. To gaze into the eyes of a wild wolf is one of the holiest of grails for lovers of nature; some say what you see is untamed, unspoiled wildness... That day in January, something had gone out of Five's eyes; she looked worried. Always before her gaze had been defiant.'

And then there's the story of Rick Swope and the chimpanzee JoJo. When Rick was asked why he risked his life to save JoJo who had fallen into a moat in the Detroit Zoo he answered: 'I looked into his eyes. It was like looking into the eyes of a man. And the message was: Won't *anybody* help me?' Recently, three men near my hometown of Boulder tried to save a young mountain lion who'd been hit by a car. The lions' eyes begged them to do so. And I stopped killing cats as part of a doctoral research project when Speedo, a very intelligent cat, looked at me and asked, 'Why me?'

Eyes tell it all and, if we can stand it, we should look into the fear-filled eyes of animals who suffer at our hands, in horrible conditions of captivity, in slaughter houses and in zoos, rodeos and circuses. Dare to look into the sunken eyes of animals who are afraid or feeling other sorts of pain, and then try to deny to yourself and to others that these individuals aren't feeling *anything*.

Writing about the importance of eyes makes a great case for some of our intuitions being borne out by hard science. In the prestigious journal *Nature*, there was a very interesting study called 'Staring fear in the face'. It turns out that the eyes are of paramount importance in knowing that another human is feeling fear; people tend to look at the eyes, and more so when the face is fearful. A study of a woman with a specific deficit in recognizing fearful facial expressions due to damage to a region of her brain called the amygdala showed that that she couldn't perceive fear because she didn't look spontaneously towards the eyes. Rather, she judged the face as having a neutral expression. It's also likely that the eyes are not only important in perceiving fear but also other emotions. The results of the study made me think that perhaps one reason that so many people can't look into the eyes of an animal who is afraid or otherwise suffering is because the people 'know' just what the animal is feelings and it's easier to deny this if one doesn't look at their eyes and feel the fear emanating from the poor beast.

The 'A' words – anecdote, anthropomorphism and activism

First let's consider the first two of what I call the three 'A' words, *anecdote*, *anthropomorphism* and *activism*. I've argued over and over again that the plural of 'anecdote' is 'data' and that we *must* be anthropomorphic. Anecdotes and stories drive much of science although, of course, they aren't enough on their own. But to claim they aren't a useful heuristic flies in the face of how hard science and soft science are conducted.

Anthropomorphism has survived a long time because it is a necessity, but it must be done carefully and biocentrically, making every attempt to maintain the animal's point of view by asking 'What is it like to be that individual?' Claims that anthropomorphism has no place in science or that anthropomorphic predictions and explanations are less accurate than behaviourist or more mechanistic or reductionistic explanations are *not* supported by any data. This is an empirical question for which there are no data. Anthropomorphism is alive and well, as it should be. But, let me stress again that it must be used with care.

Some people argue against the use of the 'A' words without seeming to know that they too are using them. For example, a representative of the American Zoo and Aquarium Association (AZA) recently claimed that we mustn't be anthropomorphic and that it's bad science to attribute human-like feelings to animals. He was critical of people who claimed that an elephant at the Los Angeles Zoo 'wasn't doing well', but in the same breath he claimed that the elephant was 'doing well' and shouldn't be sent to an elephant sanctuary. What he meant is that *he* can be anthropomorphic but others can't be. He can say that an animal in a particular zoo is doing well, but others can't say the elephant is *not* doing well. We must not let people get away with such sloppy and self-serving claims. In view of that sort of inconsistency (and hypocrisy), it's also important to note that the AZA itself has concluded in its *own* executive summary that: 'Little to no systematic research has been conducted on the impact of visits to zoos and aquariums on visitor conservation knowledge, awareness, affect or behavior'. So much for their claims that zoos are important for purposes of education and conservation.

Science isn't value-free: Three more 'A' words

Science isn't value-free. We agree and disagree about the best way to study animal emotions and animal sentience, just as we agree and disagree about what is the best bank in which to place our money. Science is but one way of knowing and is not the only show in town. We need to dispense with the three 'A' words that often characterize science – *arrogant, authoritarian and autonomous.*

I love being a scientist and doing science, but remaining open to other ways of knowing enriches me and makes me think 'out of the box'. I don't think it's a matter of science *or* subjectivity but rather science *and* subjectivity. We also need to be able to live with uncertainty and give up control. Science and scientists must be dynamic, open and compassionate. Asking questions about science is *not* to be anti-science.

What does it mean to 'know' something?

It's important to blend 'science sense' with common sense. I maintain that we *know* that some non-human animals feel *something* some of the time, just as do human animals. It's nonsense to claim that we don't know if dogs, pigs, cows or chickens feel pain or have a point of view about whether they like or don't like being exposed to certain treatments. Who are we kidding? Frankly, I think we're kidding ourselves.

The privacy of mind and the use of a double standard: It's 'just science'

The minds and feelings of individuals other than oneself are private. Access is limited because we can't really get into the head or heart of another being. Sceptics often use this solipsistic line of reasoning, but it really can be a dead end when practical matters are of primary concern. Of course other minds are private, but that doesn't stop us trying to understand what another human is thinking or feeling or stop us using this information to make future compassionate decisions.

When considering the emotional lives of animals, sceptics can be rather sanguine concerning the notions of proof or what is actually known, often employing a double standard. In practice this means that they require greater evidence for the existence of animal emotions than they do in other areas of science, a point stressed by the late Donald Griffin. But because subjective experiences are private matters, residing in the brains (and hearts) of individuals and inaccessible in their entirety to others, it's easy for sceptics to claim that we can never be sure about animal emotions and to declare the case closed. Nonetheless, a cursory glance at many studies in animal behaviour, behavioural ecology, neurobiology and biomedicine shows clearly that only rarely do we ever come to know *everything* about the questions at hand, yet this does not stop us from making accurate predictions concerning what an individual is likely to do in a given situation or from suggesting the use of a wide variety of treatments to help alleviate different diseases. This is all in the patent absence of incontrovertible proof, in the absence of total certainty, something that few scientists can ever offer.

It's also important to consider the power of prediction. No one has yet shown that one form of prediction is better than others and this is still an open question (Bekoff, 2004, 2006). Is science sense a better predictor than common sense in the study of animal emotions and sentience? I can't find any hard data on this question (even if people once thought the world was flat). Clearly, even when scientific data are available, individuals interpret them differently and they may not even be used. This is so in other fields as well. Sandra Andelman has shown that scientific data about species' abundance actually plays little or no role in determining which species are placed on the endangered species list in the US. Opportunism and other factors play more of a role.

No science is perfect, it's 'just science'. But 'just science' is not a pejorative phrase. We need to come clean about what science is, what we can prove and not prove, and how good the scientific data really are. Scientists are responsible not only for sharing their findings with the public but also for letting them know that science *is* a value-laden and imperfect enterprise. Scientists shouldn't make science something that it isn't.

Arguing against speciesism and for evolutionary continuity

> I have stressed the degree to which perceived animal/human differences in the brain's organization of feeling and emotion are probably due to artefacts rather than to a real gap between primates (including humans) and other mammalian orders. But that is not to say there is no real difference at all between humans and other animals. There may indeed be a real difference in brain organization of emotion. If so, however, it is quantitative in nature and moderate in degree – not a qualitative or massive difference.
>
> (Berridge 2003, p41)

> Neural substrates of feeling and emotion are distributed throughout the brain, from front to back, and top to bottom. The same brain

structures are implicated in affective reactions for both humans and other animals.

(Berridge 2003, p42)

Now, what about *speciesism*? Are we really the only species in which emotions have evolved. It's not a matter of 'them' versus 'us'. Over the years a variety of criteria has been used to separate 'them' from 'us' – tool use, language, culture, rationality, consciousness and a sense of self – and all have failed. Maybe we're the only species that cooks food. There are differences but there are also many similarities between humans and non-human animals. Evolutionary continuity is important to consider, the idea that there are differences in *degree* rather than differences in *kind* in behavioural phenotypes and in cognitive and emotional capacities among animals and between humans and other animals. This is an idea – descent with modification – that Charles Darwin argued long ago. There isn't a great divide as some argue there is.

A few years ago I was reading the prestigious journal *Science* and saw the following quotation: 'More than any other species, we are the beneficiaries and victims of a wealth of emotional experience.' Professor R. J. Dolan, who wrote this, cannot know that this statement is true. Indeed, it just might be that other animals experience more vivid emotions than we do. This sort of humanocentrism is what plagues the study of animal emotions. Why are we so special, why are we such deeply feeling animals whereas other animals aren't? I find it difficult to accept that we should be the standard against which other animals should be compared. Just look at the state of the world today.

They dock pigs, don't they? Does a whimpering dog feel something? Who are we kidding?

Surely a whimpering or playing dog, or a chimpanzee in a tiny cage or grieving the loss of a friend, or a baby pig having her tail cut off – 'docked' as this horrific and inexcusable procedure is called – or having her teeth ground down on a grindstone, feels something. Recent data show that chronic pain is associated with docking (United States Department of Agriculture, 2005). *Is this really surprising? Who are we kidding?* Cows also can be moody, hold grudges and nurture friendships. *Is this really surprising*? Animals aren't unfeeling objects. They don't like being shocked, cut up, starved, chained, stunned, crammed into tiny cages, tied up, ripped away from family and friends, or isolated.

Numerous pigs (and other farm animals) are mistreated daily in factory farms. Scientific research shows that pigs suffer from stress, anxiety and depression. Surely it's not a big jump to claim that they don't like having their tails cut off and their teeth ground down. Their squealing tells us that, doesn't it? Michael Mendl notes that pigs can be stressed by *normal* farm management procedures. Indeed, this and other findings support the idea that all too often what is called 'good welfare' simply is not good enough.

Of course animal emotions are not necessarily identical to ours and there's no reason to think they must be. Their hearts and stomachs and brains also differ from ours and from those of other species, but this doesn't stop us from saying they have hearts, stomachs and brains. There's dog-joy and chimpanzee-joy and pig-joy, and dog-grief, chimpanzee-grief and pig-grief.

'Oh, I harm animals "In the name of science"'

Some people justify what they do to animals 'in the name of science' or in the name of 'this' or 'that'. This is unacceptable. There is no reason to continue to harm and to kill billions of animals and we must take to task those who claim that there is.

'I do what I do because there are no adequate non-animal substitutes': The three 'E's

This is a lame excuse with no force whatsoever. Numerous organizations list non-animal substitutes that fit what I call the 'E' category – they are surely more *ethical*, and at least as good or more *educational* and *economical*. And of course, there is much evidence that many non-animal scientific procedures yield results that are as good as or better than procedures that use animals. A search on Google resulted in more than 1,300,000 'hits' for the phrase 'humane education', 1,120,000 for the phrase 'humane science' and about 23,800 for the phrase 'non-animal alternatives'. Needless to say, there is much information out there!

Where to from here? A potpourri of ideas and shifting the paradigm

We need to take the sceptics to task and turn the tables and have sceptics 'prove' that animals don't have emotions rather than our having to prove that they do. I recall an event at a symposium that was held at the Smithsonian Institution in October 2000 to celebrate the publication of *The Smile of a Dolphin*, a book about animal emotions that I edited. Cynthia Moss talked about elephants and showed a wonderful video of these highly intelligent and emotional beasts. During the question and answer period a former programme leader from the National Science Foundation asked Cynthia 'How do you know these animals are feeling the emotions you claim they are?' and Cynthia aptly replied 'How do you know they're not?'

This was a very important exchange because of course he couldn't answer his own question with certainty and neither could Cynthia. However, science sense, along with common sense and solid evolutionary biology, would favour her

Figure 3.1 *Four members of an elephant herd that is being studied by Iain Douglas-Hamilton and his colleagues in the Samburu Reserve in Northern Kenya*

Source: Photo by Jan Nystrom

Note: Elephants form social groups called matriarchies and individuals of different ages (who clearly vary in size, as shown here) form very close social bonds with one another. Elephants experience a wide range of emotions ranging from joy when they play to grief when they lose a friend. They also empathize with other individuals. Joyce Poole, a seasoned expert in elephant behaviour wrote about a mother who had lost her newborn: 'As I watched Tonie's vigil over her dead newborn, I got my first very strong feeling that elephants grieve. I will never forget the expression on her face, her eyes, her mouth, the way she carried her ears, her head, and her body. Every part of her spelled grief.' Poole also wrote: 'It is hard to watch elephants' remarkable behaviour during a family or bond group greeting ceremony, the birth of a new family member, a playful interaction, the mating of a relative, the rescue of a family member, or the arrival of a musth male, and not imagine that they feel very strong emotions which could be best described by words such as joy, happiness, love, feelings of friendship, exuberance, amusement, pleasure, compassion, relief, and respect.' I had the pleasure of visiting Iain Douglas-Hamilton in Samburu in July 2005 and was amazed by my first-hand experience of the deep emotional lives of these magnificent animals who form extremely close social bonds with other group members. Clearly, elephant social groups should never be broken up so that individuals can be shipped here and there to live miserable lives in captivity.

view over his. It's wonderful that mainstream journals are publishing essays on animal emotions. For example, the article 'Elephant breakdown' about social trauma in elephants recently appeared in *Nature*. And the *New York Times* editorial 'My little chickadee' (New York Times, 2005) is also a most welcomed event.

Just because something seemed to work in the past doesn't mean it works now. We need a paradigm shift in how we study animal emotions and animal sentience and what we do with what we 'know' and feel about animal emotions and animal sentience. The herd instinct must be strongly resisted, as must thinking such as 'Well, it worked for my mentor and his mentor, so it must be right'. Historical momentum in methodology and in interpretation and explanation need to be reassessed critically. We also need to change funding priorities by not buying into the zeitgeist of 'science over all'.

It's essential that we do better than our ancestors and we surely have the resources to do so. My optimism leads me in no other direction. But I am personally ashamed at how humans abuse animals. I am sure future generations will look back on us with shock and horror about our treatment of other animal beings and wonder how we missed what is so very obvious about animal emotions, and how much harm and suffering we brought to billions upon billions of individuals. How could we ever do the things that we did to individuals who clearly were suffering at our hands for our, and not their, benefit? How could we ever allow so many individual beings to suffer horrific pain just so that we could study them or eat them? I just don't know. I really just don't know.

I often imagine a dinner table conversation between a parent (a scientist) and his or her child concerning, for example, studies in which the nature of mother–infant bonds are studied by taking the infant away from their mother.

> Child: So, what did you do today?
>
> Parent: Oh, I removed two baby chimpanzees from their mother to see how they reacted to this treatment.
>
> Child: Hmm, do you think the baby minded being taken from her mother?
>
> Parent: Well, I'm not sure so that's why I did it.
>
> Child: Oh, but what do you think that the baby's fighting to get back to her mother and her writhing and screaming meant? Surely she didn't like it. We already knew that, didn't we? Why do you do this to young animals and their mom?
>
> Parent: It's getting late, isn't it time for bed?

Of course, this sort of conversation could be had for the innumerable situations in which we subject millions of individual animal beings to suffering. I apologize to each and every individual animal and hope that my scientific colleagues and I can make a difference in their lives.

Getting out and doing something: All we need is love

We must continue to be the voices for voiceless animals and add to their 'vociferous voices of suffering' as the philosopher Graham Harvey puts it. Numerous animals really are crying for help and they are not truly 'voiceless'.

As we change the paradigm and move forward we are in a good position to use the precautionary principle. Basically, this principle maintains that a lack of full scientific certainty should not be used as an excuse to delay taking action on some issue. So, in the arena of animal emotions and animal sentience, I have argued that we *do* know enough to make informed decisions about animal emotions and animal sentience and why they matter. We shouldn't tolerate a double standard of proof. Sceptic's stories aren't any better or truer than ours. And even if we might be wrong *some* of the time this does not mean we're wrong *all* of the time. And so what if we're wrong some of the time or unsure about how to proceed? At least we won't be adding more cruelty to an already cruel world. And I (and others) have argued that when in doubt we should err on the side of the individual animal.

It's okay to be sentimental and to go from the heart. We need more compassion and love in science, more heartfelt and heartful science. Simply put, we must 'mind' animals and redecorate nature very carefully. All we need is love...

Often 'good welfare' simply isn't 'good enough'. Animals deserve more and we can *always* do better.

Acknowledgement

I thank Jan Nystrom, Gay Bradshaw, Graham Harvey, and Jessica Pierce for comments on this essay.

References and further reading

Andelman, S. J. (2005) 'The science of land conservation', Lecture, University of Utah, 4 March 2005

AZA, Executive summary, 'Visitor learning in zoos and aquariums', available at, www.aza.org/ConEd/VisitorLearning/Documents/VisitorLearningExecutiveSummary. pdf

Bekoff, M. (1994) 'Cognitive ethology and the treatment of non-human animals: How matters of mind inform matters of welfare', *Animal Welfare*, vol 3, pp75–96

Bekoff, M. (ed) (2000) *The Smile of a Dolphin: Remarkable Accounts of Animal Emotions*, Random House/Discovery Books, Washington, DC

Bekoff, M. (2000) 'Animal emotions: Exploring passionate natures', *BioScience*, vol 50, pp861–870

Bekoff, M. (2002) *Minding Animals: Awareness, Emotions, and Heart*, Oxford University Press, New York

Bekoff, M. (2004) 'Wild justice and fair play: Cooperation, forgiveness, and morality in animals', *Biology and Philosophy*, vol 19, pp489–520

Bekoff, M. (2006) *Animal Passions and Beastly Virtues: Reflections on Redecorating Nature*, Temple University Press, Philadelphia

Bekoff, M. and Nystrom, J. (2004) 'The other side of silence: Rachel Carson's views of animals', *Zygon*, vol 39(4), pp861–883

Berridge, K. (2003) 'Comparing the emotional brains of humans and other animals', in Davidson, R. J., Scherer, K. R. and Goldsmith, H. H. (eds) *Handbook of Affective Sciences*, Oxford University Press, New York, pp25–51

Bradshaw, G. A., Schore, A. N., Brown, J. L., Poole, J. H. and Moss, C. J. (2005) 'Elephant breakdown', *Nature*, vol 433, p807

Darwin, C. (1872/1998) *The Expression of the Emotions in Man and Animals*, third edition, Oxford University Press, New York, (with an introduction, afterword and commentaries by Paul Ekman)

Dawkins, M. S. (1992) *Through Our Eyes Only?* Oxford, New York

Dolan, R. (2002) 'Emotion, cognition, and behavior', *Science*, vol 298, pp1191–1194

Duncan, I. J. H. (2002) 'Poultry welfare: Science or subjectivity?' *British Poultry Science*, vol 43, pp643–652

Goodall, J. and Bekoff, M. (2002) *The Ten Trusts: What We Must Do to Care for the Animals We Love*, HarperCollins, San Francisco, California

Griffin, D. R. (2001) *Animal Minds*, University of Chicago Press, Chicago

Laville, S. (2005) 'Lab monkeys "scream with fear" in tests', *The Guardian*, Internet Edition, 8 February, available at ww.guardian.co.uk/uk_news/story/0,3604,1407818,00.html

Leake, J. (2005) 'The secret life of moody cows', *The Sunday Times*, Internet Edition, 27 February, available at www.timesonline.co.uk/article/0,,2087-1502933,00.html

Lorenz, K. Z. (1991) *Here I am – Where Are You?* Harcourt Brace Jovanovich, New York

McMillan, F. D. and Lance K. (2004) *Unlocking the Animal Mind: How Your Pet's Feelings Hold the Key to His Health and Happiness*, Rodale, Emmaus, Pennysylvania

McRae, M. (2000) 'Central Africa's orphaned gorillas: Will they survive the wild?', *National Geographic*, February, pp86–97 (source of Jody McConnery's quotation)

New York Times (2005) 'My little chickadee', Internet Edition, 3 March, available at www.nytimes.com/2005/03/03/opinion/03thu4.html?n= Top%2fOpinion%2fEditorials%20and%20Op%2dEd%2fEditorials

Papineau, D. (2005) 'Looking ahead to future brain studies', a review of '*The new brain sciences: Perils and prospects*', Rees, D. and Rose, S. (eds), *Nature*, vol 433, p803

Poole, J. (1998) 'An exploration of a commonality between ourselves and elephants', *Etica & Animali*, vol 9, pp85–110

Preston, S. D. and de Waal, F. B. M. (2002) 'Empathy: Its ultimate and proximate bases', *Behavioral and Brain Sciences*, vol 25, pp1–72

Rollin, B. E. (1998) *The Unheeded Cry: Animal Consciousness, Animal Pain and Science*, Iowa State University Press, Ames, Iowa

Smith, D. W. (2005) 'Meet Five, Nine, and Fourteen, Yellowstone's heroine wolves', *Wildlife Conservation*, February, pp28–33

Sneddon, L. U. (2003) 'The evidence for pain in fish: The use of morphine as an analgesic', *Applied Animal Behaviour Science*, vol 83, pp153–162

UFAW Symposium (2001) 'Consciousness, cognition and animal welfare', *Animal Welfare*, vol 10 supplement

United States Department of Agriculture (2005) 'Settling doubts about livestock stress', *Agricultural Research*, March, vol 53, no 3, available at www.ars.usda.gov/is/AR/archive/mar05/stress0305.htm

Vuilleumier, P. (2005) 'Staring fear in the face', *Nature*, vol 433, pp22–23

Wemelsfelder, F. and Lawrence, A. B. (2001) 'Qualitative assessment of animal behaviour as an on-farm welfare-monitoring tool', *Acta Agriculturae Scandinavica, A*, vol 51, supplement 30, pp21–25

4
Animal Welfare: What is the Role of Science?

Peter Sandøe, Stine B. Christiansen
and Björn Forkman
Royal Veterinary and Agricultural University, Denmark

> They administered beatings to dogs with perfect indifference, and
> made fun of those who pitied the creatures as if they had felt pain.
> They said that the animals were clocks; that the cries they emitted
> when struck, were only the noise of a little spring which had been
> touched, but that the whole body was without feelings. They nailed
> poor animals up on boards by their four paws to vivisect them and see
> the circulation of the blood which was a great subject of conversation.
> (Fontaine, 1968/1738)

The 18th century scientists described in these comments, made by Nicolas
Fontaine, were influenced by the French philosopher René Descartes. Descartes
defended the view that animals are unable to have conscious experiences – that
animals are in this respect like machines. What is noticeable about the quotation
is not only the vivid way in which the attitudes of the scientists are portrayed but
also the fact that the eyewitness does not share the scientists' attitudes. Instead
he displays common-sense compassion for the 'poor' animals.

Psychological schools of animal behaviour with an interest in the study of
cognitive processes existed at the beginning of the 20th century, but mainstream biological science only started to take animal sentience seriously in the
second half of the 20th century. Moreover, the growth in scientific study of the
welfare of farm animals in the 1970s was mainly due to external pressures. In
the mid-1960s, Ruth Harrison, with her book *Animal Machines*, triggered a
public debate about the way animals are treated in modern intensive production systems. In response to this debate, governments in (primarily)
Northern Europe began funding research on farm animal welfare. Out of
existing disciplines such as ethology, veterinary pathology, veterinary epidemiology and stress physiology, animal welfare evolved as a new field of
biological research.

Four decades of research into animal welfare have produced a huge number of results: these both assist, contradict and qualify our common-sense views about how animals are affected by their treatment in agricultural production, animal-based research, zoos, circuses and other contexts. However, it is important not to lose sight of the common sense with which the whole process began. Our main message in this paper is therefore twofold: on the one hand, common sense needs to be informed by the results of scientific research, but on the other, we should make sure, in the future, that we take scientific views of animal sentience with a pinch of salt.

Applied and disciplinary science

Animal welfare science is a form of *applied science*. It more or less takes as its starting point problems that have been defined by society. For example, one of the problems raised by Ruth Harrison's book was whether it is bad for hens to live in battery systems rather than free range systems. To deal with this question, animal welfare science has to draw on methods and results from traditional, *disciplinary* science. As a result of this, the discipline of ethology, the scientific study of animal behaviour, has so far had a major impact on the development of animal welfare science – so much so, that people with a scientific interest in animal welfare often call themselves applied ethologists.

In basic science the primary aim is to understand the world. Basic science is normally disciplinary, so that it is possible to understand why a scientific problem is being studied without going beyond the specific discipline in which the scientist is working. Most disciplines have a high degree of specialization, and indeed this tendency is becoming more and more pronounced with time. The result is that, increasingly, each discipline has its own history and logic. Specialization helps to determine not just what questions are interesting but also how they should be answered and what types of answer are of value.

Where an applied ethologist might ask 'Do sows need nest building material or not?', a scientist doing basic work in ethology would probably find the question 'Why is the domestic pig one of the few hoof-bearing animals that constructs a nest?' much more interesting. In basic science, questions become more interesting the more generally applicable they are. The first question above is very restricted. As formulated, it applies only to sows kept in captivity. It follows that answers to it will not help us to understand the behaviour of other species, nor will they shed light on the behaviour of pigs under other circumstances. The second question, on the other hand, puts the behaviour of the pig into a wider perspective by looking at many different species of hoof bearing animals.

Other disciplines that have proved relevant to the study of animal welfare are stress physiology, in which chronic stress reactions, in particular, have been taken to signal decreased welfare, and veterinary pathology, in which disease is treated as an indicator of welfare problems. Often veterinary pathology is used in combination with veterinary epidemiology to investigate the prevalence of welfare problems in flocks or larger populations of animals.

The disciplines mentioned here are quite broad. Particularly in the case of ethology, the scope is much too wide for one scientist to master the whole field. This means that researchers going into the study of animal welfare will typically specialize in different sub-disciplines. Each of these will have a very narrow focus and hence involve the study of a very limited aspect of the world. The following analogy may be useful:

Imagine a group of people standing in a large house trying to look at the world through small windows. Some of the people can see out, although each of these people has just one window to look through. Sighted people typically view the parts of the world they can see in an extremely accurate way, and each tends to think that he or she has a better view of the world than other people with a view. However, when it comes to questions about how the world as a whole is, this has to be found out by a group of blind people who speak to the sighted people and try to build a coherent picture out of their different descriptions. Moreover, there are various power relations between the people. Some of the seeing people are more powerful than others, although the power may shift over time. And the blind people are generally underdogs who survive partly by making alliances with the seeing people. Each seeing person represents a scientific sub-discipline. The blind people are applied scientists.

To illustrate the point that disciplinary boundaries affect the way animal welfare is assessed one can examine the case of battery hens and free range hens. To make a very long and very complex story short and simple, one could say that two principal approaches have developed here. That is, some applied scientists have based their views on ethology. They have arrived at the conclusion that free range hens have a better life than battery hens in traditional barren cages because they can exercise a number of behaviours that battery hens cannot (e.g. dust bathe, scratch and lay their eggs in a nest). Other applied scientists have based their views on veterinary pathology. They have come to the conclusion that battery hens have the better life because their mortality rates are much lower than those of free range hens.

Animal welfare science

Applied animal welfare science is a form of problem solving. A problem or question is raised by society or some more limited constituency within it – for example, do sows need nesting material? The task of the animal welfare scientist is then to find the answer to that specific question. Now, the applied scientists may reach their conclusions in different ways, be it through physiological or be it through behavioural measures. In fact in many cases results supported from various sources are ideal. This means that applied research tends to rely more on interdisciplinary studies than basic science does. Overall the applied sciences rely heavily on advances made in the more basic sciences. These advances are put to use in new ways, and/or are shown to have implications not originally foreseen.

Like the basic sciences, the study of animal welfare has developed its own set of rules and assumptions. Although an interdisciplinary approach is widely taken, not all disciplines or approaches are accepted to the same extent. This is perhaps because, amongst most scientists working in animal welfare, there has been a greater readiness to accept novel approaches from some fields (e.g. biology) than others.

In the mid-1990s, fluctuating asymmetries/developmental instability became a popular field in behavioural ecology and numerous articles were published as a result (Polak, 2002). Essentially the theory is that animals have genotypes that code for symmetry in various characters, and that any deviation from this symmetry is caused by environmental stress. Hence animals of high quality, or which have not been exposed to stressors, should be symmetric for these characters. The notion that one can measure the intensity of the stressors an animal has experienced by measuring its symmetry was picked up in applied ethology and, while there are numerous problems with this application, it has been considered a serious possibility and various researchers have considered the idea (Klingenberg, 2003; Tuyttens, 2003).

About five years later, Françoise Wemelsfelder and her team published an article on qualitative assessment of the welfare status of pigs (Wemelsfelder et al, 2000). In such assessments the observer applies their own words to the behaviour of the animal, using labels such as 'timid', 'inquisitive' or 'active' – rather than trying to measure the behaviour by (say) counting the animal's number of steps. Wemelsfelder and her team have published a number of articles since 2000, but despite this, few attempts appear to have been made by others to use or evaluate her methodology. The qualitative approach is, however, similar to one that is well established in human personality research as well as sensory research (Oreskovich et al, 1991; Muir et al, 1995). Thus it cannot be dismissed as an approach lacking general scientific recognition.

While there might be other explanations, it is probable that the differing reactions to these two approaches are rooted in a scientific tradition within applied ethology. Quantitative methods are much more common in the various disciplines in biology, whereas qualitative methods are used sparsely there if at all. The choice of scientific method is a conservative one. This is not necessarily a negative trait, it is merely something of which we should be aware.

Equally, in basic biology there is a tendency for research areas to become popular at one time and unpopular at another. Stereotypies were much studied during the latter years of the 1980s and the early years of the 1990s, but interest has since tapered off. The study of individual differences in animals took off at the beginning of the 1990s, but later (with some exceptions) interest in it declined, and so on. This does not mean that what is found is any less genuinely interesting, nor does it mean that the relevant scientific propositions are untrue. It does suggest, however, that we ought to recognize that very probably, at any given moment, a number of problems will not be studied simply because they do not fall within the current sphere of interest.

Assessing animal welfare – beyond science

So far it has been argued that science shapes our understanding of animal welfare as a result both of the assumptions we make about underlying scientific disciplines and of the changing fashions (so to speak) within these discipline. It may be important to challenge scientific assumptions to obtain a full and rich understanding of what life is like for the animals. However, it is also important to be aware that more than science is called for when it comes to the assessment and management of animal welfare.

It is now widely recognized that assessments of animal welfare involve a number of assumptions that are *ethical* in nature (e.g. Tannenbaum, 1991; Sandøe et al, 2003). Notably, and most obviously, it matters a great deal how animal welfare is defined in the first place – whether in terms of animal function, of the balance of enjoyment or pleasure and suffering or pain, of preference satisfaction or of natural living (Duncan and Fraser, 1997; Appleby and Sandøe, 2002; Fraser, 2003).

The issue of how to define animal welfare is just one among several ethical issues that underlie discussions of animal welfare. To accept that animals may be used, for example, for farming purposes, is to agree that some restriction on the animals' lives is legitimate. At the same time, the farm may offer benefits to the animals, such as shelter and food, but what is a fair deal for the animals? When, or rather under what conditions, is it acceptable to keep farm animals? How would one go about showing that 'the deal' is fair? The answer depends in part on one's moral perspective on the relationship between humans and animals (Sandøe et al, 1997). Consider the following kinds of perspectives.

From an *animal rights* perspective, individual animals have a basic right to be treated with respect. It is only acceptable to kill animals for food in extreme circumstances (e.g. if human beings cannot survive without eating meat). Thus, from this point of view, it is fair to keep animals for production only in exceptional circumstances, and when doing so, we must ensure that each animal has a fair deal.

From an *ethics of care* perspective, livestock farming is acceptable as an activity that allows relationships to develop that benefit both humans and animals. That is, it is fair to keep animals for production purposes as long as people on the farm maintain a caring attitude to the animals in their care. Again, each animal must be part of this relationship in order for the deal to be fair.

Finally, from a *utilitarian* perspective, we must balance human and animal interests. Thus, if we can improve animal welfare with little cost to humans, we have an obligation to do so: only then will 'the deal' be fair. Here, in contrast with the previous two perspectives, although the interests of all individuals must be considered, the scores in human and animal interests are pooled into an overall estimate. It follows that a deal may be fair where the cost to a few individuals is high so long as the benefit to others is even higher. From this point of view, for example, the use of animals for vital biomedical research may be seen as acceptable even when the research animals are caused significant suffering.

It is clear from this quick glance at different ethical viewpoints, that there is no single correct answer to the question of what fair or morally acceptable treatment of animals requires. Answers will inevitably be related to one's moral point of view. At the same time, it is fair to say that in countries where animal welfare is a publicly discussed issue, the debate about animal treatment has so far proceeded on a more or less utilitarian basis.

In policy-making, in particular, discussion has been utilitarian in the sense that the focus has been on weighing costs to animals – in terms of reduced welfare – against human benefits. It has, however, been less utilitarian in the sense that human interests are rarely compared directly and on a par with the interests of animals. In other words, the discussion has displayed a 'speciesist' bias: in it, human interests seem to count for more than the interests of animals. Thus, for example, when rather trivial economic interests of farmers and consumers in rich countries are compared with the interests of animals in avoiding stress and suffering, the human interests often prevail.

On a more positive note, it is important to notice that under the heading of 'animal welfare', the interests of animals are now brought into public discussion in their own right. And it is also worth noting that the cut-off point between acceptable and unacceptable is gradually moving towards a stronger emphasis on animal welfare. However, there is great deal of confusion about how to draw the line, and about the role of science in this exercise.

What is the role of science in drawing the base-line?

In discussions about animal welfare, comparison is often made with the way animals were kept before modern intensive farming systems were introduced. The critics of intensive farming systems typically argue that the lives of today's animals are poorer than those of their ancestors, while those with a more positive view of modern animal farming point to improvements in animal welfare. In both cases the comparison is problematic. First, both seem to have a point. The life of farm animals has indeed improved, for example, in respect of health and nutrition, but at same time it has deteriorated as a result of stocking densities and production pressures. Secondly, even if it could be shown that the net welfare of farm animals is better now than it used to be, this offers no excuse for any failure to improve conditions where that is still possible. In connection with vulnerable humans, such as the mentally ill, the fact that their conditions were worse many years ago is not presented as an argument against further improvements. Rather, the issue seems to be whether the conditions have been improved sufficiently, taking into consideration what is technically and economically possible today. A similar argument would seem to apply to farm animals.

Legislation serves to specify a base-line for acceptable ways of keeping animals. Long ago the Council of Europe issued a Convention for the Protection of Animals Kept for Farming Purposes (CoE, 1976). The Convention was adopted by the European Union, which then followed it up with an EU Directive (CEU, 1998). The details of base-lines for various farm animals are specified in a number of recommendations and directives. But even so there is room for interpretation when the legislation is applied, and national implementation of such recommendations and directives may result in different initiatives in different countries.

Scientists are sometimes asked to define a cut-off point. This has happened in the EU, where animal welfare initiatives for a number of years have been based on input from scientific committees. Thus the EU Scientific Committee on Animal Health and Animal Welfare (SCAHAW) has produced a number of reports, and these have served as a basis for animal welfare legislation in the EU. In 2002, recognizing the need for a new independent body to provide scientific advice on all matters relating to food production and safety, the European Food Safety Authority (EFSA) was established by the EU. The work of SCAHAW is continued by a scientific panel under the EFSA that specializes in animal health and welfare. The panel has published reports on the keeping of laying hens, the castration of piglets, stunning and killing, and transport. (See http://europa.eu.int/comm/food/fs/aw/aw_scahaw_en.html for the SCAHAW reports and www.efsa.eu.int/science/ahaw/ahaw_opinions/catindex_en.html for the EFSA reports.)

Scientific input is very important when it comes to giving a comprehensive account of the various problems that animals may face when in farm animal production or other kinds of animal use. However, it is unclear when scientific information is sufficient to show that too much pressure is being put on the animals in connection, for example, with weaning age or stocking density.

This is illustrated by the case of stocking densities for broiler production. (Stocking density is usually expressed as the total weight of birds (in kg) per square metre of floor space in the shed; a lower total weight implies that there is more space per bird.) In a report by the Scientific Committee on Animal Health and Animal Welfare on the welfare of broilers, the following argument is made: 'The effects of stocking density on broiler welfare vary according to the slaughter age, the slaughter weight, the ventilation rate or quality of ventilation equipment and the climatic conditions. It therefore appears that the problems of high stocking rates are fewer in buildings where good indoor climatic conditions can be sustained, and any recommendations on stocking rate should take that into account. *When stocking rates exceed approximately 30kg/m², it appears that welfare problems are likely to emerge regardless of indoor climate control capacity...*' (SCAHAW, 2000, our emphasis). However, in the literature on which this recommendation is based there is no clear cut-off point at 30kg/m² for the stocking density of broilers. In fact, the report states: 'It is clear from behaviour and leg disorder studies that the stocking density must be 25kg/m² or lower for major welfare problems to be largely avoided...' One could thus argue that the cut-off point should, from a scientific point of view, be 25kg/m², and that densities beyond this will increase the risk of welfare problems with a more or less linear connection obtaining between stocking density and the level of problems faced by the broilers.

Note that the point being made here is not that it would be wrong to require a maximum stocking density of 30kg/m²; rather, it is that scientific data will have only a limited role in helping reach this decision. Besides science, economics, ethics and, not least, common sense will play a significant role in reaching this decision. It endangers transparency in public decision-making to portray this decision as if it is based purely on scientific considerations.

Interaction between common sense and science

It has so far been argued that science cannot stand alone when it comes to understanding animal welfare. However, this does not mean that science can be ignored – quite the contrary. Rather, the conclusion is that common sense and science depend on each other to reach sound conclusions about animal welfare. The case of piglet castration can be used to illustrate how common sense may depend on science to get things right.

The castration of young male piglets is commonly performed without anaesthetics or analgesics. This might seem strange, but for a very long time it was commonly believed that the newly born, animal or human, could not feel pain (Darwin, 1872; Anand and Hickey, 1987). This led to newborn infants being operated on without anaesthetics or analgesics. As late as 1985 a young infant 'had holes cut on both sides of his neck, another cut in his right chest, an incision from his breastbone around to his backbone, his ribs pried apart, and an extra artery near his heart tied off'. The infant was awake throughout and only paralyzed with a curare compound. He died a month later. When the mother asked about the operation, the anaesthesiologist said that 'it had never been demonstrated to her that infants feel pain' (from Lee, 2002). In a study some ten years later more than 6 per cent of the mothers were still not sure if the infant could feel any pain at all (Berthier et al, 1996).

In light of this, the belief that recently born piglets cannot feel pain is less surprising. In addition, when a piglet is lifted up its natural reaction is to start screaming and it will do so irrespective of whether it is castrated or not. The fact that the readily observed behaviour of castrated and non-castrated piglets does not differ makes it easy and convenient to assume that there is no difference in their welfare.

However, research as early as 1985 found that the scream of the piglet is higher in frequency at the moment of cutting the funicles (Wemelsfelder and van Putten, 1985). This research has later been refined and expanded demonstrating that there is a difference in the way piglets scream depending on whether they are being castrated or 'sham castrated' (e.g. Weary et al, 1998; Taylor et al, 2001). There is also physiological evidence that castration is a stressful event, and that it is more stressful if the castration is performed without anaesthetics (e.g. White et al, 1995).

In this case, a common sense view that was prevalent even in medical and veterinary circles has been, and continues to be, modified by scientific findings. On the other hand, there are cases in which common sense can afford insight and direction in the absence of established scientific evidence. One such case is perhaps the force-feeding of ducks and geese as part of foie gras production. This is prohibited in some countries, where the production method is considered unacceptable from an animal welfare point of view. The question is, however, what this conclusion is based on.

The production of the fatty liver in ducks and geese for foie gras involves force-feeding the animals for a few weeks prior to slaughter. The force-feeding is achieved using an auger or a pneumatic device. The farmer catches the bird, inserts the pipe 20–30cm into its throat and then starts the food pumping procedure. If an auger is used, the time taken to deliver the food is 45–60s; with a pneumatic device, only 2–3s is needed.

In a report by the Scientific Committee on Animal Health and Animal Welfare on force-feeding in ducks and geese it was concluded that '...it is very important for the further development of foie gras production to introduce alternative techniques that do not require force feeding' (SCAHAW, 1998). But a later study seems to contradict the need for alternative techniques: there is '...no significant indication that force-feeding is perceived as an acute or chronic stress by ...ducks ...' (Guémené et al, 2001). Closer examination of the reports reveals that the conclusion reached by SCAHAW was known not to be based on solid scientific evidence: '*The committee is aware that many of the facts mentioned in the report are based on a relatively small number of scientific publications or on individual observations of experts deriving from visits of farms. The evidence however suggests that* it is very important for the further development of foie gras production to introduce alternative techniques that do not require force feeding' (SCAHAW, 1998, our emphasis). Guémené et al's conclusion also has acknowledged limitations: '... *we observed* no significant indication that force-feeding is perceived as an acute or chronic stress by *male mule* ducks *in our experimental conditions. Nevertheless it remains to be shown that their adreno-corticotropic axis is responsive to acute stressors*' (Guémené et al, 2001, our emphasis).

Thus, rather than relying on science to provide a basis for taking a stand, SCAHAW gives the animals the benefit of the doubt – probably on the basis of the common-sense thought that it would be unpleasant to be force-fed. This thought is not supported, but it cannot be disproved by the more recent findings made by Guémené and colleagues. Here it is perhaps worth noting in passing a more general truth: science can only prove a difference, i.e. prove that some kind of reaction (behavioural, physiological or pathological) occurs in animals given a certain kind of treatment; it cannot prove a non-difference. This means that you can show, scientifically, that there is a difference between force-fed and non-force-fed ducks, but you cannot in the same way demonstrate that there is no difference. It may be possible to find another variable to measure, or to increase the sample size, and this will increase the likelihood of finding *some* effect.

Two kinds of uncertainty will always remain. First, if there is some kind of reaction, there may be uncertainty about how to interpret it in terms of animal welfare. For example, there is a long-running and still undecided debate about the interpretation of occurrences of various kinds of stress hormone. Secondly, if there is no reaction, it may be the case that the measurement of some other variable, or a change in the sample size, will reveal a reaction. To deal with these kinds of uncertainty we will have to rely to a considerable extent on common sense.

Conclusions

The arguments above have a number of practical implications for research policy and the role of science in giving advice on animal welfare.

In funding research, it is important to maintain a balance between animal welfare science and the relevant areas of disciplinary science. Without disciplinary science, with its focus on basic research, applied science will lack new ideas and tools. Without funding for applied animal welfare research, there will be inadequate focus on issues of practical relevance. It is also very important to ensure that different research approaches are allowed to coexist and compete fruitfully with each other.

In committees or other bodies that deliver advice on animal welfare, it is important to combine both scientific and ethical perspectives – for example, by involving ethicists and lay people. Only in this way will it be possible to encourage the right kind of dialogue between science and common sense. Science has an important role to play, and so there may be a need for more of it; but there is also a need for more than science.

The present paper derives from a talk given at a meeting at which the organizers put the following question as a working title: does science take sentience seriously? This question suggests that the main issue about the role of science in the study and practical management of animal welfare is whether science is taking sentience seriously enough. However, perhaps this is not quite right. Perhaps the problem is rather that science is expected to deliver *all* the answers, and thus that we expect too much from it. It may well be, therefore, that the on we need to ask is: do we take science too seriously?

References

Anand, K. J. S. and Hickey, P. R. (1987) 'Pain and its effects in the human neonate and fetus', *New England Journal of Medicine*, vol 317, no 21, pp1321–1329

Appleby, M. C. and Sandøe, P. (2002) 'Philosophical debate on the nature of well-being: Implications for animal welfare', *Animal Welfare*, vol 11, pp283–294

Berthier, M., Sacheau, V., Cardona, J., Paget, A. and Oriot, D. (1996) 'Évaluation des connaissances de 189 mères concernant les capacités sensorielles du nouveau-né. L'information peut-elle être un outil de prévention?' *Archives de Pédiatrie*, vol 3, pp954–958

CoE (Council of Europe) (1976) *European Convention for the Protection of Animals Kept for Farming Purposes*, European Treaty Series no 87

CEU (Council of the European Union) (1998) 'Council Directive 98/58/EC concerning the protection of animals kept for farming purposes', *Official Journal of the European Communities* (L221/23), 20 July

Darwin, C. A. (1872) *The Expression of Emotions in Man and Animal*, John Murray, London

Duncan, I. J. H. and Fraser, D. (1997) 'Understanding animal welfare', in Appleby, M. C. and Hughes, B. O. (eds) *Animal Welfare*, CAB International, Wallingford, UK, pp19–31

Fontaine, N. (1738) Mémoires pour servir à l'histoire de Port-Royal, quoted from Rosenfield, L. C. (1968) *Beast–Machine to Man–Machine*, Octagon Books, New York

Fraser, D. (2003) 'Assessing animal welfare at the farm and group level: The interplay of science and values', *Animal Welfare*, vol 12, pp433–443

Guémené, D., Guy, G., Noirault, J., Garreau–Mills, M., Gouraud, P. and Faure, J. M. (2001) 'Force-feeding procedure and physiological indicators of stress in male mule ducks', *British Poultry Science*, vol 42, no 5, pp650–657

Klingenberg, C. P. (2003) 'Fluctuating asymmetry and animal welfare. How far are we? And how far should we go?', *Veterinary Journal*, vol 166, pp5–6

Lee, B. H. (2002) 'Managing pain in human neonates – applications for animals', *Journal of the American Veterinary Medical Association*, vol 221, no 2, pp233–237

Muir, D. D., Hunter, E. A., Banks, J. M. and Horne, D. S. (1995) 'Sensory properties of hard cheese: Identification of key attributes', *International Dairy Journal*, vol 5, pp157–177

Oreskovich, D. C., Klein, B. P. and Sutherland, J. W. (1991) 'Procrustes analysis and its applications to free-choice and other sensory profiling', in Lawless, H. T. and Klein, B. P. (eds) *Sensory Science: Theory and Applications in Foods*, Marcel Dekker, New York, pp353–393

Polak, M. (2002) *Developmental Instability. Causes and Consequences*, Oxford University Press, Oxford

Sandøe, P., Crisp, R. and Holtug, N. (1997) 'Ethics', in Appleby, M. C. and Hughes, B. O. (eds) *Animal Welfare*, CAB International, Wallingford, UK, pp3–17

Sandøe, P., Christiansen, S. B. and Appleby, M. C. (2003) 'Farm animal welfare: The interaction between ethical questions and animal welfare science', *Animal Welfare*, vol 12, pp469–478

SCAHAW (Scientific Committee on Animal Health and Animal Welfare) (1998) *Welfare Aspects of the Production of Foie Gras in Ducks and Geese*, report of the European Commission Scientific Committee on Animal Health and Animal Welfare, available at http://europa.eu.int/comm/food/fs/aw/aw_scahaw_en.html

SCAHAW (Scientific Committee on Animal Health and Animal Welfare) (2000) *The Welfare of Chickens Kept for Meat Production (Broilers)*, report of the European

Commission Scientific Committee on Animal Health and Animal Welfare, available at http://europa.eu.int/comm/food/fs/aw/aw_scahaw_en.html

Tannenbaum, J. (1991) 'Ethics and animal welfare: The inextricable connection', *Journal of the American Veterinary Medical Association*, vol 198, pp1360–1376

Taylor, A. A., Weary, D. M., Lessard, M. and Braithwaite, L. (2001) 'Behavioural responses of piglets to castration: The effect of piglet age', *Applied Animal Behaviour Science*, vol 73, pp35–43

Tuyttens, F. (2003) 'Measures of developmental instability as integrated, a posteriori indicators of farm animal welfare: A review', *Animal Welfare*, vol 12, pp535–540

Weary, D. M., Braithwaite, L. A. and Fraser, D. (1998) 'Vocal responses to pain in piglets', *Applied Animal Behaviour Science*, vol 56, pp161–172

Wemelsfelder, F. and van Putten, G. (1985) 'Behaviour as a possible indicator for pain in piglets', Instituut voor Veeteltkundig Onderzoek 'Schoonoord', Zeist, The Netherlands, IVO Report B–260

Wemelsfelder, F., Hunter, E. A., Mendl, M. T. and Lawrence, A. B. (2000) 'The spontaneous qualitative assessment of behavioural expressions in pigs: First explorations of a novel methodology for integrative animal welfare measurement', *Applied Animal Behaviour Science*, vol 67, pp193–215

White, R. G., DeShazer, J. A., Tressler, C. J., Borcher, G. M., Davey, S., Waninge, A., Parkhurst, A. M., Milanuk, M. J. and Clemens, E. T. (1995) 'Vocalization and physiological response of pigs during castration with or without a local anesthetic', *Journal of Animal Science*, vol 73, pp381–386

PART 2

Ethics, Law and Science

5
Educating Scientists About Ethics

Michael J. Reiss

Institute of Education, University of London, UK

Introduction

There was a time when in most countries, those learning to become scientists would not formally have been taught anything about ethics. But that is changing. It is not just medical students who learn about ethics; engineers learn about environmental ethics, agricultural and veterinary higher education students learn about issues to do with animal ethics and so on. This broadening of educational aims and content reflects a growing societal expectation that graduates in applied science disciplines should know something of ethics in their field, rather than merely being expected to 'pick it up' during the course of their professional lives (Reiss, 2005).

Why should scientists study ethics?

But what precisely might be the aims of teaching ethics to scientists (Figure 5.1)? Based on Davis (1999), at least four can be suggested (Reiss, 1999).

First, such teaching might heighten the ethical *sensitivity* of participants. For example, scientists (and those training to be scientists) who have never thought about whether laboratory rats deserve the same standard of care as laboratory dogs or whether there is a right age at which calves should be permitted to be removed from their mothers might be encouraged to think about such issues. Such thinking can result in scientists becoming more aware and thus more sensitive. It is not unusual, as a result, to find science students saying 'I hadn't thought of that before'.

Secondly, such teaching might increase the ethical *knowledge* of scientists and science students. The arguments in favour of this aim are much the same as the arguments in favour of teaching any knowledge – in part that such knowledge is worth possessing in itself, in part that possession of such knowledge has useful consequences. For example, appropriate teaching about the issue of rights might help scientists to distinguish between legal and moral rights, to understand something of the connections between rights and duties, and to be able to identify fallacies in arguments for or against the notion of animal rights.

Figure 5.1 *Appropriate ethical teaching about, for example, chimpanzees, might make scientists more sensitive to issues affecting chimpanzees, more knowledgeable about chimpanzees, better able to make ethical judgements about chimpanzees or better people in the sense of making better decisions about how chimpanzees should be regarded and treated.*

There is in any science discipline concerned with animals a tremendous amount of relevant knowledge for scientists to review. Consider, for example, the issue of whether we should be concerned, on welfare grounds, about fish farms. Relevant considerations include the possibilities of pain detection by fish and the extent to which fish are conscious of such pain. To understand such issues requires knowledge of animal behaviour, of neurophysiology and of psychology (cf. Kaiser, 1997; Lymbery, 2002; Rose, 2002). If scientists are to think through the consequences of permitting, prohibiting or regulating fish farms, then they also need knowledge of such matters as disease transmission (as farmed fish generally have higher rates of parasites and infectious diseases), pollution (from the various chemicals used to treat the parasites and infectious diseases) and employment in rural economies (as there are a lot of people employed in some countries on such fish farms).

Thirdly, such teaching might improve the ethical *judgement* of scientists. As Davis, writing about students at university, puts it:

> The course might, that is, try to increase the likelihood that students who apply what they know about ethics to a decision they recognize as ethical will get the right answer. All university courses teach judgment of one sort or another. Most find that discussing how to apply general principles helps students to apply those principles better; many also find that giving students practice in applying them helps too. Cases are an opportunity to exercise judgement. The student who has had to decide how to resolve an ethics case is better equipped to decide a case of that kind than one who has never thought about the subject.
>
> (Davis, 1999, pp164–165).

Fourthly, and perhaps most ambitiously, such teaching of ethics might make scientists *better people* in the sense of making them more virtuous or otherwise more likely to implement morally right choices. For example, a unit on ethics for student veterinarians might lead the students to reflect more on the possibilities open to them when people bring puppies to have their tails docked, leading them to be less pressured (consciously or otherwise) by the views of others and so resulting in improved animal welfare. There is, within the field of moral education, a substantial literature both on ways of teaching people to 'be good' and on evaluating how effective such attempts are (e.g. Wilson, 1990; Carr, 1991; Noddings, 1992). Here it is enough to note that while care needs to be taken to distinguish between moral education and moral indoctrination, there is considerable evidence that moral education programmes can achieve intended and appropriate results (e.g. Straughan, 1988; Bebeau et al, 1999).

What sort of ethics should scientists study?

Ethics might be taught to scientists at various points in their careers. It might be taught, for example, during undergraduate or postgraduate courses; it might be taught to professional scientists as part of continuing professional education; it might be learnt informally throughout life. What sorts of ethics should be taught to scientists? I suggest the following:

- ethics that connects to fundamental issues of ethics – that is, issues not specific to science. For example, the principles of consequentialism, Kantian ethics and virtue ethics, the contribution of religious traditions, feminist approaches, etc;
- ethics that arises especially in science (including use of animals, relations to the natural environment and duties to future generations);
- appropriate professional codes of ethics.

Ethics that connects to fundamental issues of ethics

Ethics is the branch of philosophy concerned with how we should decide what is morally wrong and what is morally right. We all have to make moral decisions daily on matters great or (more often) small about what is the right thing to do: Should I intervene if I see someone bullying someone else in a shop? Should I offer my seat on a crowded train to someone who seems to need it more than I? May I park my car in a disabled parking area if I am in a rush to catch a train and there are plenty of spaces available? We may give much thought, little thought or practically no thought at all to such questions. Ethics is a specific discipline that tries to probe the reasoning behind our moral life, particularly by critically examining and analysing the thinking that is or could be used to justify our moral choices and actions in particular situations (Reiss, 2003).

The way ethics is done

One can be most confident about the worth of an ethical conclusion if three criteria are met: first, if the arguments that lead to the particular conclusion are convincingly supported by reason; secondly, if the arguments are conducted within a well established ethical framework; and thirdly, if a reasonable degree of consensus exists about the validity of the conclusions, arising from a process of genuine debate.

It might be supposed that reason alone is sufficient for one to be confident about an ethical conclusion. However, there still does not exist a single universally accepted framework within which ethical questions can be decided by reason (O'Neill, 1996). Indeed, it is unlikely that such a single universally accepted framework will exist in the foreseeable future, if ever. This is not to say that reason is unnecessary but to acknowledge that reason alone is insufficient. For instance, reason cannot decide between an ethical system that looks only at the consequences of actions and one that considers whether certain actions are right or wrong in themselves, whatever their consequences. Then feminists and others have cautioned against too great an emphasis upon reason. Much of ethics still boils down to views about right and wrong that are informed more about what seems 'reasonable' than what follows from logical reasoning.

Given the difficulties in relying solely on any one particular ethical tradition, we are forced to consider the approach of consensus (Moreno, 1995) when considering ethical questions, particularly when trying to discern ways forward on the ground at local level. It is true that consensus does not solve everything. After all, what does one do when consensus cannot be arrived at? Nor can one be certain that consensus always arrives at the right answer – a consensus once existed that women should not have the vote.

Nonetheless, there are good reasons both in principle and in practice for searching for consensus. Such consensus should be based on reason and genuine debate and take into account long-established practices of ethical reasoning. At the same time, it should be open to criticism, refutation and the possibility of change. Finally, consensus should not be equated with majority voting. Consideration needs to be given to the interests of minorities, particularly if they are especially affected by the outcomes, and to those – such as young children, the mentally infirm and non-humans – unable to participate in the decision-making process. At the same time it needs to be borne in mind that while a consensus may eventually emerge, there is an interim period when what is more important is simply to engage in valid debate in which the participants respect one another and seek for truth through dialogue (cf. Habermas, 1983).

Looking at consequences

The simplest approach to deciding whether an action would be right or wrong is to look at what its consequences would be. No one supposes that we can ignore the consequences of an action before deciding whether or not it is right. Even when complete agreement exists about a moral question, consequences will have been considered. The deeper question is whether that is all that we need to do. Are there certain actions that are morally required – such as telling the truth – whatever their consequences? Are there other actions – such as betraying confidences – that are wrong irrespective of their consequences?

Consequentialists, including utilitarians, believe that consequences alone are sufficient to let one decide whether a course of action would be ethically right. Utilitarianism begins with the assumption that most actions lead to pleasure (typically understood, at least for humans, as happiness) and/or displeasure. In a situation in which there are alternative courses of action, the desirable (i.e. right) action is the one that leads to the greatest net increase in pleasure (i.e. excess of pleasure over displeasure), where displeasure means the opposite of pleasure, that is, hurt or suffering.

Utilitarianism now exists in various forms. For example, preference utilitarians argue for a subjective understanding of pleasure in terms of an individual's own conception of his/her well-being. After all, if I like to spend my holidays participating in mud wallowing competitions (permission to use photograph declined), who are you to say that there are other more pleasurable ways in which I could spend my time?

There are two great strengths of utilitarianism. First, it provides a single ethical framework in which, in principle, any moral question may be answered. It doesn't matter whether we are talking about the introduction of identity cards, the permissibility of private education, whether there should be women bishops or the cloning of race horses; a utilitarian perspective exists. Secondly, utilitarianism takes pleasure and happiness seriously. People sometimes suppose that ethics is all about telling people what not to do. Utilitarians proclaim the positive message that people should simply do what maximizes the total amount of pleasure in the world.

However, there are difficulties with utilitarianism. For one thing, there is the question as to how pleasure can be measured. Is pleasure to be equated with well-being, happiness or the fulfilment of choice? And, anyway, what are its units? How can we compare different types of pleasure, for example sexual and aesthetic? Then, is it always the case that two units of pleasure should outweigh one unit of displeasure? Suppose two people each need a single kidney. Should one person (with two kidneys) be killed so that two may live (each with one kidney)?

Utilitarians (e.g. Singer, 1993) claim to provide answers to all such objections. For example, rule-based utilitarianism accepts that the best course of action is often served by following certain rules – such as 'Tell the truth', for example. Then, a deeper analysis of the kidney question suggests that if society really did allow one person to be killed so that two others could live, many of us might spend so much of our time going around afraid of being kidnapped for such purposes at any moment that the sum total of human happiness would be less than if we outlawed such practices.

Intrinsic ethical principles

The major alternative to utilitarianism is when certain actions are considered right and others wrong in themselves, that is intrinsically, regardless of the consequences. There are a number of possible intrinsic ethical principles. Currently, and in the west, perhaps the most important such principles are thought to be those of autonomy and justice.

People act autonomously if they are able to make their own informed decisions and then put them into practice. At a common-sense level, the principle of autonomy is why people need to have access to relevant information, for example, before consenting to a medical procedure such as a surgical operation.

There has been a strong move in many countries in recent decades towards people having increased autonomy. Until recently, for example, most doctors saw their role as simply providing the best medical care for their patients. If a surgeon thought, for instance, that a patient would find it upsetting to be told that there was a slight chance that an operation might lead to unwanted side effects, they generally did not tell them. Nowadays, doctors withholding such information might find themselves sued. Society increasingly feels that important medical decisions should be made not by doctors alone but should involve patients (or their close relatives in the case of children or adults unable to make their own informed decisions).

Of course, such autonomy comes at a cost. It takes a doctor time to explain what the various alternative courses of action are – time that could be spent treating other patients. In addition, some doctors feel deskilled, while some patients would simply rather their doctor made the best decision on their behalf. Overall, though, the movement towards greater patient autonomy seems unlikely to go away in the near future. However, autonomy is not a universal good. A youth can autonomously choose to shoot at people's pets. If society grants people the right to be autonomous, society generally also expects people to act responsibly, taking account of the effects of their autonomous decisions on others.

Autonomy is concerned with an individual's rights; justice is construed more broadly. Essentially, justice is about fair treatment and the fair distribution of resources and opportunities among moral subjects, including sentient non-humans. Considerable disagreement exists about what precisely counts as fair treatment and a fair distribution of resources. For example, some people accept that an unequal distribution of certain resources (e.g. educational opportunities) may be fair provided certain other criteria are satisfied (e.g. the educational opportunities are purchased with money earned or inherited). At the other extreme, it can be argued that we should treat all people equally in all regards. However, as Nietzsche and others have pointed out, it is surely impossible to argue that people should (let alone believe that they will) treat absolute strangers as they treat their children or spouses.

Feminist ethics and virtue ethics

Feminist ethics is one of the many products of feminism, which starts from the belief that women have been and still are being denied equality with men, both intentionally and unintentionally. This inequality operates both on an individual level (e.g. discrimination in favour of a male candidate over an equally good female candidate for a senior job) and at a societal level (e.g. poor access to state child care makes it extremely difficult for women in certain careers to return to full-time work after having a child).

Feminist ethics, in the words of Rosemary Tong 'is an attempt to revise, reformulate, or rethink those aspects of traditional western ethics that depreciate or devalue women's moral experience' (Tong, 1998, p261). Feminist philosophers fault traditional western ethics for showing little concern for women's as opposed to men's interests and rights. There has, for example, been a lot more written about when wars are just than about who should care for the elderly. Then there was the discovery that some of the best known and most widely used scales of moral development tend to favour men rather than women because the scoring system favours the application of impartial, universal rules over more holistic judgements aimed at preserving significant relationships between people (Gilligan, 1982). In addition, there is the feminist argument that moral philosophers have tended to privilege such 'masculine' traits as autonomy and independence over 'feminine' ones such as caring, striving for community, valuing emotions and accepting the body. Feminist ethics, with its analysis of the use and abuse of power in relationships, can help shed light on the way that we relate to and use animals.

Virtue ethics holds that the motives and characters of people are of central moral significance as well as what they actually 'do'. The emphasis within virtue ethics is therefore more on traits that are fairly stable over time and which define the moral nature of a person. For example, we might hope that people, whether friends, employers, politicians or farmers, would be honest, caring, thoughtful, loyal, humane, truthful, courageous, reliable and so on. We might expect different categories of people to have somewhat different virtues (contrast a nurse and a soldier) but good people are likely to differ far more in their skills than in their virtues.

Of course, as Aristotle pointed out almost two and a half thousand years ago, any virtue can be taken to excess. Loyalty to one's friends is generally a good thing but it is better to report your friend to the police if you have reasonable cause to think that he or she has murdered someone.

In practice, working out precisely what the virtuous thing to do in a situation is can be difficult. Consider euthanasia. Is it more caring absolutely to forbid euthanasia or to permit it in certain circumstances? Despite such difficulties – difficulties that attend every ethical set of principles – there seems little doubt that the world would be a better place if we were all even a bit more virtuous.

Ethics that arises especially in science

Traditionally, ethics has concentrated mainly upon actions that take place between people at one point in time. In recent decades, however, moral philosophy has widened its scope in two important ways. First, intergenerational issues are recognized as being of importance (e.g. Cooper and Palmer, 1995). Secondly, issues concerning species other than humans are now increasingly taken into account (e.g. Rachels, 1991).

Issues concerning species other than humans are of obvious importance in animal science. Consider, for example, the use of new practices (such as the use of growth promoters or embryo transfer) to increase the productivity of farm animals. Nowadays, probably the majority of people feel that the effects of such new practices on the farm animals need to be considered as at least part of the ethical equation before reaching a conclusion. This is not, of course, necessarily to accept that the interests of non-humans are equal to those of humans.

Accepting that issues concerning species other than humans need to be considered leads one to ask 'How?' Need we only consider animal suffering? For example, would it be right to produce, whether by conventional breeding or modern biotechnology, a chicken unresponsive to other birds and less able to detect pain? Such a chicken would probably suffer less and its use might lead to significant productivity gains. Someone arguing that such a course of action would be wrong would not be able to argue thus on the grounds of animal suffering. Other criteria would have to be invoked. It might be argued that such a course of action would be disrespectful to chickens or that it would involve treating them only as means to human ends and not, even to a limited extent, as ends in themselves.

Appropriate professional codes of ethics

The insufficiency of reason is a strong argument for conducting debates within well established ethical frameworks, when this is possible. Professional codes of ethics can be useful in this regard. Traditionally, the ethical frameworks most widely accepted in most cultures arose within systems of religious belief. Consider, for example, the questions 'Is it wrong to lie? If so, why?' There was a time when the great majority of people in many countries would have accepted the answer 'Yes. Because scripture forbids it'. Nowadays, though, not everyone accepts scripture(s) as a source of authority. Another problem is that while the various scriptures of the world's religions have a great deal to say about such issues as theft, killing people and sexual behaviour, they say rather less that can directly be applied to the debates that surround many of today's ethical issues, particularly those involving modern biotechnology. A further issue is that we live in an increasingly plural society. Within any one western country there is no longer a single shared set of moral values. Instead there is a degree of moral fragmentation: one cluster of people has this set of ethical views; another has that.

Nevertheless, there is still great value in taking seriously the various traditions – religious and otherwise – that have given rise to ethical conclusions. People do not live their lives in isolation: they grow up within particular moral traditions. Even if we end up departing somewhat from the values we received from our families and those around us as we grew up, none of us derives our moral beliefs from first principles, *ex nihilo*, as it were.

In the particular case of moral questions concerning science, a tradition of ethical reasoning has accumulated and continues to accumulate (e.g. Spier, 2002). Indeed, there is a strong possibility that an internationally agreed code of ethics for scientists may soon be agreed. The World Commission on the Ethics of Scientific Knowledge and Technology (COMEST) was established in 1998 as an independent advisory body to the United Nations Educational, Scientific and Cultural Organization (UNESCO) in response to the growing ethical challenges posed by scientific and technological progress. With respect for the rights, freedoms and responsibilities of the human individual, it sets out ethical principles and formulates recommendations for the international community. At a recent meeting the UNESCO Board commissioned a study, in cooperation with the International Council for Science (ICSU), on 'the advisability of elaborating an international declaration on science ethics to serve as a basis for an ethical code of conduct for scientists'. There are over 850 codes of professional ethics listed at the Center for the Study of Ethics in the Professions, University of Illinois, at www.iit.edu/departments/csep/Public WWW/codes/ and another useful website for science and engineering codes is at www.onlineethics.org/

How might ethics be taught to scientists?

In discussing strategies for how ethics might be taught to scientists, considering some of the advantages and disadvantages of each, a useful distinction can be made between learning that occurs while someone is a student learning to become a scientist and learning that occurs subsequently, 'on the job', when one is a scientist.

Teaching fundamental ethical approaches

Teaching ethics by going through such fundamental ethical approaches as consequentialism, deontology, virtue ethics, feminist ethics and so forth provides a rigorous and valid grounding. But the approach can appear abstract and may give too optimistic a view of the ease of making ethical decisions in reality. If it is used – and this approach can be used as part of a course of applied ethics – it is particularly important, in my view, for the approach to be even-handed. There are some consequentialists who, both in their writing and in their talks, seem more evangelical about their position than are many religious people about their faith. Similarly, in some quarters the principalist approach has reached the level of a mantra. Equally, virtues are culturally laden. Consider, for example 'honour'; what is the right way for me to behave if you insult me? The answer varies greatly from culture to culture.

Studying case studies

Case studies can be highly motivating for learners. They are seen to be 'relevant' (the highest accolade for some students) and allow learners to contribute their own views and to discuss the views of others, whether of their peers, their lecturer(s) or academics in the field. They have considerable flexibility, taking as little as 20 minutes or occupying months of study.

However, some care is needed. Too much background information or too complicated a dilemma may be overwhelming; too superficial an introduction to a case study and learners may not engage; too many case studies and learners may fail to see connections between cases or get bored. Teachers (e.g. higher education lecturers) may need to help students 'debrief' at the end of a case study, so that more general lessons can be drawn out and learnt – even if the lesson is only that sometimes general lessons can't be learnt!

Role plays

Role plays, though rarely used in teaching about ethics, can be memorable and allow for a lived experience rather than students just engaging in talk. They can also increase empathy so that students see more deeply how others may perceive a situation. Indeed, it can be worth encouraging (but not forcing) students to take on a role different from that which they would occupy themselves. My own view is that it's not a particularly good idea to get students to role play being non-humans (e.g. farm animals); a better idea is to get some of them to act the role of someone who argues that animals have rights, shouldn't be kept in captivity, eaten or whatever.

However, role plays do make particular demands on both lecturers and students. Role plays can polarize attitudes and it is always a good idea to 'de-role' at the end of one, so that participants come out of role and get the chance to say anything they want to now that they are again 'themselves'.

Imitation of lecturers

In a higher education course, students inevitably get to know something of the views of their lecturers and the degree to which their lecturers' actions are consonant with these views. The extent to which students gain such knowledge depends on the structure of the course. If all your teaching is delivered in 50-minute lectures to groups of more than 100 students, they will learn far less about you than if you take them on outings or a residential field trip.

Imitation of lecturers is an apprenticeship model in which lecturers are seen as role models. It is a form of embodied learning and is likely to happen to a certain extent in any event. However, awareness of it can make especial demands on lecturers. Similarly, students learn from the whole ethos and structure of an institution as well as from individual lecturers. What sorts of relationships between staff and students are encouraged and which forbidden? What provision is made for students' diets (e.g. vegetarian, vegan, kosher or halal)? Are students allowed to keep pets on campus? And so on.

Students act authentically by changing their own actions during the course

Do students get the chance to learn authentically by changing their own actions during their course? This is a type of enacted learning that involves getting into the habit of being good through the manifestation of agency. Of course, it requires courses to provide opportunities for students to make such authentic decisions, and so makes demands on course administrators, lecturers and technicians – as well as on the students! What opportunities do students get to choose the subject matter of their project work and other assignments? Do they have any control over the use of animals in their establishment; for example, which species are kept, how they are kept and whether and under what circumstances they are killed?

Scientists reflect on ethical issues in the course of their work

Finally, ethics can be and is learnt by scientists themselves in the course of their work. In many ways this can be one of the most powerful sources of learning.

I know at least three people who changed careers because they felt increasingly uncomfortable about working with animals in laboratory settings in which the experiments were invasive and caused suffering and were conducted not for the benefit of the animals themselves but for the ultimate benefit, it was hoped, of humans.

Of course, education at an earlier educational stage (e.g. school or university) can help all of us as adults subsequently to reflect on the ethical acceptability of various practices. As discussed above, teaching about ethics can aim to enhance ethical sensitivity, knowledge or judgement or to make people morally better (Davis, 1999; Reiss, 1999). Given the number of new ethical issues that scientists are facing, and are likely to face in the future, it is particularly important that formal education provides learners with the tools to enable them to make their own, valid ethical analyses subsequently in new situations. After all, ten years ago few prospective scientists were taught about the ethics of xenotransplantation or therapeutic cloning. Ten years hence there will be new, presently unexpected ethical issues.

References

Bebeau, M. J., Rest, J. R. and Narvaez, D. (1999) 'Beyond the promise: A perspective on research in moral education', *Educational Researcher*, vol 28, no 4, pp18–26

Carr, D. (1991) *Educating the Virtues: An Essay on the Philosophical Psychology of Moral Development and Education*, Routledge, London

Cooper, D. E. and Palmer, J. A. (1995) (eds) *Just Environments: Intergenerational, International and Interspecies Issues*, Routledge, London

Davis, M. (1999) *Ethics and the University*, Routledge, London

Gilligan, C. (1982) *In a Different Voice*, Harvard University Press, Cambridge, MA

Habermas, J. (1983) *Moralbewusstsein und Kommunikatives Handeln*, Suhrkamp Verlag, Frankfurt am Main

Kaiser, M. (1997) 'Fish farming and the precautionary principle: Context and values in environmental science for policy', *Foundations of Science*, vol 2, pp307–341

Lymbery, P. (2002) *In Too Deep: The Welfare of Intensively Farmed Fish*, Compassion in World Farming, Petersfield

Moreno, J. D. (1995) *Deciding Together: Bioethics and Moral Consensus*, Oxford University Press, Oxford

Noddings, N. (1992) *The Challenge to Schools: An Alternative Approach to Education*, Teachers College Press, New York

O'Neill, O. (1996) *Towards Justice and Virtue: A Constructive Account of Practical Reasoning*, Cambridge University Press, Cambridge

Rachels, J. (1991) *Created from Animals: The Moral Implications of Darwinism*, Oxford University Press, Oxford

Reiss, M. J. (1999) 'Teaching ethics in science', *Studies in Science Education*, vol 34, pp115–140

Reiss, M. J. (2003) 'How we reach ethical conclusions', in Levinson, R. and Reiss, M. J. (eds) *Key Issues in Bioethics: A Guide for Teachers*, Routledge Falmer, London, pp14–23

Reiss, M. J. (2005) 'Teaching animal bioethics: Pedagogic objectives', in Marie, M., Edwards, S., Gandini, G., Reiss, M. and von Borell, E. (eds) *Animal Bioethics:*

Principles and Teaching Methods, Wageningen Academic Publishers, The Netherlands, pp189–202

Rose, J. D. (2002) 'The neurobehavioural nature of fishes and the question of awareness and pain', *Reviews in Fisheries Science*, vol 10, pp1–38

Singer, P. (1993) *Practical Ethics*, 2nd edn, Cambridge University Press, Cambridge

Spier, R. E. (ed) (2002) *Science and Technology Ethics*, Routledge, London

Straughan, R. (1988) *Can We Teach Children to be Good? Basic Issues in Moral, Personal and Social Education*, 2nd edn, Open University Press, Milton Keynes

Tong, R. (1998) 'Feminist ethics', in Chadwick, R. (ed) *Encyclopedia of Applied Ethics*, Academic Press, San Diego, vol 2, pp261–268

Wilson, J. (1990) *A New Introduction to Moral Education*, Cassell, London

6
What Prevents Us from Recognizing Animal Sentience?

Andrew Linzey

University of Oxford, UK

I propose to identify and illustrate what might be described as 'the powers that be' – four mechanisms that prevent us from recognizing sentience in animals – and to indicate the challenges that should follow for future work in this field.

Misdescription

The first is what Denys Turner has recently called 'that most powerful of human tools, *the power of misdescription*'. In a paper, provocatively titled 'How to kill people', he argues:

> Let me tell you how to kill people efficiently; or rather, here's how to get yourself, and, if you are in the business of doing so, here's how to get others to kill people. First you have got to call your proposed victims names ... if we propose to kill a fellow human being and justify it, we have to redescribe him in such a way that he no longer belongs to us, becomes an alien being ... and in that way the inhibition against killing is effectively weakened.

He provides the examples of how some newspapers, in the time of the Falklands/Malvinas war, described the Argentinians as 'Argies' or 'wops', and how, in the Vietnamese war, US soldiers called the North Vietnamese 'Gooks' (Turner, 2002). In order to kill or abuse we need to create an *artificial* distance from the one who is to be killed or abused.

Similarly, we have created an artificial distance between ourselves and other animals. There are differences, sometimes important ones, both between and among species. It is not difference *per se*, but rather the *denigration* of difference that is significant morally. It is how we *use* differences to justify unjust treatment and, specifically, how these are embodied in our language. Consider the historic language we use about animals: 'brutes', 'dumb brutes', 'unfeeling brutes', 'critters', 'sub-humans', 'beasts' and 'wild beasts'. Also consider the adjectives, 'brutal', 'beastly' and 'bestial'. The Anglican *Book of Common Prayer*, which is still in use, recommends that marriage should not be undertaken 'to satisfy men's carnal lusts and appetites, like brute beasts that have no understanding'. By definition, it is difficult to champion the rights (though some undoubtedly have) of 'beastly', 'brutal' or 'bestial' life.

So pervasive is this language that it is difficult even for 'animal advocates' (itself not an unambiguous term) to find an alternative nomenclature. 'Our Dumb Friends' League' was the title of an animal-friendly organization that was set up in the late 19th century. And the term 'non-human animals' (used by pioneering animal advocates in the 1970s) is hardly unprejudicial either. In a class on sexual ethics at Oxford University, I recall one student saying how much he opposed adultery because it was 'ratting on one's partner'. I had to point out that some rats are more monogamous than some human beings. In doing so, I had, as it were, 'to take the bull by the horns', not let 'sleeping dogs lie', 'be as sly as a fox' and even act as 'a snake in the grass'; the point to be grasped is that these are not just libels on human beings.

Unless we address the power of misdescription, we shall never be able to *think* straight, let alone *see* straight (that is, impartially, or, at least, with some measure of objectivity). Even 'animals' itself is a term of abuse (which hides the reality of what it purports to describe, namely, a range of differentiated beings of startling variety and complexity). The language we use is the language of *past* thought. We shall not possess a new understanding of animals unless we actively challenge the language we use, which is the language of historic denigration. The challenge is how to create a nomenclature – born of moral imagination and a sense of fellow feeling – that does justice to animals.

Misrepresentation

The second mechanism that prevents us from recognizing sentience in animals is the *power of misrepresentation*. It is important to grasp that the artificial distance between ourselves and other animals does not arise from nowhere. It has been fuelled by both religious and scientific ideologies. In Christianity, that ideology is Cartesianism – the doctrine largely originating with the 17th century French philosopher Descartes that animals are unthinking automata. The reasoning goes like this: because animals possess no rational (and therefore immortal) soul they cannot therefore think, possess self-consciousness and language, and, therefore, they cannot experience pain. In short: they cannot feel pain because they do not have the mental wherewithal to do so.

In other words (and at the very least), animals are unthinking organisms that operate by instinct. We cannot assume that their organs, though similar to our own, carry the same, or even similar, sensation since this is the function of the rational soul, which is unique to human beings. The argument is entirely *a priori*. It is difficult to see how any empirical evidence could count against it. The effect of Cartesianism was to devastate earlier Christian traditions of kindness to animals. It is doubtful whether the Jesuit Joseph Rickaby could have written that 'we have no duties of charity, nor duties of any kind to the lower animals, as neither to stocks or stones' (Rickaby, 1889) without the influence of Cartesianism.

Cartesianism was paralleled by a scientific doctrine called 'behaviourism'. Behaviourist ideology – which has so influenced American and British psychology – only allows for descriptions of *learned* behaviour. Subjectivity in animals was jettisoned. In order to preserve scientific objectivity, scientists 'totally ignored any subjective dimension of feeling, and dealt only with the neurological and chemical substratum, the "plumbing" of pain'. The result, as Bernard Rollin indicates (Rollin, 1990, 2006), was an extreme scepticism about the existence of animal pain. 'Animal anaesthesia was known only as "chemical restraint" throughout most of the 20th century, and the first textbook of veterinary anaesthesia, published in the United States in the middle of the 1970s, does not list control of felt pain as a reason for anaesthetic use' (Rollin, 2006).

In fact, there is no good reason to deny that all mammals are sentient. 'Sentience' is defined in some dictionaries as 'sense perception', but it is commonly used by philosophers to denote the capacity for pain and pleasure. The issue is not just about pain, however. Pain may be defined as an 'adverse physical stimuli', but there is ample evidence that all mammals experience not just pain, but also mental suffering, that is, stress, terror, shock, anxiety, fear, trauma and foreboding, and that only to a greater or lesser degree than we do ourselves. Animals and humans exhibit a common ancestor, show similar behaviour and have physiological similarities. Because of these triple conditions, these shared characteristics, it is perfectly logical to believe that animals experience many of the same emotions as humans. Logic tells us this. Thus we do not need scientific data to believe in the suffering of animals. Rather, the onus should be on those people who try to deny that animals have such emotions. They must explain how nerves act in one way in one species and completely differently in another. They must explain why we believe that a child who cries and runs away from us after we have trodden on his or her foot is unhappy, while a dog who behaves in the same manner is said to present us with insufficient information for us to make a judgement.

That is not to deny, however, that the scientific evidence is not there for those who want it. As early as 1872, Darwin devoted a whole book to *The Expression of Emotions in Man and Animals* (Darwin, 1872). Since then, there has been a wide range of scientific findings, especially ethological and episte-mological findings, on animal learning, tool making and self-consciousness. The conclusion is clear: 'The available evidence suggests that most or all verte-brates, and perhaps some invertebrates, can suffer' (DeGrazia, 1996).

The misrepresentation of animals is paralleled by the misrepresentation of their advocates. The British TV presenter Jeremy Paxman introduced an item on BBC2's 'Newsnight' concerning the Great Ape Project, by asking: 'Should we give *human* rights to apes?' In fact, no animal advocate (to my knowledge) wants to give apes *human* rights. The notion conjures up – as one suspects it was designed to do –

visions of apes in polling booths, ape MPs, apes demonstrating for better pay, ape trade unions and so on. By the misuse of *one* word, the case for not harming apes was subject to public ridicule. The power of the media to misrepresent can frighten us out of most moral sensibilities. Who wants to be known as a 'bunny hugger', a 'Bambi lover' or a 'friend of the dumb brutes', or, less benignly, a 'sentimentalist', an 'extremist', a 'fanatic' or even (most regrettably of all) a 'terrorist'?

The second challenge, then, is to seek non-pejorative, even convivial, representations of animals, and less than partial labels for those who try to protect them.

Misdirection

The third mechanism is *the power of misdirection*. I mean by that, the way in which suffering in animals, even when acknowledged, is minimized, obfuscated or its moral significance belittled. There are several arguments.

The 'we can't really know' argument

Academics frequently exhibit the 'scepticism of the wise' tendency, that is, when presented with what to most ordinary mortals appears as a case of abuse, if not downright cruelty, they invariably inflate uncertainty and in so doing misdirect our attention away from the harm inflicted. Here is an example:

TV interviewer: 'Don't pigs suffer when immobilized in these crates?'

Respected scientist: 'You are assuming of course that pigs suffer just like we do. We do not really know that. It's a very complex question.'

TV interviewer: 'But don't most animals have the need to turn around?'

Respected scientist: 'But, again, you're assuming that the needs of pigs are identical to our own. We have to move beyond naïve anthropomorphism.'

TV interviewer: 'So you're saying that they aren't suffering then?'

Respected scientist: 'I think we would need a great deal more research in order to reach a definite conclusion about such a complex question. We can't simply assume that pigs suffer in circumstances that would make us suffer.'

TV interviewer: 'So what do you think should be done?'

Respected scientist: 'I think we need much more research. We don't know how animals feel because they can't tell us about it. We should set up a scientific committee to explore this question, make experiments, obtain research grants and find really objective ways of measuring what may be at issue here.'

TV interviewer: 'Thank you, Professor, for your fascinating insights.'

The interview is imaginary, but not wholly fictional. Such are the legacies of Cartesianism and behaviourism that academics find it as difficult to talk about emotion in animals as 19th century clergymen found it difficult to talk about sex. It is something that they cannot easily do without blushing. They would have to live with the most dreaded accusation that can be levelled at any academic, namely, being a 'sentimentalist'. What is worrying is that this professional scepticism (which, in other contexts, we should welcome) is increasingly taken over by government ministers, officials and especially by their committees (who are usually packed full of appropriately appointed academics) so that government policy becomes itself unreasonably sceptical about animal sentience.

Philosophers have sometimes compounded the scepticism of scientists by reason of their own agnosticism. Modern discussion has been influenced by Thomas Nagel's well known essay, 'What is it like to be a bat?' (Nagel, 1979) His answer (not surprisingly) is that we cannot know much – actually nothing – about what it is like to be a bat. But we do not need to know precisely how a bat thinks or feels or mentally encounters the world in order to know basic things about how it can be harmed, for example, by mutilation, by deprivation of its instincts, by isolation from its peers, by subjecting it to invasive procedures and by the infliction of adverse physical stimuli. We can, and do, know these things without scientific evidence and without knowing everything possible, philosophically or scientifically, about the mental consciousness of a bat. We can know these things, at least, as reasonably as we know them in the case of most humans. The same is also true of the many millions of mammals that we regularly harm in research, recreation and farming. We should not allow not knowing everything to prevent us from acting ethically on what we can reasonably know.

The 'we must have scientific evidence before we can make a judgement' argument

The desire for data, for evidence of all kinds, rather than simply assertion, is to be welcomed in moral debate, but when it comes to animals this desire is hardened into a precondition of judgement. The Burns Report on Hunting with Dogs in England and Wales provides an example. Commissioned post-mortem evidence showed that hunted foxes died from 'massive injuries to the chest and vital organs'. Yet, the Report concludes that there is 'a lack of firm scientific evidence about the effect on the welfare of a fox of being closely pursued, caught and killed above ground'. Hunting is judged to 'seriously compromise the welfare of the fox' (Burns Report, 1999) but it is not 'cruel'. Lord Burns, in a subsequent speech in the House of Lords, explains why:

> Naturally, people ask whether we were implying that it was cruel ...
> The short answer to that question is no. There was no sufficient

verifiable evidence or data safely to reach views about cruelty. It is a complex area ... One cannot ask an animal about its welfare or know what is going on inside its head.

(Burns, 2001)

But the idea that there must be 'sufficient verifiable evidence' before we can know that a fox suffers when it is being disembowelled by dogs is as unreasonable as supposing that we cannot know that a whip lashing a child's back is 'cruel'. If Burns's attitude of extreme scepticism were maintained in the face of similar evidence of cruelty to children, the noble Lord would justifiably be the subject of public ridicule, even though infants cannot tell us 'what is going on inside their heads' either.

The 'we mustn't be anthropomorphic' argument

There is a bad as well as a good anthropomorphism. Bad includes the attempt to project obviously human needs and emotions onto animals as when, for example, we enter the Beatrix Potter world of animals dressed up in human clothes and enjoying gardening. But these fantasies should not detract from the truth of good anthropomorphism, which accepts as a reasonable assumption that, in their own individual manner, mammals suffer only to a greater or lesser extent than we do. The 'anthropomorphic' view was ably expressed by the 'ethical approach' of the former Farm Animal Welfare Advisory Committee in 1970: 'The fact that an animal has limbs should give it the right to use them; the fact that a bird has wings should give it the right to spread them; the fact that both animals and birds are mobile should give them the right to turn around, and the fact that they have eyes should give them the right to see' (FAWAC, 1970).

In fact, it is a very reasonable assumption that animals denied use of most, or all, of their natural instincts – without any compensating factors – are 'unhappy'. That is exactly what we *can* – and *should* assume. We do not need science to know that intensive farming harms animals, deprives them of their natural life and makes them liable to suffering. We have seen a 30-year industry in which academics have been paid sometimes huge sums to investigate whether animals in intensively farmed conditions are 'suffering'. But if anthropomorphism is so 'unscientific' and so flawed, why is it that subsequent research has vindicated almost all the objections to factory farming, based on 'naïve anthropomorphism'? The very systems that attracted criticism – battery cages, sow stalls, veal crates – have all been shown to make animals liable to harm or to engender suffering. The words of Konrad Lorenz cannot be gainsaid: 'The similarity [between humans and animals] is not only functional but historical, and it would be an actual fallacy not to humanize' (Lorenz, 1966).

The 'they may feel pain, but not as we do' argument

This is reminiscent of Mr Spock's famous line in *Star Trek*, 'yes, it's life, but not as we know it'. The origin of this view is the idea, so central to Cartesianism, that animals are incapable of rational thought and therefore cannot really suffer like us. But the moral issue is not whether their suffering is identical in all respects to our own, but rather whether their suffering is *as important to them as ours is to us*. Rationality may, plausibly, increase suffering if there is anticipation or foreboding involved. It may be, for example, that animals have no concept of death and therefore cannot fear it. But it does not follow that the suffering of non-rational beings (if that is what mammals are) is always less intense.

If animals are (as we are told) devoid of rational thought and therefore live closer to their instincts, then it may be that a calf immobilized in a crate or a lion caged up in a zoo experiences a mental kind of torment that we can only imagine. Terry Waite, who suffered five terrible years in captivity, said that in order to alleviate his suffering he, *inter alia*, composed novels in his head (Waite, 1993). But such consolations are not available to animals. If animals are not rational, then it follows that their suffering cannot be softened by an intellectual comprehension of the circumstances – they just experience the raw terror of not knowing what has happened, why it has happened and how long it will endure. If, as some philosophers have claimed, animals are not intelligent like us, it is possible that some forms of suffering are actually *worse* for them than they would be for us. Rationality requires (of us), at least, an attempt at even-handedness.

The 'animals experience pain, but it's not morally important like our pain' argument

Looked at objectively there are good rational grounds for regarding the suffering of animals as especially significant morally. Consider the case of children, specifically infants. In recent years there has been an increase of sensitivity towards children, which is rather remarkable in the light of their low status historically. Is this sensitivity well founded philosophically? I think it is. Consider further that infants are, strictly speaking, morally innocent, they are vulnerable and powerless in relation to us, they cannot fully represent themselves or articulate their needs, and they are subjects of a special trust. All these considerations make the infliction of suffering upon them not *easier* but *harder* to justify.

Now, these considerations also apply to animals, perhaps even more so. Animals also are morally innocent – they cannot morally be bettered by pain or be improved by it; no pain in animals can be 'deserved' (as some have argued may be true in the case of some humans); they are also, at least mostly, vulnerable and powerless in relation to us and they are incapable of representing themselves, of giving 'informed' consent or articulating their needs. They are also subjects of a special trust in that they are (in the case of domestic animals) wholly dependent upon us; we have (in most cases) deliberately chosen to make them so dependent. It is precisely these considerations that should mark out both infants and animals as justifying special moral solicitude (Linzey, 1994).

In short: we need to reject the common rationalizations that animal pain, even when acknowledged, is not morally important like *our* pain. On the contrary, not only is human pain not the only morally significant pain in the world, but there are also rational grounds for supposing that suffering in animals, like suffering in children, should make a special moral claim upon us. There is something particularly poignant about the sheer vulnerability and helplessness both of infants and animals. When we grasp that fact, it should inform our moral reckoning.

In addition to these philosophical considerations, there is an underlying theological one. It concerns the Christ-like nature of animal suffering. What should 'move our very hearts and sicken us', according to John Henry Newman, is the realization that animals are morally innocent, 'that they have done no harm. Next, that they have no power of resisting; it is the cowardice and tyranny of which they are the victims that makes their suffering so especially touching … there is something so dreadful, so satanic [sic] in tormenting those who have never harmed us, and who cannot defend themselves, who are utterly in our power, who have weapons neither of offence nor defence that none but very hardened persons can endure the thought of it.' And he concludes: 'Think then, my brethren, of your feelings at cruelty practiced upon brute animals, and you will gain one sort of feeling which the history of Christ's Cross and passion ought to excite within you' (Newman, 1868).

The third challenge, then, is to find the moral and intellectual resources to face the full reality of animal sentience without trivialization or obfuscation.

Misperception

I turn, lastly, to the *power of misperception (or, rather, to the power of perception)*. I begin with an example that I have used before (Linzey, 1999). The university where I once used to work as chaplain was situated in acres of 18th century parkland. From my office, I was able to look out over the undulating hillside populated with rabbits. At first, I used to just notice things moving here and there as I occasionally looked up from my computer. But as the weeks and months progressed, I slowly began to marvel at the complexity, intricacy and beauty of their lives. I used to say – only half jokingly – that it 'was worth coming to the university to see the rabbits'. Whenever visitors came I used to point out the rabbits, and some would indeed say, 'How wonderful', but for many others it was as if I had pointed out the dust on the carpet or the faded colour of the paint. Whatever they saw they did not *see* rabbits.

Many people still do not *see* animals. They may have seen things moving, objects out there, even 'pests' that invade 'their' territory. But they have not yet seen other living, sentient beings. Our language, our philosophy, our science, our history, our theology and our culture, by and large, prevent us from seeing. I recall after lecturing one day in Oxford, a student came up to me and said: 'Well, Dr Linzey, I found all your arguments very interesting, but there's something I don't understand. What are animals for, if they are not to be eaten?' The person concerned was being perfectly serious and sincere. She just had not seen animals as anything more than lumps of meat. We have to move from an anthropocentric – indeed gastrocentric – view of animals.

The change of perception – or rather insight – can be stated quite simply: it is the move away from ideas that animals are commodities, machines, tools, things or resources here for us, to the idea that animals have their own value – what we may call an 'intrinsic value'. Animals are not just 'objects' out there; they are – in the words of Tom Regan – 'subjects-of-a-life' (Regan, 1983; Linzey, 1987). As I have put it elsewhere, 'this is a moral and spiritual discovery that is as objective and important as any other fundamental discovery, whether it be the discovery of the stars or the discovery of the human psyche' (Linzey, 1998). It is the 'Eureka!' experience, the 'Aha!' experience, 'the moment when the penny drops' experience. It is when we make the *moral* discovery that animals matter in themselves, that they have value in themselves and that their suffering is as important to them as ours is to us.

There are still many human beings out there who have not had this experience, this insight. They do not think that animals matter or that there are other creatures of value in the world. They think that human beings matter, but that the rest is just 'the environment', the theatre or backdrop to what really matters, namely themselves. They suffer, theologically, from the terrible delusion that God only cares for the human species – among the millions of species that she has made.

The educational agenda

Now, this insight cannot be programmed or, even worse, indoctrinated. But it should, at least, be on the educational agenda. There are few examples of where the possibility of seeing animals differently forms part of the curriculum at any level of education: primary, secondary, tertiary or higher. In many courses, whether they be in animal husbandry, animal conservation, animal science or even sometimes in animal welfare, students are not required to challenge, or at least address, the dominant perceptions of animals as commodities, resources, tools, machines or things.

Indeed, courses in animal conservation seem to miss the point entirely. For they often presuppose that animals are not individuals, but just collectivities or species. Hence, so-called 'conservationists' are in the forefront of killing ruddy ducks, hedgehogs or grey squirrels in order to preserve other species. Conservationists see species, but they fail to see *individual* animals that deserve our protection. Similarly, courses in animal science are often so 'scientific' that they fail to see animals as anything more than objects of dissection or complex machines. It never seems to occur to zoologists, any more than to conservationists, that animals are not just animals but *individual* animals – each with their own unique, morally significant, individuality.

History, it has been said, is the province of the winners; what we see all around is the embodiment of what was once thought. Think of what a zoo or a factory farm is – it is not just a building or a piece of geography – it is a living embodiment of the past view, the historic view, that sees animals as commodities to be put on display or simply bred for human use. Education needs to give people the chance to think and imagine differently, to conceive of other, better worlds for humans and animals.

The final and most important challenge, then, is to find ways of institutionalizing, embodying and incarnating new perceptions of animals so that as a matter of course all students in education – at whatever level – are encouraged to rethink the dominant intellectual paradigm. Only then shall we be in a position to effectively counter the moral and spiritual impoverishment revealed in our maltreatment of animals. 'We need another, and wiser, and perhaps more mystical, concept of animals' wrote the enlightened conservationist Henry Beston; 'they are not brethren, they are not underlings, they are other nations, caught with ourselves in the net of life and time, fellow prisoners of the splendour and travail of the earth' (Beston, 1928).

Acknowledgement

I am grateful to Professor Priscilla Cohn of Penn State University for her comments on an earlier draft of this paper.

References

Beston, H. (1928) *The Outermost House: A Year of Life on the Great Beach of Cape Cod*, Penguin Books, Harmondsworth, p25 (I am grateful to Brian Klug for this reference)

Burns, Lord (2001) 'Debate on the hunting bill', *Hansard*, 12 March, p533

Burns Report (1999) *Committee of Inquiry into Hunting with Dogs*, chaired by Lord Burns, HMSO, London, para 6.49, p117

Darwin, C. (1872) *The Expression of Emotions in Man and Animals*, University of Chicago Press, Chicago and London, reprinted from the authorized edition of D Appleton and Company, New York and London (I am grateful to Priscilla Cohn for this reference)

DeGrazia, D. (1996) *Taking Animals Seriously: Mental Life and Moral Status*, Cambridge University Press, Cambridge, p123 (Chapters 4–7 survey and analyse the empirical evidence about animal consciousness and sentiency)

FAWAC (1970) *Codes of Recommendations for the Welfare of Livestock*, report by the Farm Animal Welfare Advisory Committee, MAFF, London, p5

Linzey, A. (1987) *Christianity and the Rights of Animals*, SPCK, London, pp82f

Linzey, A. (1994) 'The moral priority of the weak', in *Animal Theology*, SCM Press,

London, pp28–44

Linzey, A. (1998) 'Foreword' to Stephen H. Webb, *On God and Dogs: A Christian Theology of Compassion for Animals*, Oxford University Press, New York, pxi

Linzey, A. (1999) *Animal Gospel*, Hodder and Stoughton, London, pp45–46

Lorenz, K. (1966) *On Aggression*, trans by Latzke, M., Methuen, London, p54; cited and discussed in Clark, S. R. L. (1977), *The Moral Status of Animals*, Clarendon Press, Oxford, pp38–39

Nagel, T. (1979) 'What is it like to be a bat?' in *Mortal Questions*, Cambridge University Press, Cambridge, pp164–180

Newman, J. H. (1868) 'The crucifixion', in *Parochial and Plain Sermons*, vol 8, Rivingtons, London, vol II, pp136–137

Regan, T. (1983) *The Case for Animal Rights*, Routledge and Kegan Paul, London, pp243–248

Rickaby, J. (1889) *Moral Philosophy*, Longman, London, p249

Rollin, B. E. (1990) *The Unheeded Cry: Animal Consciousness, Animal Pain and Science*, Oxford University Press, Oxford

Rollin, B. E. (2006) 'Animal pain' in Linzey, A. (ed) *Animal World Encyclopedia*, Kingsley, Plymouth, forthcoming 2006

Turner, D. (2002) *Faith Seeking*, SCM Press, London, p61

Waite, Terry (2003) *Taken on Trust*, Hodder and Stoughton, London

7
Sentience and Rights

Tom Regan
North Carolina State University, US

Some defining characteristics of moral rights

Like many others, I am a proponent of moral rights, including the moral rights of other-than-human animals. Moreover, I believe that sentience has an important role to play when it comes to understanding these rights. Here, I want to explore this nexus of ideas: moral rights, sentience and the latter's relevance to the former. I begin by highlighting some of the defining characteristics of moral rights.[1]

No trespassing

To possess moral rights is to have a kind of protection we might picture as an invisible 'No Trespassing' sign. What does this sign prohibit? Two things. First, others are not morally free to harm us; to say this is to say that others are not free to take our life or injure our body as they please. Second, others are not morally free to interfere with our free choice; to say this is to say that others are not free to limit our free choice as they please. In both cases, the 'No Trespassing' sign is meant to protect our most important goods (our life, our body and our liberty) by morally limiting the freedom of others.

Things are different when people exceed their rights by violating ours. When this happens, we act within our rights if we fight back, even if this does some serious harm to the aggressor. However, what we may do in self-defence does not translate into a general permission to hurt those who have not done anything wrong.

Equality

Moral rights breathe equality. They are the same for all who have them, differ though we do in many ways. This explains why no human being can justifiably be denied rights for arbitrary, prejudicial or morally irrelevant reasons. Race is such a reason. To attempt to determine which humans have rights on the basis of race is like trying to sweeten tea by adding salt. What race we are tells us nothing about what rights we have.

The same is no less true of other differences between us. My wife Nancy and I trace our family lineage to different countries; she to Lithuania, I to Ireland. Some of our friends are Christians, some Jews and some Muslims. Others are agnostics or atheists. In the world at large, a few people are very wealthy; many more are very poor. And so it goes. Humans differ in many ways. There is no denying that.

Still, no one who believes in human rights thinks these differences mark fundamental moral divisions. If we mean anything by the idea of human rights, we mean that we *have them equally*. And we have them equally regardless of our race, gender, religious belief, comparative wealth, intelligence, or date or place of birth, for example.

Trump

Every serious advocate of human rights believes that our rights have greater moral weight than other important human values. To use an analogy from the card game bridge, our moral rights are trump. Here is what this analogy means:

A hand is dealt. Hearts are trump. The first three cards played are the queen of spades, the king of spades and the ace of spades. You (the last player) have no spades. However, you do have the two of hearts. Because hearts are trump, your lowly two of hearts beats the queen of spades, beats the king of spades and even beats the ace of spades. This is how powerful the trump suit is in the game of bridge.

The analogy between trump in bridge and individual rights in morality should be reasonably clear. There are many important values to consider when we make a moral decision. For example, how will we be affected personally as a result of deciding one way or another? What about our family, friends, neighbours or people who live somewhere else? It is not hard to write a long list. When we say, 'rights are trump', we mean that respect for the rights of individuals is the most important consideration in 'the game of morality', so to speak. In particular, we mean that the benefits others derive from violating someone's rights never justify violating them.

Respect

In a general sense, the rights mentioned above (life, liberty and bodily integrity) are variations on a main theme, that theme being respect. I show my respect for you by respecting these rights in your life. You show your respect for me by doing the same thing. Respect is the main theme because treating one another with respect *just is* treating one another in ways that respect our other rights. Our most fundamental right, then, the right that unifies all our other rights, is our right to be treated with respect.

Understanding moral rights

It is one thing to say what moral rights are and quite another to explain why *we* have them whereas sticks and stones do not. Given the constraints of space, it will not be possible for me to offer anything like a complete explanation, even if I could. But permit me to offer a rough sketch of the answer that I favour.

Subjects-of-a-life

Earlier we noted some of the many ways humans differ from one another – in terms of gender, race and ethnicity, for example. Despite our many differences, there are some ways in which all humans who have rights are the same. I do not mean because we all belong to the same species (which is true but not relevant). And I do not mean because we all are persons (which may be relevant but is not true). What I mean is that we are like one another in relevant ways, ways that relate to the rights we have: our rights to life, liberty and bodily integrity.

Think about it. Not only are we all in the world, we all are aware of the world, by which I mean we perceive tables and chairs, meadows and sunshine, and colours and odours and sounds. In addition, we are aware of what happens to us, and what happens to us – whether to our body, or our freedom or our life itself – matters to us because it makes a difference to the quality and duration of our life, as experienced by us, whether anybody else cares about this or not. Whatever our differences, these are our fundamental similarities.

We have no commonly used word that names this particular family of similarities. 'Human being' does not do the job (a deceased human being is a human being but is not aware of the world, for example). Neither does 'person' (human infants are aware of what happens to them but are not persons, at least not in the way philosophers understand this idea). Still, these similarities are important enough to warrant a verbal marker of their own. I use the expression 'subject-of-a-life' to refer to them. Given this usage, the author of these words, Tom Regan, is a subject-of-a-life, and so are the people who read them.

Which humans are subjects-of-a-life? All those humans who have the family of similarities mentioned above. And who might these be? Well, somewhere in the neighbourhood of *six billion* of us, regardless of where we live, how old we are, our race or gender or class, our religious or political beliefs, our level of intelligence and so on through a very long inventory of our differences.

Why is being the subject-of-a-life an important idea? Because the family of characteristics that define this idea *makes us all the same* in a way that makes sense of our moral equality. Here is what I mean.

As implied in the preceding sections, human subjects-of-a-life differ in many ways. These differences are real, and they matter. However, when we think about the world in terms of fundamental moral equality, these differences make no difference. Morally considered, a genius who can play Chopin etudes with one hand tied behind her back does not have a 'higher' rank than a serious mentally impaired child who will never know what a piano is or who Chopin was. Morally, we do not carve up the world in this way, placing the Einsteins in the 'superior' category, 'above' the 'inferior' Homer Simpsons of the world. The less gifted do not exist to serve the interests of the more gifted. The latter are not mere things when compared to the former, to be used as means to their ends. From the moral point of view, each of us is equal because each of us is equally a somebody, not a something, the subject-of-a-life, not a life without a subject.

So why is the idea of being the subject-of-a-life important? Because it illuminates our moral sameness, our moral equality:

- As subjects-of-a-life, we are all the same because we are all in the world.
- As subjects-of-a-life, we are all the same because we are all aware of the world.
- As subjects-of-a-life, we are all the same because what happens to us matters to us.
- As subjects-of-a-life what happens to us matters to us because it makes a difference to the quality as well as the duration of our life.
- As subjects-of-a-life, there is no superior or inferior, no higher or lower.
- As subjects-of-a-life, we are all morally the same – all morally equal.

Needless to say, the forgoing does not constitute a strict proof of our rights. My intention, rather, has been to explain how our being subjects-of-a-life illuminates (how it helps us understand) the underpinnings of our rights, especially our moral equality. It should come as no surprise that I believe that what I have just said about our rights is no less true of the rights of other animals.

Animal rights

Are any other-than-human animals subjects-of-a-life? Yes, of course. All mammals, at least. All birds, at least. All fish, at least. Why? Because these beings satisfy the conditions of the kind of subjectivity in question. Like us, they are in the world, aware of the world and aware of what happens to them. Moreover, what happens to them (to their body, their freedom and their life) matters to them, whether anyone else cares about this or not. Thus do these beings share the rights we have mentioned, including the right to be treated with respect.

I am all too painfully aware that some people deny or contest this way of thinking. Animals do not experience anything, some maintain. Or they experience very little, hardly enough to ground the kind of subjectivity I have described. Or (to mention objections from another quarter) no one, human or otherwise, has rights. And so on.

I have addressed these and other relevant challenges on many occasions in the past and do beg leave of them on this one.[2] Here I wish only to mention that respect for the rights of those animals to whom I have referred will have profound, one might even say revolutionary, consequences. Respect for these rights means (among other things) more than cutting back on the amount of meat we eat, or avoiding pale veal, or eating only chicken and fish, or being satisfied with providing farmed animals with larger cages. It means an end to commercial animal agriculture, whether intensive or free range. We do not respect the rights of cows and pigs, chickens and geese, and tuna and trout by ending their life prematurely, however 'humane' the methods used. These animals have a right to life no less certainly than we do. Or so I believe, even as I hope the reader will agree. It remains to be asked what role sentience might play in helping us understand human and animal rights to life, liberty and bodily integrity.

Two meanings of 'sentience'

Some people favour a broad understanding of sentience, one that equates being sentient with consciousness in any of its myriad manifestations.[3] Given this understanding, beings who think, imagine, remember, act purposefully, feel emotions and experience pleasure and pain are sentient. More, the same is true of beings who lack all these capacities but who are able to see, hear and in other ways perceive objects in their immediate environment. They are sentient beings, too.

Now, some of these same thinkers maintain that sentience, in any of its forms, is both necessary and sufficient for having rights. In their view, in other words, all sentient beings have rights *because* they are sentient, and (again) only sentient beings have rights *because* they are sentient.

I do not think this is correct. There is no plausible reason to think that having the capacity to hear or smell in itself confers rights on anybody or helps us understand rights when they are possessed. Granted, if the beings who have such capacities *want to be free to use them,* or if being denied their use *detracts from their welfare,* then we may have the beginnings of an argument for recognizing their rights. However, this is not what the broad interpretation of sentience maintains. It maintains that possession of these perceptual capacities themselves, independent of any other capacity, including wanting or desiring, is sufficient for having rights. Speaking for myself, this seems more than false. It seems plainly false.

Some thinkers prefer a narrow interpretation of sentience, one that limits it to the capacity to experience pleasure and pain, to suffer and enjoy.[4] Would the presence of this capacity, unlike the capacity for sense perception, help us understand why sentient beings have the rights we have been discussing?

One could argue – in fact I have made this argument in the past[5] – that sentience in the narrow sense plays a central role in explicating why sentient beings have the right to be spared gratuitous suffering, suffering that cannot be morally justified. Just as it is wrong to cause such suffering in others, so (it can be argued) these others have a right not to be the victims.

Suppose this much is granted. Even if it is, it is hard to understand how the mere capacity to experience pleasure and pain can help us understand why sentient beings all have rights to life, liberty and bodily integrity. If the basis of rights is sentience in the narrow sense, then sentient beings whose lives are taken, whose freedom is stolen or whose bodies are injured have no right violated if these assaults are done painlessly, a consequence no serious animal rights advocate would embrace. As is true of the broad interpretation of sentience, therefore, the narrow, hedonic one fails to illuminate (fails to help us understand) why sentient beings have the rights we have been discussing.

Where, then, if not the broad or the narrow interpretation, should we turn for greater understanding? Perhaps further reflection on being the subject-of-a-life will offer the needed assistance.

Sentient beings and subjects-of-a-life

Notice, to begin with, that while all subjects-of-a-life are sentient, not all sentient beings are subjects-of-a-life. Beings who are aware of the world (who perceive things in their immediate environment) are sentient, in the broad sense; but having this capacity is not sufficient for being a subject-of-a-life (for having an experiential welfare, for example).

Notice, too, that the same is true of having sentience in the narrow sense. In our case, our mental life has continuity and unity over time. We are the same subjects-of-a-life today as we were yesterday and (assuming all goes well) as we will be tomorrow. In the normal course of events, moreover, we perceive the world around us, remember some of our past experiences, learn from them and use our knowledge to anticipate what will happen in the future. It is entirely possible that some sentient beings (in the narrow sense) are not like this. We might picture their way of being in the world as akin to soap bubbles. They are here one moment and gone the next. In their case, there is no one they were yesterday and there will be no one for them to be tomorrow. In their case, as well, there is no perception of the things that surround them, no memory of past experience, no learning, no anticipation.

Logically, there is no reason why some sentient beings, in the narrow sense, cannot be like this. Severely brain damaged and sensory impaired humans are one possible example. One moment something is done to them and they experience something pleasant; then, like a burst soap bubble, they are gone. The same thing happens when it comes to their experience of pain. One moment something is done to them and they experience something painful; then, like a burst soap bubble, they are gone. They perceive nothing around them. They remember nothing. Neither do they learn or anticipate.

Beings meeting this description, though sentient, are not subjects-of-a-life. And they are not subjects-of-a-life for the simplest of reasons: they are not aware of (they do not perceive) objects in the world around them. In fact, they have no understanding that there is a world 'out there', so to speak, that is open to their awareness.

So, yes, again, while all subjects-of-a-life are sentient, not all sentient beings are subjects-of-a-life, whether sentience is understood broadly or narrowly. The reverse, however, is true: all subjects-of-a-life are sentient, given both the broad and narrow interpretations of sentience. For in so far as subjects-of-a-life are aware of the world (they have sensory perception), the broad understanding captures this capacity shared by all subjects-of-a-life. And in so far as what happens to them matters to them because it makes a difference to the quality of their life, this characteristic of subjects-of-a-life is captured by the narrow understanding as well.

Now, one could say (and perhaps some readers will say) that being the subject-of-a-life represents a third way to interpret sentience. We might even think of it as a middle way, not as broad as the broad interpretation but also not as narrow as the narrow one, a way that helps us better understand why we and other animals have the rights we do. Given this way of thinking, subjects-of-a-life *just are* sentient beings, and sentient beings *just are* subjects-of-a-life.

Myself, I have no objection to thinking in these terms provided we are clear about what we are doing if we do so. To put the main point as simply as possible: we would be *prescribing* a new way to use an old word, not *describing* how it already is used. If we look up 'sentient' and its cognates in any diction-ary, we never find words like 'what happens to us – whether to our body or our freedom, or our life itself – matters to us' as part of the definition. What we find instead is very much in keeping with the broad interpretation, as in this example: 'Sentient ... 1. Capable of sensation or at least rudimentary consciousness ... 2a: consciously perceiving: aware ...'[6]

The plain fact is, 'sentient' and its cognates already have established mean-ings that give 'sentient being' a different meaning than 'subject-of-a-life'. Of course, we can, if we choose to do so, *stipulate* that we will henceforth give 'sentient being' a new meaning. As to whether we should go down this path, that is a question I leave for each person to consider as future time and circum-stances permit.

In conclusion, investigating and understanding the many forms of sentience found in animals is important for many reasons, including the cause of their liberation from the hands of human tyranny. The great mass of humanity will never change their views about how animals should be treated unless or until they change their views about who these (non-humans) are. For this very reason, all of us who spend sleepless nights waiting for this day to dawn must be forever grateful to the many scientific and other advances being made in our understanding of animal sentience.

Notes

1   My remarks in this section are adapted from Regan, T. (2004) *Empty Cages: Facing the Challenge of Animal Rights*, Rowman and Littlefield, Lanham, MD

2   See, for example, Regan, T. (2004) *The Case for Animal Rights*, 2nd edn, University of California Press, Berkeley

3   Joan Dunayer is a proponent of the broad interpretation. See Dunayer, J. (2005) *Speciesism*, Lantern Books, New York

4   Peter Singer is a proponent of the narrow interpretation. See Singer, P. (1975) *Animal Liberation*, Avon Books, New York (and later updated editions of the book)

5   See, for example, Regan, T. (1975) 'The moral basis of vegetarianism', *Canadian Journal of Philosophy*, vol 5, pp181–214

6   Webster (1961) *Third New International Dictionary of the English Language*, Mirriam-Webster, Inc, Springfield, MA

8

Entitling Non-human Animals to Fundamental Legal Rights on the Basis of Practical Autonomy

Steven M. Wise

Center for the Expansion of Fundamental Rights,
Florida, US

What are legal rights?

Before we argue that non-human animals should be accorded fundamental legal rights, we must first be clear what we are arguing for. During World War I, Yale law professor Wesley Hohfeld cogently set out what legal rights are.[1] A right, he explained, was an advantage conferred by legal rules upon a legal person. One legal person has a legal advantage (that's the right). Another legal person bears a corresponding legal disadvantage. Neither person can stand alone, and Hohfeld defined their rights in relation to each other.[2]

There are four kinds of legal rights.[3] A 'liberty' allows us to do as we please, but no one need respect what we do. A 'claim' demands respect, for it can constrain another's liberty by requiring one to act, or not act, in certain ways towards someone with a claim.[4] A 'power' can affect another's legal rights; the power to sue being perhaps the most important.[5] Last, the 'immunity' legally disables one person from interfering with another.[6] Claims say what one should not do; immunities what one cannot legally do. You cannot enslave me because human slavery is prohibited; humans are *immune* from enslavement.[7] Such immunities as freedom from slavery and torture are the most basic kind of legal rights. It's these to which at least some non-human animals are most strongly entitled, and immunity rights are likely to be achieved first.[8]

How legal change occurs

I argue that legal change follows a 'round hole, square peg' theory. The round hole is the legal rule that non-human animals are rightless things, chattels, property. The square peg is the potential legal rule that at least some non-human animals are, to some extent, persons entitled to basic legal rights. To attain these rights, one must either square the hole or round the peg. I usually write to advocate change in a legal system that derives from the English common law, in which judges play a more central role than they do in civil or Roman law systems. But much of what I write about common-law judges applies in civil law systems, sometimes for judges, but more often for legislatures.

Judges, and legislators, may have different values. Judges with 'formal visions' look backwards and think judges should decide the way judges have decided, because judges have decided that way. The most formal of these judges – I call them 'Precedent (Rules) Judges' – think it better that law be certain than it be correct. Valuing stability, certainty and predictability, they see law as a system of narrow and consistent rules from which they can glean rules that they can more-or-less mechanically apply. 'Precedent (Principles) Judges' look to a different past. Prior decisions set out broad principles to guide judges who need not confine themselves to the specific ways in which these principles have been applied, but can operate at a higher level of generality.

'Substantive' judges may weigh social considerations, moral, economic and political.[9] Law, they believe, should express a community's present sense of justice, not that of another age.[10] Courts should keep law consonant with public values, prevailing understandings of justice, morality and new scientific discoveries. They don't want issues settled, but settled correctly. Substantive Judges who try to predict the future are 'Policy Judges', who try to predict the effects of their rulings and think law should be used to achieve important goals, such as economic growth, national unity or the health or welfare of a community. On the other hand, 'Principle Judges' value principles and moral rightness when deciding cases, principles they may borrow from religion, ethics, economics, politics or even literature.[11]

Fundamental rights

In 2000, US Circuit Judge Richard Posner, the leading scholarly judge in the US, reviewed my book *Rattling the Cage – Toward Legal Rights for Animals* in the *Yale Law Journal*. In that book I set forth some of the arguments I make here. Posner found it 'not an intellectually exciting book'.[12] But he did 'not say this in criticism. Remember who Wise is: a practicing lawyer who wants to persuade the legal profession that courts should do more to protect animals'.[13]

This was perceptive. In arguing for the basic legal rights of non-human animals, I rely upon first principles of western law, liberty and equality. These are hoary enough to be enshrined in the American Declaration of Independence: 'We hold these truths to be self-evident, that all men are created equal, that they are endowed by their Creator with certain unalienable Rights, that among these rights are Life, Liberty, and the pursuit of Happiness.' French Revolutionaries demanded liberté and egalité. They appear in Article I of the Universal Declaration of Rights: 'All human beings are born free and equal in dignity and rights'; explicitly or implicitly in Articles 1, 2, 7, 9, 13, 16, 17, 18,

19, 21, 24, 25, 26, 27 and other articles of the Portuguese Constitution; and in Articles 2, 3, 4, 5 and 14 of the European Convention on Human Rights.

Equality demands that likes be treated alike. Equality rights therefore depend upon how one rightless animal compares to another with rights. An animal might be entitled to basic equality rights, even if she isn't entitled to liberty rights, because she is 'like' someone with basic liberty rights. Liberty rights entitle one to be treated a certain way because of how one is constructed, especially one's mental abilities. Since World War II, nations have agreed that the liberty to act as one pleases stops somewhere; they don't always agree where.[14] But some absolute and irreducible degree of bodily liberty and bodily integrity are everywhere considered sacrosanct. If we trespass upon them we inflict the gravest injustice, for we treat others as things.[15] We may not enslave or torture. Yet these sacred places are the front line in the battle for the rights of non-human animals.

One important aspect of liberty is autonomy, or self-determination. If a being has it, she is entitled to basic liberty rights. Things don't act autonomously; persons do. Things can't self-determine; persons can. Things lack volition; persons don't. Persons have wills.[16] Philosophers often understand autonomy as Kant did two centuries ago. I call Kant's version of autonomy, 'full autonomy'. Non-human animals, and probably children, act from desire, Kant believed.[17] Fully autonomous beings act completely rationally and should therefore be treated as legal persons.[18]

Kant is not the only philosopher to try to knit hyper-rationality into the fabric of liberty.[19] The most honest concede what philosopher Carl Wellman calls a 'monstrous conclusion': a great many human beings are not entitled to fundamental legal rights.[20] Most normal adults lack full autonomy. Infants, children, the severely mentally retarded or autistic, the senile and the persistently vegetative never come close. Were judges to accept full autonomy as prerequisite for personhood, they would exclude most humans.

Judges who deny personhood to every non-human animal act arbitrarily. They don't say they do, of course. Instead they use legal fictions, transparent lies they insist we believe, which allow them to attribute personhood to humans lacking consciousness, sometimes lacking brains, to ships, trusts, corporations, and even to religious idols.[21] They pretend that these have autonomy. Legal scholar John Chipman Gray couldn't see any difference between pretending that will-less humans have a will and doing the same for non-human animals.[22] Because legal fictions may cloak abuses of judicial power, Jeremy Bentham characterized them as a '*syphilis* ... (that) carries into every part of the system the principle of rottenness'.[23]

A fair and rational alternative exists: most moral and legal philosophers, and just about every common-law judge, recognize that less complex autonomies exist and that a being can be autonomous if she has preferences and the ability to act to satisfy them; or if she can cope with changed circumstances; or if she can make choices, even if she can't evaluate their merits very well; or if she has desires and beliefs and can make at least some sound and appropriate inferences from them.[24]

The sorts of autonomies are 'realistic' or 'practical'.[25] 'Practical autonomy' is not just what most humans have, but what most judges think is *sufficient* for basic liberty rights, and it boils down to this: a being has practical autonomy, and is entitled to personhood and basic liberty rights, if she:

- can desire;
- intentionally tries to fulfill her desire;
- possesses a sense of self sufficient to allow her to understand, even dimly, that she wants something and is trying to get it.[26]

Consciousness, but not necessarily self-consciousness, and sentience are implicit in practical autonomy.

But human newborns, foetuses and even ova sometimes have legal rights, even though they lack all autonomy. This might be explained as resulting from legal fictions or sheer arbitrariness. But it might also have something to do with autonomy. They may not have it now, but it's believed they have the potential. And if they have the potential, we should treat them as if they have it now.

But the potential for autonomy no more justifies treating someone as if he has autonomy than does the fact that someone's potential for dying justifies treating him as if he were already dead.[27] Philosopher Joel Feinberg thought allocating rights based on potential was simply a logical error. Potential autonomy gives rise to potential rights, while actual autonomy gives rise to actual rights.[28] And even the potentiality argument fails to explain how the common law can grant basic rights to adult humans who never had and never will have autonomy.

Isaiah Berlin wrote, 'if the essence of men is that they are autonomous beings... then nothing is worse than to treat them as if they were not autonomous, but natural objects, played on by causal influences at the mercy of external stimuli'.[29] The same is true for any being who meets the requirements for practical autonomy. He is entitled to basic liberty rights. But an animal may be entitled to equality rights even if he lacks practical autonomy.

A scale of practical autonomy

What are the chances that any animal feels or wants or acts intentionally or thinks or knows or has a self?[30] The more certain we are the answer to any of these questions is 'yes', the closer is the probability to 1.0. If 'no' is certain, the probability is 0.0. If we think the answer impossible to know, or it's possible, but we just don't anything, the probability is exactly 0.50.

The more exactly the behaviour of any non-human animal resembles ours and the taxonomically closer he is, the more confident we can be that he possesses desires, intentions and a sense of self resembling ours, and that we can fairly assign him an autonomy value closer to ours. Practical autonomy is hard to quantify and we should consider not just those mental abilities that directly reveal it, but mental complexity in general, on the assumption that some rough association between general mental complexity and practical autonomy exists.

When a range of behaviours in an evolutionary cousin, such as a chimpanzee, closely resembles ours, we can confidently assign him a value near 1.0. Let's place any animal with an autonomy value of 0.90 or greater into Category One. These animals clearly possess practical autonomy sufficient for basic liberty rights. They are probably self-conscious and pass the mirror self-recognition (MSR) test, which was developed by psychologist Gordon Gallup, Jr, in the 1970s while working with chimpanzees. Gallup placed red marks on the heads of anaesthetized chimpanzees, then watched to see if they touched the marks when peering into a mirror. He assumed that if they did, they were self-aware.[31] Gallup's MSR test, and variants adapted for other non-human species and human infants, are widely used as a marker for visual self-recognition, though there is disagreement about what it signifies and whether failures mean that self-awareness is lacking. But if one passes, one should be placed into Category One. These animals often have some or all the elements of a theory of mind (they know what others see or know); understand symbols; use a sophisticated language or language-like communication system; and may deceive, pretend, imitate or solve complex problems.

Into Category Two are animals who fail MSR tests. They may lack self-consciousness and every element of a theory of mind, but possess a simpler consciousness; mentally represent and are able to act insightfully; think; perhaps use a simple communication system; have a primitive, but sufficient, sense of self; and are not too evolutionarily distant from humans.

The strength of each animal's liberty rights will turn upon what mental abilities she has and how certain we are she has them. Category Two covers the immense cognitive ground of every animal with an autonomy value between 0.51 and 0.89. Whether an animal should be placed in the higher (0.80–0.89), middle (0.70–0.79) or lower (0.51–0.69) reaches of Category Two depends upon whether she uses symbols, conceptualizes (mentally represents) or demonstrates other sophisticated mental abilities. Her taxonomic class (e.g. mammal, bird, reptile, amphibian, fish or insect) and the nearness of her evolutionary relationship to humans (which are related) may also be important factors.

We can assign taxonomically and evolutionarily remote animals, whose behaviour scarcely resembles ours and who may lack all consciousness and be nothing but living stimulus–response machines, an autonomy value below 0.5. The lower the value the more certain we are that they utterly lack practical autonomy. We'll place them all into Category Four. Finally, we do not know enough about many, perhaps most, non-human animals reasonably to determine whether their autonomy values should be above or below 0.5. Perhaps we have never taken the time to learn about them or our minds are not sufficiently keen to understand them. We'll place them to Category Three.

Taking precaution

How should we assign an autonomy value to an animal about whose mental abilities we know something, but are uncertain? Scientific uncertainty exists whenever data is incomplete or absent, because we can't or don't know how to measure accurately, we sample improperly, our theoretical models are simply wrong or because we confuse cause and effect.[32] Moreover, scientists recognize that absolute scientific truth doesn't exist. Much of what they do is to try to gain more certainty.

Uncertainty is no less common in law. But judges and legislatures may lack the scientist's luxury of deferring judgment until the data are more complete. In the face of uncertainty and chance of error, they content themselves with deciding on which side they wish to err. In Anglo–American law a criminal defendant is presumed to be innocent until and unless a jury of 12 unanimously finds him guilty of committing the crime charged beyond a reasonable doubt. Every reasonable doubt is therefore resolved in the defendant's favour.

A so-called 'precautionary principle' is finding a home in US law and German law; emerging in English, Australian and European law; and even evolving as a customary rule of international environmental law.[33] For example, the United States Endangered Species Act requires federal agencies to give a benefit of the doubt to any threatened or endangered species when determining how to act, while the Marine Mammal Protection Act permits takings (killing or capturing) of marine mammals 'only when it is known that the taking would not be to the disadvantage of the species'.[34] The World Charter for Nature says 'activities which are likely to pose a significant risk to nature shall be preceded by an exhaustive examination; their proponents shall demonstrate that expected benefits outweigh potential damage to nature, and where potential adverse effects are not fully understood, the activities should not proceed'.[35]

For centuries law followed an 'exploitation principle' in our dealings with non-human animals. All were erroneously thought to lack most, perhaps every, sophisticated basic mental ability – desire, intentionality, self, perhaps even consciousness – and were categorized as legal things, and mercilessly exploited.[36] But evidence is clear that, for at least some, this is untrue. In light of what we know, it is time to apply a precautionary principle to at least some non-human animals. Depriving any being with practical autonomy of basic liberty rights is a most terrible injustice. When there is doubt and serious damage is threatened, we should err on the cautious side where evidence of practical autonomy exists. And some evidence is required, for every version of the precautionary principle instructs 'how to respond when there is some evidence, but not proof, that a human practice is damaging the environment'.[37] Speculation is not enough.[38]

The precautionary principle has at least seven senses.[39] At its weakest, it merely requires a decision-maker to think ahead and act cautiously. A stronger version requires a decision-maker carefully to regulate her actions, even in the face of insufficient scientific evidence of a threat. Stronger still is the demand that the proponent of a potentially harmful act prove its harmlessness to an unusually stringent degree.[40] This shifting of the normal burden of proof may be tantamount to forbidding the act, for the more uncertain the evidence, the more likely it will be that whoever has the burden of proof will lose.[41] A kind of precautionary principle has been argued as a reason for not using seriously defective human beings in painful biomedical research. The reason, philosopher Christina Hoff wrote, is not because they are human, for Hoff concedes that is insufficient. It is because we cannot 'safely permit anyone to decide which human beings fall short of worthiness. Judgments of this kind and the creation of institutions for making them are fraught with danger and open to grave abuse.'[42] When rights for non-human animals are involved, there is a compelling reason to apply the precautionary principle that goes beyond what Hoff says and doesn't exist in environmental law.

Assigning autonomy values

After reviewing the evidence, a judge or legislature may assign an autonomy value to any non-human animal. A value of 0.9 or higher will place any animal in Category One; she will be presumed to have practical autonomy sufficient for basic liberty rights. A Category Four animal, scored at less than 0.5, will be presumed to lack practical autonomy. Any animal given a score of 0.5 means we haven't a clue.

There may be vast differences among Category Two animals, whose autonomy values range from 0.51 to 0.89. A refusal to apply the precautionary principle would result in every Category Two animal being disqualified from liberty rights. An expansive application of the precautionary principle would mean that any animal with an autonomy value above 0.50 should be granted some basic liberty rights. I propose an intermediate reading: any animal with an autonomy value higher than 0.70 is presumed to have practical autonomy sufficient for basic liberty rights. But how should an animal scoring higher than 0.50 but less than 0.70 be treated? By definition, some evidence exists that they possess practical autonomy, but it is weak, either because at least one element is missing, or the elements together are feebly supported.

More than a million animal species exist. While Darwinian evolution postulates a natural continuum of mental abilities, the animal kingdom is incredibly diverse. At some taxonomic point, the elements of practical autonomy begin to evaporate: self, intentions, desire, sentience and finally consciousness. We don't know precisely where. I have stood on the summit of Cadillac Mountain on Mount Desert Island in Maine watching the summer sun rise. At four o'clock in the morning, it was indisputably night, at seven o'clock indisputably day. When did night become day?

We could deal with this problem in one of two ways. Not using the precautionary principle would allow a judge or legislature to draw a line. Any animal beneath it would not be entitled to liberty rights. However, there is another way that is consistent with even a moderate reading of the precaution-ary principle. Personhood and basic liberty rights should be given in proportion to the degree that one has practical autonomy. If you have it, you get rights in full. But if you don't, the degree to which you *approach* it might make you eligible to receive some proportion of liberty rights.[43]

This idea of receiving proportional liberty rights accords with how judges often think. They may give *fewer* legal rights to humans who lack autonomy. But they don't make her a legal thing. A severely mentally limited human adult or child who lacks the mental wherewithal to participate in the political process may still move freely about. They may give *narrower* legal rights to her. A severely mentally limited human adult or child might not have the right to move in the world at large, but may move freely within her home or within an institution. They may give *parts* of a complex right (remember that what we normally think of as a legal right is actually a bundle of them). A severely mentally limited human might have a claim to bodily integrity, but lack the power to waive it, and be unable to consent to a risky medical procedure or the withdrawal of life-saving medical treatment.[44]

Consistent with a moderate use of the precautionary principle, we need not grant basic liberty rights to a non-human animal who has just a shadow of practical autonomy; that is, we grant even animals with an autonomy value of 0.51 some tiny right. But it would be consistent with such a reading for an animal with an autonomy value of 0.65, perhaps even 0.60, to be given strong consideration for some proportional basic liberty rights.

Fundamental equality rights for non-human animals

Liberty means you receive rights because of what you are, without comparing you to anyone. Equality is different. It requires a comparison. Since likes should be treated alike, something can only be equal *to* something or to someone else. Equality, the idea that likes should be treated alike, is among the highest values and principles of western law.[45] Because courts and legislatures are forever making distinctions and drawing lines, and necessarily so, equality can be hard to apply.[46] Early on, the European Court of Human Rights turned back the argument that every difference in treatment violates the European Convention on Human Rights.[47] European discrimination is legal only if some objective and reasonable justification exists. It must further some legitimate aim and there must be a reasonable relationship between that aim and the means employed to attain it.[48] This is essentially how the US Supreme Court normally applies the equality provision of the Constitution.[49] But both Euro-pean and American judges closely scrutinize distinctions based on race, sex or illegitimacy.[50]

In September 2000, physiology professor Colin Blakemore, Britain's most outspoken proponent of the use of all non-human animals in biomedical research, told the Fifth International Congress on Bioethics that humans must use apes and monkeys in biomedical research because they are so like us. Why? Because '[r]esearch on a species which is similar to humans is more likely to generate results which are relevant. It is a dilemma that we all have to acknowledge.'[51] The similarities to which Blakemore refers are mental. When one hears the word 'similarity', one should think about equality.

The strongest argument for equality rights incorporates the argument for dignity-rights and goes like this: A normal human child has dignity-rights by age eight months, perhaps even by four. Any non-human animal with practical autonomy is similar to this child in ways highly relevant to the possession of basic legal rights. As a matter of equality, a chimpanzee who knows a language, often signed, is certainly entitled to them. In many ways her mind resembles the mind of a toddler, even a preschool child. She has a developed sense of self, can pass a mirror self-recognition test, imitate, form complex mental represent-ations, understands hundreds of signs, intentionally communicates and deceives, and demonstrates elements of a theory of mind. Every Category One animal has a strong equality argument for basic rights.

As the minds of more distant non-human animals less and less resemble the minds of human preschool children, then toddlers and infants, either because they become more simple or just different, the argument for equality rights weakens. It may still remain strong, just not as strong. But at some point our minds are no longer sufficiently alike to trigger equality rights at all. Where that point lies is no more clear for equality than it is for liberty, but a moderate application of the precautionary principle suggests generosity.

At some point, all autonomy disappears and with it any non-arbitrary entitle-ment to liberty rights on the ground of possessing practical autonomy. But judges and legislators might still decide to grant even a completely non-autonomous being basic liberty rights. To the extent they confer rights arbitrarily, the argument that, as a matter of equality, non-autonomous animals of many species should be entitled to basic rights is strengthened too.

Judges and legislators actually do this. There are humans with little or no autonomy who have legal rights. In Massachusetts, Joseph Saikewicz, a 67-year-old man with an IQ of ten, and Beth, a ten-month-old girl born in a permanent vegetative state were both given fundamental legal rights.[52] The American state of Louisiana has enacted a statute that designates a fertilized *in vitro* ovum a legal person before it is implanted in a womb.[53] Louisiana judges may appoint curators to protect its rights and the fertilized ovum can even sue and be sued.[54]

The bestowal of rights upon a Joseph Saikewicz, a Beth or a fertilized embryo strengthens the argument for equality rights for not just Category One animals, but also Category Two animals. On what non-arbitrary ground could a judge find that Beth has a fundamental right to bodily integrity that forbids her use in terminal biomedical research, but that a chimpanzee has not, without violating basic notions of equality? Only a radical speciesist could accept a baby girl lacking consciousness, sentience or even a brain having legal rights just because she's human, while the 'thinkingest, 'talkingest', 'feelingest' apes have no rights at all, just because they're not human.[55]

It is the extreme disparity, the utter arbitrariness, of the distinction that powers the argument for equality rights for all Category One and some Category Two animals. This distinction is so extreme, so arbitrary, that it obviously violates the principle of equality at its most fundamental level. The disparity decreases as an animal's autonomy value lessens. As the value approaches 0.50, the disparity becomes small enough to allow a judge rationally to distinguish between that creature and a severely retarded man or a girl in a vegetative state. And, finally, at some point the psychological and political barriers to equality for a non-human animal with a low autonomy value become insuperable.

Notes

1   Wesley Newcomb Hohfeld, *Fundamental Legal Conceptions as Applied in Judicial Reasoning* 64 (Walter Wheeler Cook ed., Yale University Press 1919). See W.L. Morison, *John Austin* 164 (Edward Arnold, 1982); Joseph William Singer, 'The Legal Rights Debate in Analytical Jurisprudence from Bentham to Hohfeld', 1982 *Wisconsin Law Review* 975, 989 note 22; Walter J. Kamba, 'Legal Theory and Hohfeld's Analysis of a Legal Right', *Juridical Review* 249, 249 (1974).

2   David Lyons, 'Correlativity of rights and duties', 4 *Nous* 46 (1970).

3   Rex Martin, *A System of Rights* 31 (Oxford University Press, 1993).

4   Wesley Newcomb Hohfeld, *supra* note 1, at 38, 39

5   *Virani v. Jerry M. Lewis Truck Parts and Equipment, Inc.*, 89 F. 3d 574, 577 (9th Cir. 1996), quoting Judith Jarvis Thomson, *The Realm of Rights* 9 (Harvard University Press, 1990); P.J. Fitzgerald, *Salmond on Jurisprudence* 229 (12th ed., Sweet and Maxwell, 1966).

6   Walter J. Kamba, *supra* note 1, at 256.

7   Rex Martin, *supra* note 3 at 3; L.W. Sumner, *The Moral Foundation of Rights* 37–8 (Oxford University Press, 1987).

8   Steven M. Wise, *Rattling the Cage – Toward Legal Rights for Animals* 59 (Perseus Publishing, 2000).

9   Robert S. Summers, 'Form and Substance in Legal Reasoning', in *Legal Reasoning and Statutory Interpretation* 11 (J. van Dunne, ed., Gouda Quint, 1989).

10   P. S. Atiyah and R. S. Summers, *Form and Substance in Anglo–American Law* 5 (Oxford University Press, 1987).

11   Melvin Aron Eisenberg, *The Nature of the Common Law* 26–37 (Harvard University Press, 1988); Robert S. Summers, 'Two Types of Substantive Reasons: The Core of a Theory of Common Law Justification', 63 *Cornell Law Review* 707, 717–8, 722–724 (1978); Harry H. Wellington, 'Common Law Rules and Constitutional Double Standards: Some Notes on Adjudication', 83 *Yale Law Journal* 221,

223–5 (1973).

12 Richard A. Posner, 'Animal Rights', 110 *Yale Law Journal* 527, 527 (2000).

13 *Id.*

14 *Id.* at 235.

15 *Id.* at 194, 196, 197, 198, 199, 203, 232, 236, 237.

16 See IV Roscoe Pound, *Jurisprudence* 194–199 (West Publishing Co., 1959).

17 Ellen Langer, *The Power of Mindful Learning* 4 (Addison Wesley 1997); Barbara Herman, *The Practice of Moral Judgment* 229 (Harvard University Press, 1993).

18 Immanuel I. Kant, *Groundwork of the Metaphysic of Morals* 114–131 (H. S. Papp, trans., Harper Torchbooks, 1964). *See* Barbara Herman, *supra* note 17, at 227–228.

19 Isaiah Berlin, *supra* note 18, at 216. *See* Michael Allen Fox, 'Animal Experimentation: A Philosopher's Changing Views', in 3 *Between the Species* 260 (spring, 1987).

20 Carl Wellman, *Real Rights* 113–4 (Oxford University Press, 1995). *See* Daniel A. Dombrowski, *Babies and Beasts* 45–140 (University of Illinois Press, 1997) (discussing many modern philosophers); H. L. A. Hart, 'Are There Any Natural Rights?' in *Theories of Rights* 79, 82 (Jeremy Waldron ed., Oxford University Press, 1984); R. G. Frey, *Interests and Rights – The Case Against Animals* 30 (1980). *See also* A. John Simmons, *The Lockean Theory of Rights* 201 note 93 (Princeton University Press, 1992) (listing modern philosophers who claim that children cannot have rights because they lack the capacities for agency, rationality, or autonomy); Katherine Hunt Federle, 'On the Road to Reconceiving Rights for Children: A Postfeminist Analysis of the Capacity Principle', 42 *DePaul Law Review* 983, 987–999 (1993) (Hobbes, Locke, Rousseau, Bentham, and Mill).

21 For example *Guardianship of Doe*, 583 N.E. 2d 1263, 1268 (Mass. 1992); *id.* at 1272–3 (Nolan, J., dissenting); *id.* at 1275 (O'Connor, J., dissenting); *International Shoe Co. v. Washington*, 326 U.S. 310, 316 (1945); *Tauza v. Susquehanna Coal Co.*, 115 N.E. 915, 917 (N.Y. 1917); *Pramatha Nath Nullick v. Pradyumna Kumar Mullick*, 52 Indian L. R. 245, 250 (India 1925). *See* Roscoe Pound, *supra* note 16, at 195, 197, 198.

22 John Chipman Gray, *The Nature and Sources of the Law* 43 (Second edn, The MacMillan Co., 1931).

23 Jeremy Bentham, 'Elements of Packing as Applied to Juries', in 5 *The Works of Jeremy Bentham* 92 (J. Bowring, ed., 1843) (emphasis in the original).

24 Tom Regan, *The Case for Animal Rights* 84–5 (Temple University Press, 1983); James Rachels, *Created From Animals* 140, 147 (Oxford University Press, 1990); William A. Wright, 'Treating animals as ends',

Journal of Value Inquiry 353, 357, 362 (1993); Christopher Cherniak, *Minimal Rationality* 3–17 (MIT Press, 1985).

25 XII *Oxford English Dictionary* 269–270, definitions A.I.1.a and b; A.I.2.a, b, and c; A.I.3. A.I.4 (2nd edn 1989).

26 If I were Chief Justice of the Universe, I might make the capacity to suffer, not practical autonomy, sufficient for personhood and dignity-rights as well. For why should even a non-autonomous being be forced to suffer? But the capacity to suffer appears irrelevant to common-law judges in their consideration of who is entitled to basic rights. Practical autonomy appears sufficient. This may be anathema to disciples of Bentham and Singer. I may not like it much myself. But philosophers argue moral rights; judges decide legal rights. And so I present a legal, and not a philosophical, argument for the dignity-rights of non-human animals.

27 Eric Rakowski, *Equal Justice* 359 (Oxford University Press, 1991).

28 Joel Feinberg, 'Potentiality, Development, and Rights', in *The Problem of Abortion* 145 (2nd. edn., Joel Feinberg, ed., Wadsworth Publishing 1984) (emphases in the original). See H. Tristram Englehardt, Jr., *The Foundations of Bioethics* 143 (2nd ed. Oxford University Press, 1996). See Stanley I. Benn, 'Abortion, Infanticide, and Respect for Persons', in Joel Feinberg, ed., *supra* note 27, at 143.

29 Isaiah Berlin, 'Two concepts of liberty', in *The Proper Study of Mankind* 208 (Henry Hardy and Roger Hausheer, eds, Farrar, Straus and Giroux, 1997).

30 Donald R. Griffin, *Animal Minds – Beyond Cognition to Consciousness* 11 (University of Chicago Press, 2001).

31 Gordon G. Gallup, Jr., 'Chimpanzees: Self-recognition', 167 *Science* 86 (1970).

32 James E. Hickey, Jr. and Vern R. Walker, 'Refining the precautionary principle in international environmental law', 14 *Virginia Environmental Law Journal* 423, 448 (1995).

33 Michele Territo, 'The precautionary principle in marine fisheries conservation and the U.S. Sustainable Fisheries Act of 1996', 24 *Vermont Law Review* 1351, 1352–1358 (1999); Charmian Barton, 'The status of the precautionary principle in Australia: Its emergence in legislation and as a common law doctrine: 12', *Harvard Environmental Law Review* 509, 514, 518 (1998); Chris W. Backes and Jonathan M. Verschuren, 'The precautionary principle in International, European, and Dutch wildlife law', 9 *Colorado Journal of International Environmental Law and Policy* 43 (1998); David Bodansky, 'The precautionary principle in US environmental law', in *Interpreting the Precautionary Principle* 203–228 (Tim O'Riordan and James Cameron, eds, Cameron May, 1996); Sonja Boehmer-Christiansen, 'The precautionary principle in Germany – enabling Government', in *id.* at 31–60; Nigel Haigh, 'The introduction of the precautionary principle in the UK', in *id.* at

229–251; Ronnie Harding, 'The precautionary principle in Australia', in *id.* at 262–283; James Cameron, 'The status of the precautionary principle in international law', in *id.* at 262–283.

34 *Roosevelt Campobello International Park v. Environmental Protection Agency*, 684 F. 2d 104, 1049 (D.C. Cir. 1982) (Endangered Species Act); *Committee for Humane Legislation v. Richardson*, 540 F. 2d 1141, 1145 (D.C. Cir. 1976) (Marine Mammal Protection Act).

35 World Charter for Nature, A/Res/37/7 art. 11/b (October 28, 1982).

36 *See* Steven M. Wise, *supra* note 8, at 9–22.

37 Barnabas Dickson, 'The precautionary principle in CITES: A critical assessment', 39 *Natural Resources Journal* 211, 213 (1999).

38 James E. Hickey, Jr. and Vern R. Walker, *supra* note 32, at 448–449

39 Jonas Ebbeson, *Compatibility of International and National Environmental Law* 119 n. 73 ((Kluwer Law International, 1996).

40 Charmian Barton, *supra* note 33, at 520, 550; David Freestone, 'The precautionary principle', in *International Law and Global Climate Change* 25 (Robin Churchill and David Freestone, eds, International Environmental Law and Policy Series, 1991); J. Cameron and J. Abouchar, 'The precautionary principle: A fundamental principal of law and policy for the protection of the global environment', 14 *Boston College International and Comparative Law Review* 1, 20–23 (1991). See, e.g. David Pearce, 'The precautionary principle and economic analysis,' in *id.* at 132, 144.

41 William Rogers, 'Benefits, costs and risks: Oversight of health and environmental decision-making', 4 *Harvard Environmental Law Review* 191, 225 (1980).

42 Christina Hoff (Summers), 'Immoral and moral uses of animals', 302 *New England Journal of Medicine* 115, 117 (1980).

43 Carl Wellman, *supra* note 20, at 129; Alan Gewirth, *Reason and Morality* 111, 121 (University of Chicago Press, 1978).

44 Carl Wellman, *supra* note 20, at 130–1.

45 *See* Peter Westen, *Speaking of Equality – An Analysis of the Rhetorical Force of 'Equality' in Moral and Legal Discourse* xiv note 2 (Princeton University Press 1990).

46 For example, Eric Rakowski, *Equal Justice* (Oxford University Press, 1991); Peter Westen, *supra* note 5; Douglas Rae, *Equalities* (Harvard University Press, 1981).

47 *The Belgian Linguistics Case*, A6., at para. 34 (Eur. Ct. Hum. R. 1968) (final judgment).

48 *Darby v. Sweden*, A. 87, at para. 31; *The Belgian Linguistics Case*, *supra* note 8, at 34.

49 See, e.g. *Romer v. Evans*, 517 U.S. 620, 634–635 (1996); *Rinaldi v. Yeager*, 384 U.S. 305, 308–309 (1966).

50 Race (*Korematsu v. United States*, 323 U.S. 214 (1944); *East African*

Asians Cases; 3 EHRR 76 (1973)); sex (*United States v. Virginia*, 116 S.Ct. 2264, 2277–2278 (1996); *Abdulaziz, Cabales, and Balkandali v. UK*, A.94, at para. 78 (Eur. Ct. Hum. R. 1985)); illegitimacy (*Trimble v. Gordon*, 430 U.S. 762 (1977); *Marckx v. Belgium*, A 19, at para. 48 (Eur. Ct. Hum. R. 1975)). Compare *Weinburger v. Salfi*, 422 U.S. 749, 785 (1975) with *Cleveland Board of Education v. LaFleur*, 414 U.S. 632 (1974); *Stanley v. Illinois*, 405 U.S. 645 (1972).

51   Excerpt from presentation of Colin Blakemore to the Fifth International Congress on Bioethics, London, September 23, 2000, reported in Catherine Pepinster, *Independent Digital (UK)*, September 24, 2000.

52   Steven M Wise, *supra* note 8, at 244–245.

53   La. Rev. Stat. Ann. Sec. 9:123 (1990).

54   La. Rev. Stat. Ann. Sec. 9:124 and 9:126 (1990).

55   Daniel Dombrowski, *Babies and Beasts – The Argument from Marginal Cases* 14, 21, 22, 23, 26, 34, 49–50, 52, 54, 63, 76, 77, 90, 92, 106, 116, 127, 152, 155, 159, 167, 168, 169, 182–183 (University of Illinois Press, 1997). See, e.g. Carl Cohen, 'The Case for the Use of Animals in Biomedical Research', 315 *New England Journal of Medicine* 865, 867 (1986); Richard A. Epstein, 'The Next Rights Revolution?' *National Review* 44, 45 (November 8, 2000).

9

Animal Welfare Legislation in China: Public Understanding and Education

Song Wei

University of Science and Technology of China

Complementarity of legislation and education

This chapter is mainly concerned with public understanding, publicity and specialized education in relation to animal welfare laws in China. However, the question of legislation needs to be mentioned first because legislation and popular acceptance are mutually complementary. Popular understanding and popular acceptance must precede legislation; after legislation has been enacted, they are the crucial link in the process of enforcement.

First, even the most perfect modern systems of laws, guidelines and regulations are merely skeletons. If a nation lacks the mental basis to give those empty systems real life, if the people expected to carry them out have not moved towards modernization in their psychology, thinking, viewpoint and behaviour, then failure is tragically unavoidable. No matter how good the legal and regulatory systems may be, no matter how advanced the technology is, they will become a pile of waste paper in the hands of the conservatives. For these systems to be successful and to have the desired effect, the quality of the people involved is crucial; a country will never realize modernization in any area of life, unless its people are able to advance in psychology, thinking and behaviour in parallel with economic development, and to work effectively with each other.

Secondly, from a sociological point of view, legislation, or the establishment of laws, is a process designed to raise social and economic activity in a particular area of activity to the level of those particular legal standards and regulations. This process occurs through understanding of and compliance with the legal requirements involved. During the process of the establishment of laws, the legal consciousness of society forms the bridge between economic realities and legal regulations. It directly determines the purposes and the values embodied in the legislation.

Thirdly, laws must be realized in society. Unrealizable laws are nothing but meaningless sheets of paper. This is a distortion of the essence of legislation. Legislation cannot be realized effectively without a universal spirit among the citizens to abide by the law, and this spirit must be based on the recognition by all citizens of the rule of law in a modern society. It is this tradition of abiding by the law that can really prevent crimes, and this tradition has to be rooted in the belief that legislation is not merely a policy instrument, but is also relevant to the ultimate goals of human life.

Therefore, the concept of animal welfare needs to be publicized and disseminated among all citizens in order to raise the level of social behaviour, and to ensure that the public can understand, accept and carry out the animal welfare legislation.

Publicity is not enough – legislation is fundamental

First, publicity and education are only effective at the moral level. Animal welfare will therefore be dependent on public awareness and the public conscience to ensure its enforcement. Enforcement as a matter of individual conscience is not enough, and animal welfare needs to be enforced by law to regulate and restrain the behaviour of citizens.

Secondly, in order to establish the rule of law, to build a state equipped with legal institutions and to realize the advancement of social civilization and modernization, legislation on animal welfare is both unavoidable and desirable. A civilized nation is obliged to establish humane laws and regulations to protect animals from cruelty.

Thirdly, China has successfully joined the World Trade Organization, and has won the right to hold the Summer Olympic Games in 2008. This is both an advantageous factor and an encouragement to Chinese legislation on animal welfare. Before Korea and Japan co-hosted the World Cup in 2002, there were widespread international protests against the Korean practice of cruelly raising and killing dogs for food, and calls for the Korean government to enforce the law protecting dogs and cats from being abused and ban the consumption of dog meat. From this, it can be seen that neglect of the gaps in animal welfare legislation will definitely impair the international image of China and could damage China's relations with the rest of the world.

Fourthly, legislation is essential because popular understanding and acceptance needs to have a foundation in the law. Systematic procedures are essential to support the popular will. Legislation not only ensures animal welfare, but also plays a role in leading the will of the people. Therefore, there is an urgent need for China to enact the relevant legislation on animal welfare, especially anti-cruelty laws, to make clear the legal status of animals.

It can be concluded from the above that legislation and popular understanding of animal welfare are complementary. Both of them should be seen as equally important and equally necessary.

Some suggestions on public and specialized education related to Animal Welfare Laws in China

The essence of public acceptance of Animal Welfare Laws is education of the entire nation. This should include social education aimed at different communities; fundamental education among university, high school and primary school students; specialized courses for professionals working on animal welfare; and adult education and training in order to improve the quality of staff working in animal laboratories, zoos, livestock husbandry, circuses and other fields that have direct contact with animals.

No one is born with the concept of animal welfare, but it can be gained by learning. Thus it has to be learned through the education system, which expresses the values and nature of society as a whole. For this reason, the whole of society needs to be educated on animal welfare.

In order to achieve popular understanding and public education, we need to emphasize morality and legislation together. On the one hand, we need to put forward the ideas of cooperation, compassion for the weak and respect for life; advocate kindness to living things; and pay attention to the value and basic rights of other lives. On the other hand, we need to emphasize laws and the legal status of animals in order to make citizens aware of the difference between legal and illegal ways of treating animals. In specialized education for professionals, we need to increasingly improve research in all relevant subject areas and to cultivate ideas of animal welfare among professional staff.

The following is an outline of each of these types of animal welfare education.

Social education aimed at all social groups

The purpose of social education is to put out a positive message that will encourage a change in public consciousness leading towards greater love and care for animals. The following are some of the measures that may be taken.

In the course of time, the use of bulletin boards in streets and cultural activities in the community could make the topic of animal welfare something that becomes part of people's everyday lives. In the countryside, the idea of animal welfare could be introduced to farmers together with training in new husbandry and slaughter methods that can enhance both animal welfare and economic benefits. This is similar to the way in which scientific and technological advances have been publicized in the past. A special day could be established as Animal Welfare Day when all citizens would be exposed to publicity on moral and legal aspects of animal welfare.

Places such as zoos and specimen centres that exhibit animals are in a good position to publicize the idea of animal welfare. Presently, the information given about an animal in a zoo is limited to its distribution and habitat, natural behaviour, to what degree it is protected and even focuses on its practical value for medicine, fur and so on. Such a situation must be changed because it may create an erroneous and deep-rooted view among the public, especially among children, who enjoy visiting zoos, that animals are born to be used by man. In addition, it may leave the impression in people's minds that animals are subordinate to man in the same way that inanimate objects are, with no consideration for the feeling of animals.

China can instead follow the successful practice of other wildlife parks. For example, many notices can be seen in zoos carrying messages such as, 'Please do not feed the animals because their keepers have provided them enough balanced nutrition. Extra food will harm their health'; 'Please keep quiet so as not to frighten the animals'; 'Please do not imitate gibbons singing because it will offend them. In the wild, gibbons defend their territory and drive off invaders of the same species by such calls. If you roar at our gibbons, they will feel upset, thinking you are threatening to invade their territory.'

The zoo itself pays attention to improving the animals' living conditions, reducing their anxiety and building more suitable and safer living places for them. In order to cultivate the awareness of the need to cherish animals and nature from childhood, many zoos have educational centres to provide information on animals to visiting high school and primary school students, to help the children to imperceptibly form the habit of being close to animals and making friends with them.

Zoos can organize animal adoption programmes to increase consciousness among citizens of the need to care for animals, and also to raise more funds. A visitor needs only contribute a small amount of money a year, and then he can adopt an animal in cooperation with others. The adopter will receive a picture of the animal, a certificate of adoption and a visitor's ticket. In addition, he will be given a sense of achievement by having his name displayed.

Zoos in China could also publicize the idea of animal welfare through the information provided for visitors, by telling them about the nature and disposition of each animal, leading them imperceptibly to accept the concept of animal welfare. In this way, people would learn to care for animals from the bottom of their hearts, to avoid unnecessary pain or abuse, and to think of animal welfare first when making use of them, rather than having a purely instrumental attitude to animals. To my mind, this would be a very effective means of social education.

China also needs to organize specialized animal welfare organizations, because it is difficult to protect animal welfare effectively if one depends only on governmental executive institutions and the courts. For example, we can follow the example of the RSPCA in the UK by setting up a national charitable civic organization that is non-profit making. This would have professionals as members from all over the country. Its administrative institutions would be made up of legal and animal experts dedicated to animal welfare in China, as well as in the rest of the world. The establishment of such an organization would be very advantageous to the progress of animal welfare. Publicity and education about animal welfare would be achieved by appeals to the public, the use of the media to spread the animal welfare message, the production of free educational materials, the development of economic resources and so on.

Fundamental education aimed at university, high school and primary school students

In the kindergarten, an 'animal corner' could be set up, where some common 'pet' animals are kept and cared for, in order to cultivate an attitude of care for animals, and get to know the natural behaviour of those friends of man from childhood.

In primary schools, within the elementary science curriculum, some basic knowledge of animal welfare could be introduced to allow students to become familiar with the nature of some common animals, especially birds or pets. It would also be possible to introduce the concept of Animal Welfare Laws to students so that they may become familiar with the idea of legislation in relation to animals from childhood. The emphasis would be put on respect and love towards animals and nature. In other words, the aim would be to cultivate the consciousness of animal welfare and reduce the incidence of cruelty that results from ignorance. For example, when introducing an animal, the diction-ary for primary school students should not mention only its economic value, such as delicious meat, warm fur and so on.

Current biological courses offered in Chinese middle schools pay no attention to how a live animal becomes a dead one in the hands of the students. Such a state of affairs must be changed urgently. Biological textbooks should introduce basic but inclusive knowledge of animal welfare, because students will finally step into a society where they will have contact with more animals (such as experimental animals, working animals, farm animals, etc), and currently are likely to cause them greater harm. The education in middle school needs to encourage not only empathy and emotion but also to emphasize the binding force of morality and legislation. In addition, cruel experiments can do no good to the students' emotional development; schools should completely abandon the performance of repeated and unnecessary animal experiments.

In universities, animal welfare should be introduced as a subject of study in the same way as the subject of wildlife and environmental protection, in the form of group activities and elective courses. Education at this level should be in-depth, including seminars and practical work on topics relevant to animal welfare. It also needs to emphasize legal aspects of the subject in order to restrain the behaviour of any individual college students who may be have psychological or moral flaws in their attitude to animals. The existing subject of environmental education can provide useful examples of educational practice that animal welfare education can follow.

Specialized education in university

College students who major in law or social science should be encouraged to take animal welfare as a subject. The students need to become informed on matters such as legislation, public dissemination, enforcement and social implications of animal protection measures and to be capable of revising current Animal Welfare Laws in the future in accordance with social changes and advances in public opinion.

Students who major in medicine, chemistry, biology and agriculture should take animal welfare as a compulsory course, because their close working relationship with animals requires that they have the most comprehensive understanding of animal welfare. In addition to learning how to avoid unnecessary pain to animals, for example in experiments, these students need to be encouraged to see the improvement of animal welfare by the use of advanced science and technology as an important research subject for the future. In this connection, it should be noted that China has for the first time included animal welfare in the Experimental Animals Regulations.

Students majoring in relevant subjects could also work directly on projects to improve animal welfare: medical students could research better treatments for animal diseases; others could research alternatives to animal ingredients in medicinal products, especially ingredients from rare and valuable animals; and students of materials science could research substitutes for animal furs. Students majoring in livestock husbandry could research new animal rearing techniques based upon understanding of the physiology, ecology and natural behaviour of farm animals so that rearing practices will be in accordance with the animals' biological needs and welfare, in addition to bringing economic and social benefits. Students majoring in biological, psychological and behavioural science could research animal physiology, ecology and natural behaviour, respectively. Normal schools could specialize in animal welfare education.

Adult education and training for animal-related professions

Animal welfare training should be required for people working in animal-related jobs, such as those working in animal laboratories, zoos, in livestock husbandry, circuses or any other fields where there is direct contact with animals. It should not be possible for a person to hold such a position unless he/she has certified training and competence in animal welfare.

Case study: Flaws in the Chinese education system

Liu Haiyang, a senior student majoring in electromechanical engineering in Tsinghua University (the most famous university in China), has twice attacked five bears in Beijing Zoo by pouring a mixture of sulphuric acid and caustic soda onto the animals' bodies and into their mouths. The apparent motive was merely to test whether bears are really unintelligent or not.

Liu entered the electromechanical engineering department in Tsinghua University in 1998. He had always been among the top students in the class and passed the graduate exam with high marks. On 29 January 2002, to satisfy his 'curiosity', Liu went to the zoo with a bottle of prepared drink mixed with caustic soda stolen from a laboratory in the university. He pretended to feed the bears, and then threw the mixture onto them. He then managed to escape. But, having seen the burned bears rolling on their backs and screaming, Liu was not satisfied. He continued to prepare for his next test, or scientific experiment, as he said later.

On the afternoon of 23 February 2002, Liu bought a bottle of sulphuric acid for a dollar from a chemical shop and mixed it into two bottles of drink and a 500-ml plastic cup. Then he took a bus to the zoo with the bottles and cup in a white paper bag. There he repeated his offence. It was a fine spring Saturday. Beijing Zoo was crowded with visitors. At about 1.10pm there came a painful screaming from the bear hills. Wisps of white smoke were rising from the ground, and two bears were rolling around in pain. Among the commotion of the bystanders, a young man wearing spectacles pushed his way out, a food bag in hand, and sneaked off in a hurry. This was Liu Haiyang.

People from all walks of life have expressed a variety of opinions on this incident. The University Director Zong Chunshan thought that the punishment of Liu required further discussion, because it depended on whether the aim was purely to punish a troublemaker, or to save a talent for society. He pointed that in foreign countries an offender may be sentenced to 'community service' in order to bring home the seriousness of the offence, and that this might be more effective than a fine. Director Zong suggested that Liu should be required to take part in animal care in his spare time, especially to take care of black bears, which could lead him to appreciate the animals through close contact with them and develop his love of animals. This way would save a talent as well as reforming his attitudes.

Wu Boxin, a psycho-criminologist and Professor in China People's Public Security University, said that from the psychological point of view Liu Haiyang may have a defect in cognition that is due to problems in his personality, psychology and upbringing, leading to a propensity to commit crimes. He pointed out that a considerable number of college students are not able to deal with their current problems, so they feel uncertain or confused and suffer from emotional disturbances such as anxiety, depression and fear. Sometimes this leads to severe psychological problems and research shows that psychological health is declining year after year. Therefore, Professor Wu thought that university education should concentrate not on legal matters but on the psychological health of the students and that new educational methods need to be developed that are based on the psychological study of modern students.

Against these views, it is very hard to believe that an adult person with a high level of education could commit such an act today, when the whole of society is exposed to ideas of environmental and animal protection that even a kindergarten child could understand. In my view, Liu Haiyang is not ignorant, but morally wrong and deficient. Such an evil act cannot be covered up or simply explained as curiosity. Liu is an adult and must take responsibility for his actions. It is provided in Article 341 of the Criminal Law of the People's Republic of China that a fine and a period of imprisonment of less than five years shall be imposed on anyone who poaches or catches nationally protected endangered rare and valuable wild animals; a fine and imprisonment for from five to ten years shall be imposed according to the frequency of violation; a fine or confiscation of property and imprisonment for more than ten years shall be imposed when it is a very severe violation. Every person is equal before the law. Liu cannot be allowed special privileges just because he is a student from a prestigious university. Therefore, society should purely regard him as an adult lawbreaker, and give him the punishment he deserves. The Secretary General of the China Wildlife Protection Association, Wang Fuxing, thought that at present, in view of the deficiencies in China's animal protection law, there is an urgent need to enforce the animal protection legislation clearly. Only in this way can we put an end to similar occurrences.

Why did Liu Haiyang's case have such an impact on society? There were in general three reasons: first, instead of a bear harming a man, a man attacking a bear has great news value. Secondly, the person who attacked the animal was a college student; this is contrary to general expectations, and raised debate about the relationship between education and behaviour. Thirdly, the event involved one creature deliberately hurting another and led to reflections on the nature of mankind and the meaning of life, as well as the relationship between the individual, society and nature.

This case has given us a line of investigation to follow up: education for top grades' – personality development – understanding of life. Did Liu Haiyang's case become such big news only because of the headline 'Man attacks bear'? It is not as simple as that. The intuitive response of people is to ask why a multitude of robberies and murders do not stir society in the same way. Is it possible that the life of a man is less important than that of a bear? Is it simply that murder is commonplace and has no novelty value, or is it because people are developing a new understanding of the value of wild animals' lives? I would rather attribute the unexpected stir to the increasing awareness of Chinese citizens about animal protection. However, the following case in Qingdao Zoo received no attention. A person named Wang killed two bears and five deer as an act of retribution against his boss, who he felt had treated him unfairly. Why does the public keep quiet about the slaughter in this case? It must raise questions about the citizens' awareness of the issue of animal protection. At least it can be concluded that such awareness is not deep rooted or widely applicable, but somewhat impulsive and superficial. It can lead to nothing but a conclusion that a person of high educational level should have more aware-ness of animal protection issues.

In the Chinese view, there is a linear relationship between high educational level and personality, intelligence or even morality. However, the value of schooling has become distorted in present-day China. We not only hold to the traditional idea that excellence in education is followed by a distinguished career, but also create a situation where education is solely for the purpose of career advancement. The close relationship between a person's school record and his or her career prospects has superseded the understanding of the relationship between knowledge and personality. Learning is the sign of human civilization, but a good school record cannot replace personality. Excellence in study is not equivalent to a fine personality. Statistics show that 30 per cent of college students have some psychological problems, which can destroy the value of years of study in a moment.

Current education in China fails to encourage understanding of the value of life. Even in the field of the humanities, students study only abstractions about society, law, economics and culture without the 'human aspects' being considered. This type of knowledge may even be harmful. Before we 'condemn' Liu, we should first criticize the deficiencies in our own education system. The current competitive educational system is not a vehicle for popular education, but an education for elites. Many highly educated students created in this system are 'exam machines'. Liu should not be considered as an individual but as a type. Liu is not an extreme special case, but a product of the system. The same educational system operates in every school, creating an assembly-line similarity between its products.

Sympathy and mercy are basic psychological attributes that are needed to prevent the violation of individuals in society. How much of our education is concerned with encouraging qualities that have such lifelong importance? Liu says that he has learned the 'basic theory of legal science', and knows that wild animals are not to be killed. But he has no idea that it is also illegal to hurt animals in a zoo. If Liu had been given more understanding of life in his lessons from childhood and had developed sympathy for all living things, he would have avoided the present tragedy even if he knew nothing about the animal protection law.

It may be necessary to lower our goals for educational achievement in order to ensure that we better nurture the basic emotions and psychological qualities of students. We should make sure that students have acquired these fundamental qualities before we send them off to acquire high-level learning. We should make sure they understand that any violation of other individuals must be punished before we make them recite the articles of the law. The development of personality is based on the understanding of the value of all life. This understanding is what makes man civilized. People have asked what the motives of Liu Haiyang were. He said that he wanted to test whether bears can recognize sulphuric acid, but more than ten years' education failed to make him understand that sulphuric acid causes pain to animals. This reminds us that the understanding of lives should be the understanding of life. Similarly, the lack of education about life leads to a lack of humanity. In a society that advocates chauvinism, the citizens have more obligations than rights. To be a hero, a person must be prepared to sacrifice himself for society. If a person becomes a criminal, society can exterminate him; the abolition of the death penalty is not yet on the agenda. People should be aware that life and nature will be despised as long as the value of an individual life is of less importance than its value to society. The debate about the value of life cannot be completely separated from the free choices of individuals.

Conclusions

Making progress on animal welfare is a tough battle over a long period of time. Although it has started fairly recently in China, it has kept pace with the development of the social economy and culture. The conditions are now right for legislation on animal welfare. Therefore, we should make legislation on animal welfare come into being as soon as possible and effectively carry out the public and specialized education needed to achieve the harmonious coexistence of man and animals in a better and more civilized future.

10

The Evolving Animal Rights and Welfare Debate in China: Political and Social Impact Analysis

Peter J. Li

University of Houston-Downtown, US

In the past few years, a new debate has erupted in mainland China. This debate focuses on animal rights, animal welfare and animal treatment in general. In the not too distant past, such subjects were conveniently rejected as unworthy of serious academic attention. China's rapid economic changes, increasing societal activism on environmental issues, continuous influx of foreign ideas and a rising societal awareness of the rights for the disadvantaged, including the non-human animals, are impacting the agendas of public discussions. Directly triggering this public debate were several highly publicized animal cruelty incidents involving, for example, five bears at Beijing Zoo attacked with concentrated acid by a college student and the tragic death of a circus tiger out of sheer exhaustion. Indirectly fuelling this debate is the prevalence of cruel practices in China's farming industries, slaughtering operations, entertainment parks and other animal-holding institutions.

This chapter introduces the ongoing debate and the positions of the participants. By reviewing their respective arguments, we attempt to present the two opposing camps: the proponents of animal policy change and their opponents who oppose such a change. By examining their different perspectives, the article intends to highlight the challenges and opportunities for policy change. Importantly, we shall explore the political and social impacts of the evolving debate to shed light on the role of China's animal advocacy groups in the country's political and social evolution in the years to come.

The animal rights' discussion

Animal rights is a foreign concept introduced into mainland China in the early 1990s. In 1993, Yang Tongjin, a researcher at China's Academy of Social Sciences (CASS), published an introductory article on western ideas of animal rights and animal liberation.[1] This was arguably the first article giving a comprehensive account of the origin, arguments and counter-arguments of the western intellectual explorations of these issues. The article, however, did not spark a continuing interest in the topic. The fact that no scholars responded to this initiative can perhaps be attributed to Yang's silence on the subject's connection with policy-making. Additionally, intellectual activism in the early 1990s was subdued due to the Tiananmen crackdown in 1989.

Since the mid-1990s, however, ideas of animal rights and animal liberation have attracted more attention. A Chinese translation of Peter Singer's *Animal Liberation*, published in Taiwan, was introduced to readers in mainland China. Most noticeably, international non-governmental organizations (NGOs) began to operate on the Chinese mainland. They have played an important role in facilitating Chinese intellectual exploration of foreign animal rights and animal welfare ideas.

Qiu Renzhong and his rights arguments for animals

In 2002, Professor Qiu Renzhong of the CASS Institute of Philosophy published his seminal article 'It is high time that we discuss the question of animal rights in China'. The article was an instant hit and caused a big stir. Unlike Yang Tongjin's earlier introductory essay that stayed clear of any normative assumptions, Qiu makes it explicit at the beginning of the article that we should not only discuss the question of animal rights, we should also push for attitude and policy changes.[2]

Qiu believes that there exist a host of compelling reasons for discussing the issue of rights for animals. The favourable conditions for starting such a discussion include the awakening of the public's animal protection consciousness, the increasing media exposure of cruelty incidents, experiences acquired from animal protection work, rights awareness among the people and the society's rising standard of living. Understanding that his proposition would cause a knee-jerk reaction, Qiu expressed emphatically at the beginning that honouring the rights of the animals would also promote human rights.

On animal rights, Qiu introduces the three key elements of the rights claim: the subject of rights, the indirect objects of rights and the direct objects of rights. What follows is an analysis and dissection of the three basic positions: that humans have no obligations towards animals, that humans have indirect obligations to animals and that humans have direct obligations to animals. Qiu reviews the theological, philosophical, Confucian and ethical arguments of the three positions. In the section on animal liberation, Qiu introduces Peter Singer's concept of speciesism and its three manifestations: the use of animals in laboratories, the use of animals for food and philosophical approaches that are based on speciesism.

On the tactics for animal liberation, Qiu introduces the status quo faction, the abolitionist school and the reformers. To Qiu, the status quo position is too pessimistic and constitutes a force obstructing humane progress. He concludes,

'Therefore, on the question of animal liberation, we cannot maintain the status quo'. However, he does not believe in the abolitionist arguments. In his opinion, immediate abolition of animal use is not only unrealistic, it could even be counter-productive. 'Animal liberation will be a long historical process. It cannot be accomplished in the short term.' Qiu stands by a gradualist approach to animal liberation. Steady improvement of animal welfare, animal protection education, law enforcement and China's involvement in international animal protection work will better serve the goal of animal liberation in the future.

Zhao Nanyuan and his 'anti-humanity' thesis

Professor Qiu's article gave rise to an immediate rebuttal from Zhao Nanyuan, a professor at Tsinghua University. In his article entitled 'The essence of the animal rights argument is anti-humanity', Zhao calls on the public to be vigilant. This is because, according to Zhao, Qiu's arguments are nothing but a full shipload of 'foreign trash'.[3] According to Zhao, Qiu and his followers are not satisfied with simply propagating imported ideas, they are determined to convert their ideas into legislation.

According to Zhao, vigilance is of high necessity because of what he perceived as the dangerous ethical grounds underlying the animal rights arguments. To Zhao, ethics is a double-edged sword. 'Ethics allows the talking of nonsense and it, as a result, often leads people astray and to commit ridiculous acts contrary to their original intentions.' Ethics constitutes a limitation and a deprivation of freedom. Therefore Zhao argues that, like famine, plague and wars, moralists who propagate ethical standards are creators of human disaster. This is why the intention of moralists such as Professor Qiu is suspect.[4]

At great length, Zhao rejects the view that animals are sentient beings and that animals are self-conscious. Because they do not feel pain and do not have emotions, he argues, they are therefore not the subjects of rights. Animals cannot have rights because they cannot fulfil the corresponding obligations. People, for example pet owners, treat animals differently not because of their recognition of animal sentience but because of their own personal emotional needs.

From a broader angle, Zhao sees a more sinister image of what he calls neo-imperialism looming in the background. Zhao believes that those who advocate animal protection and discuss animal rights have connections with the west. They enjoy defaming their own motherland and cater to the interest of the west in its desire to dominate non-western civilizations. Not only does Zhao allege that China's animal protection activists have psychological, developmental, character and personality flaws, he also charges that they, like all other animal rights advocates, are 'anti-humanity' elements. Instead of acting as members of the 'fifth column' of the neo-imperialists, Zhao argues, they should learn from the South Koreans who stood firm against western protests against the Korean dog-eating culinary culture.[5]

Additional exchanges

Zhao's highly inflammatory article was responded to by other scholars. Zu Shuxian, a professor at China's Anhui Medical University, points out that non-human animals have common faculties with humans. Citing Charles Darwin, he comments that almost all mammals have emotions. They express, to a different degree, fear, frustration, jealousy, love, sympathy and respect. Moreover, some of them can even make and use tools. Zu argues that the mental difference between humans and the non-human mammals is simply one of degree.

In response to Zhao's assertion that science has so far failed to prove that animals or humans have a sense of pain and that scientists should not be misled by the emotional utterance of animal rights-advocating ethicists, Zu points out that reality cannot be defined solely by the results of scientific experiment.[6] He reminds us that such a world-renowned scientist as Albert Einstein, who spent his entire life searching for scientific truth, urged the future generation of scientists 'to free ourselves by widening our circle of compassion to embrace all living creatures and the whole of nature in its beauty'. Quoting Kant, Zu states that if we humans have not lost our humanity, we should treat the non-human animals fairly, on the grounds that those who are cruel to animals are likely also to lack sympathy for their fellow humans. Commenting on Zhao's assertion that Chinese animal protection advocates are acting as members of a 'fifth column' of western neo-imperialism, Zu rejects the charge as a 'mass criticism' type of character assassination commonly seen during the Cultural Revolution era (1966–1976).

Zheng Yi, a dissident Chinese writer who recently published *China's Ecological Winter* (2002), joined the discussion from the US. To him, Zhao really does not need to approach the question of whether animals are sentient and whether animals should have rights from the multiple angles of science, philosophy, ethics, comparative culture and jurisprudence. Instead, Zheng believes that the science of ecology should be enough to demonstrate the fundamental contribution of biodiversity to human survival. As members of a diverse ecological system, non-human life forms deserve human moral consideration because it is to them that humans owe their survival and prosperity. Zheng asks: how can we say that animals do not deserve human protection because they cannot fulfil their obligations? And, how can we assert that humans are not receiving benefits in return for their responsibilities?

The animal welfare debate

Like the concept of animal rights, the concept of animal welfare is foreign to the mainland Chinese population. Animal welfare has, however, received greater media attention in recent years. In May 2002, an international forum on animal welfare was held in Beijing. More than 20 scholars and activists from across the world attended the meeting.[7] In October of the same year, an animal protection and education conference was organized in Heifei in China's Anhui province. At the 19th International Zoological Conference, held in Beijing in August 2004, animal welfare was also the topic of two panels. In 2005 CIWF Trust and the RSPCA held a conference in Beijing on 'Animal Welfare and Meat Quality', co-sponsored by China's leading meat hygiene journal. The conference was opened by China's assistant Minister of Commerce, Huang Hai. The Chinese media has not only increased its coverage of animal cruelty incidents, it has also invited Chinese and foreign animal welfare experts on to its programmes on animal welfare. One of the several TV discussions was aired on 14 June 2004 by China's national China Central Television (CCTV). It is against this backdrop of increased societal attention to the plight of animals that the animal welfare discussion has evolved.

Welfare crisis: Myth or reality?

To the proponents of animal welfare, China is deep in crisis. In their articles, media interviews and petitions, they have cited large number of cruel practices and incidents to support their arguments that China's animal welfare crisis calls for immediate government attention.[8] The cited cruel acts include the bear attack at Beijing Zoo, a puppy microwaved alive in Sichuan,[9] a brown bear attacked by three visitors in a zoo in Northeast China,[10] a college student's diary depicting in graphic terms the entire process of a kitten tortured to death and a zoo bear missing four paws.[11] Admittedly, such random violence happens anywhere in the world. Yet, China is facing a more widespread animal welfare crisis that is connected with state-sanctioned business operations.

As the world's leading producer of poultry, pork, dairy and wildlife products, China today has a burgeoning factory-farming industry.[12] Chinese scientists have already raised questions about farm conditions. On the many peasant-owned bear farms, bears are intentionally deprived of food or water so that more bile can be extracted. Little consideration is given to the space and nutrition needs of the animals.[13] Conditions of China's zoological gardens are also a big concern to Chinese and international animal advocacy groups. In the many private and state zoos, animals are caged in small, barren and often filthy houses. A private zoo in China's southwest Guangxi province let its bears starve to death.[14]

In China, live animals are prized more than frozen meat. This eating preference has led to the flourishing of live animal markets with supplies of farm, wild and other meat animals from across the country. Animals Asia Foundation's (AAF) investigation found that wild and companion animals are shipped, for example, to Guangdong from other provinces. Many of the animals, cramped in tiny cages, are on the road for as many as 72 hours. They are often denied food and water. Many wild-caught animals are dying a slow and agonizing death from wounds inflicted by traps or snares. In live animal markets, cages of live animals are stacked one above another. To attract customers, sellers sometimes resort to cruel methods to kill the animals. In the words of Annie Mather, AAF's media director, Guangdong's live animal markets were hellholes for the animals: 'Nobody seemed to care'.[15]

Despite the introduction of western livestock slaughtering technology and techniques in China's big meat processing plants, animal slaughtering on the whole is a depressing scene. Pigs and other animals undergo a cruel forced-watering process to increase their weight before slaughter. In this procedure, a large quantity of water is pumped into their stomach through a rubber tube.[16] A recent report on China's fur animal farming also questioned the slaughtering practices on these farms.[17] Other cruel slaughtering practices include removing brains from live monkeys, skinning giant salamanders alive, and live feeding in the many wildlife parks (i.e. feeding zoo animals with live prey).

One of the extreme animal cruelty practices in China today is the state-sanctioned bear farming. This farming operation has been the target both of Chinese and non-Chinese animal welfare activists. Today, more than 7000 Asiatic black bears are incarcerated in tiny cages for the sole purpose of bile extraction from an open wound cut in their stomachs. These bears, kept in total deprivation, go through daily bile extraction for up to 22 years. Their plight has been exposed to a shocked outside world by Jill Robinson, CEO and founder of AAF. Guo Geng, a prominent animal protection activist and prolific writer on animal welfare, condemned bear farming as a practice cruel beyond description.[18] Li Xiaoxi, deputy to Beijing's Haidian District People's Congress, appealed to the Chinese leaders to end bear farming.[19] Recent scientific and welfare policy studies have documented the welfare crisis on Chinese bear farms.[20] My own visit to a small bear farm in the suburb of Tianjin and a huge farm in Northeast China confirmed the level of suffering the bile bears are subjected to.

These incidents and cases often cited by the proponents of animal welfare are considered either myth or sheer fabrications by the opponents. Qiao Xingsheng, a vocal anti-animal welfare scholar of Central Chinese College of Politics and Law, dismisses all the above-mentioned practices and incidents. He views animal suffering under conditions of mass production as a necessary evil and does not see the welfare problem developing into a crisis. In his opinion, Chinese scholars are discussing the question largely because of western pressures.[21]

Zhao Nanyuan flatly rejected the existence of an animal welfare crisis in China. He stated in articles and media interviews that animal welfare problems were sheer fabrication by hostile westerners and Chinese lunatics who allegedly loved animals more than their fellow human beings. To him, those who call for animal welfare improvements in China are making trouble out of nothing.[22] The reported acts of cruelty to animals, according to Zhao, were sensational stories made up by the media or the evil-minded animal lovers.[23] He continued, 'There is really no crisis under heaven except for the one imagined by some not too smart guys'.[24] While Zhao Nanyuan argued that the Chinese cultural tradition is flawless on questions regarding the treatment of animals, Qiao Xingsheng believed that animals in China are well taken care of by the existing welfare laws. They concluded that there was nothing China should do at the moment.[25]

Animal welfare in China's legal system

Animal welfare has received increasing attention by China's policy-making agencies in recent years. This attention was shown by the issuing of the 1997 Forestry Ministry's Tentative Implementation Regulation on the Use and Management of Black Bear Farming Technology. In this document, cage size, duration of time in the cage, veterinarian care, the method of bile extraction and the condition of bears suitable for extraction are clearly stated. In addition, the Regulation provides against bodily injuries to the farm bears.[26] Other more recent government orders such as the revised regulations on urban zoo management also includes an article requiring the designing and building of zoo facilities to meet the behavioural needs of the animals.[27] The recently revised Beijing Ordinance on the Management of Laboratory Animals also includes articles requiring the provision of appropriate cages, feed and bedding materials for different species.

In general, there are about 70 laws and government ordinances that contain articles related to animal welfare. Yet, except for the 1997 Forestry Ministry Regulations on the Management of Black Bear Farms, most only touch on the issue or are expressed in very vague terms. And, the laws and ordinances passed in the early 1980s and 1990s contained no animal welfare articles at all. For example, the Detailed Rules on Preventing Disease Outbreak in Poultry Production, passed in 1992, made no mention about cage size, ventilation, slaughtering methods, transportation amenities or other welfare requirements that also impact on the health of the animals. The Regulations on Pet Dogs enacted in November 1980 were perhaps the most draconian, treating dogs suspected of carrying rabies as open targets for extermination. Most of the 70 laws and ordinances do not contain actionable welfare stipulations. The Wildlife Protection Law passed in 1988 is the most typical in that it is completely silent on animal cruelty. Most noticeable in the Chinese legal system is the absence of an overarching anti-cruelty law.

One recent study of China's animal-related legislation has identified four main problems.[28] First, China's animal welfare laws are few in number, and these laws 'were enacted mainly to advance the interest of humans. They were primarily enacted to regulate the reasonable use of animal resources by humans. Animal welfare issues and how animals were treated were not considered.'[29] Secondly, existing Chinese laws do not cover all relevant animals. Except for the endangered species in category I and II in the Wildlife Protection Law, most other animals fall outside the protection of any laws. Thirdly, the existing laws and ordinances are disappointingly inadequate to deter acts of animal cruelty. Fourthly, articles in the existing laws are mostly stated as principles that have low enforceability. For example, on live animal transport-ation, article 31 of the regulations on fresh fruits and live animal transportation require feeding and providing water to the animals. Yet, how often food and water should be provided is not specified.

The issue of animal welfare legislation

Animal welfare legislation is the focal point of the animal welfare discussion. The two sides stand squarely opposed as a result of their conflicting positions on the question of an animal welfare crisis on the Chinese mainland.

Does China need animal welfare legislation?

The proponents of animal welfare argue that such a legislative action is long overdue. Professor Song Wei and Wang Guoyan's arguments are representative of the proponents' views. In their opinion, China has a void in this policy area and the void needs to be filled. Secondly, China's sustainable development calls for animal welfare legislation to curb the current rate of wildlife devastation. Thirdly, concern for animal welfare in legislation is a sign of progress in human civilization. Cruel practices such as live feeding, relentless exploitation of circus animals, and wildlife farming in conditions of total deprivation form a sharp contrast to the fast modernizing China. Finally, animal welfare legislation will also bring economic benefits to China. The production and export of Chinese animal products could suffer losses due to meat quality issues that are often caused by welfare problems on the farms.[30]

Similar arguments are also voiced by others. Mao Lei, a *People's Daily* reporter, agreed that 'China's animal welfare legislation cannot be postponed any longer'. Mao called for a long-term perspective on the question of animal welfare legislation in China. He states: 'For the sake of development, our legislative action on animal welfare ultimately serves the interest of us humans in the long run'. As a result, legal restrictions placed on us humans are worthwhile and necessary.[31] In her legislative proposal to the National People's Congress, Li Xiaoxi called on the national legislature to outlaw cruel hunting and cruel eating practices. 'People are generally unaware of the deterioration of social morality caused by cruel acts to animals', Li writes. She refers to severe acute respiratory syndrome (SARS) and avian flu to emphasize the need for legal construction in animal welfare. As a challenge to Chinese law-makers, Li believes that the 2008 Olympic Games present a good opportunity for anti-cruelty legislation. She ends with a call for China to be modern not only economically, but also in humane consideration of the non-human animals.[32]

Mang Ping's article 'Animal welfare challenges human morality: animals should be free from fear and distress' touches on both the practical and the philosophical aspects of animal treatment. From a practical point of view, Professor Mang points to the economic loss caused by poor animal welfare practices. Philosophically, she argues that, as sentient beings, animals should be given moral consideration on the farms, in transport and when their lives end. Rejecting the opponents' arguments that animals do not deserve moral consideration since they cannot fulfil their obligations to humans, Mang asks if there is better fulfilment of obligation than sacrificing one's own life as animals do for human use? Also importantly, Mang rejects the arguments that animal welfare legislation is incompatible with Chinese conditions. On the contrary, she argues that China has a philosophical tradition of kindness to animals.[33]

The position of the opponents is clear cut. Qiao Xingsheng rejects the proposal of animal welfare legislation. He argues that at the present time China is not materially ready for such a legislative move. And, according to Qiao, Chinese culture does not allow people to treat animals as equal to humans. Legislatively, anti-cruelty laws originated in the west and reflect western culture, western levels of production, and western legal systems. China therefore cannot adopt western legislative norms. He believes that animal welfare should be viewed as a social question rather than a legislative issue. At the present time, adopting such a law is practically unenforceable.[34] Liang Yuxia, a researcher at the Chinese Academy of Social Sciences, agrees with Qiao's views that anti-cruelty legislation at the present is premature. Yet, unlike Qiao, Liang admitted that the idea of animal welfare does have merits. In a country where animal cruelty is so widespread, anti-cruelty laws would be difficult to enforce at the present time.[35]

Zhao Nanyuan's rebuttal of animal welfare legislation is no surprise. In an article entitled 'The strange tales and absurd arguments of the animal welfare proponents', Zhao launched a frontal attack on the views of Song Wei and Yang Tongjin. First, Zhao questions the belief that animals have feelings. He argues that the way we treat animals would not elicit the same kinds of emotional reactions from the non-human animals themselves. Secondly, he questions the view that how we treat animals influences how we treat each other. He believes that humans can still be moral beings regardless of our treatment of non-human animals. Thirdly, Zhao rejects the need for anti-cruelty legislation in China. Those who argue for such legislation, in Zhao's opinion, are standing on an 'anti-humanity' position. Fourthly, he rejects the view that animal welfare impacts on human health. He argues that SARS and avian flu have nothing to do with how animals are treated. To him, factory farming has the advantage of better disease control. Fifthly, Zhao sees an irreconcilable conflict between animal welfare and human welfare. Calling for animal welfare legislation, Zhao argues, could lead to an increase of meat prices, thus depriving people of their right to eat meat. Therefore, 'advocacy of animal welfare would reduce the welfare of humans'. This is, he alleges, 'an act to be resisted because it is anti-humanity'. He asks: how could China adopt anti-humanity laws?[36]

What should be done legislatively?

In August 2003, sponsored by the International Fund for Animal Welfare (IFAW – China Office), a proposal on animal welfare legislation was submitted to the National People's Congress. The proposal called for expanding the list of wildlife animals under state protection. In addition, it suggested that four other categories of animal (farm, laboratory, entertainment and working animals) should also be protected. Some detailed recommendations were included, such as making reference to the UK's principle of the 'Five Freedoms' in animal welfare legislation. Other recommendations include the use of the 'three Rs' (reduce, refine and replace) in articles dealing with laboratory animals. The proposal emphasized the importance of drafting an enforceable law containing specific articles rather than the principle-type statements prevalent in China's current environmental laws.

Importantly, the proposal calls for a phased approach in legislation. While emphasizing the importance of immediate anti-cruelty law-making, the proposal suggests that, as a first step, revisions should be made to the existing laws and government ordinances to include or strengthen the existing welfare articles. For example, the Wildlife Protection Law does not contain any articles on animal welfare. It only penalizes acts causing death to protected species in the wild; acts causing injuries to the same species, whether in the wild or in captivity, are not legally punishable.

The legislative proposal also called for research and preparatory work for legislation on areas not legislated on in the past, with a view to enacting a comprehensive anti-cruelty law at a later date. As a concession to proponents of animal welfare, the guideline for animal welfare legislation should be changed from an emphasis on human use of animals to one that stresses the welfare needs of the animals. The proposal also suggests that the legislative process should be open to animal welfare experts and animal protection activists.[37]

Other more detailed recommendations on the contents of the welfare articles have also been advanced. Environments suitable for the display of animals' natural behaviour should be provided. Prolonged and agonizing slaughter should be outlawed. Laboratory animals should be provided with space, time to play, and adequate food and water. Live animal tests at elementary and secondary schools should be abolished. On companion animals, articles against abandonment and maltreatment were recommended. For law enforcement, the proposals refer to the British Royal Society for the Prevention of Cruelty to Animals as an example of a societal supervisory group to verify law enforcement, investigate violations, assist government enforcement and educate the public.[38]

Opponents have not let the proponents' proposals pass without responding. Jie Geng launched a point-by-point critique of the proponents' arguments. First, he rejected the need for animal welfare legislation arguing that the existence of such a law in the west does not mean that China should also have it. He throws down the challenge as to whether China should also adopt laws to legalize gun ownership or prostitution simply because such laws exist in the US and in The Netherlands. Furthermore, he argues that Korea has not been excommunicated from the WTO for its dog-eating culture.[39]

On the principle of the 'Five Freedoms', Jie Geng asks whether these freedoms have even been realized in relation to humans. According to him, efforts should be made first to improve the lot of people rather than animals. 'In China, the right thing to do is to create groups and assistance agencies that work for the rights of disadvantaged people.'[40] On Professor Song's emphasis on enforcing anti-cruelty laws, Jie believes that poverty, not animal cruelty, is China's main problem. He asks: 'When human welfare is not yet achieved, isn't it ridiculous to propose the building of special administrative agencies empowered to supervise animal welfare law enforcement?'[41]

Other recommendations

One highly noticeable, and certainly the most controversial, proposal is that China should emulate foreign countries and create special organizations complete with staff having the authority to investigate animal abuse.[42] Understanding that respect for other forms of life cannot be achieved in the short run, the proponents propose the creation of special courses, programmes and research projects at Chinese universities. The objective is to make animal welfare part of the college curriculum. Importantly, they believe it is urgent to conduct animal welfare education at elementary and secondary schools.[43] Additionally, they call on Chinese zoos to change the derogatory language used to describe the animals on display. Finally, they call on the media to increase exposure of acts of cruelty to animals and to educate the public about the need to treat other lives with respect and dignity.[44]

What does the debate tell us?

The evolving animal rights and welfare debate is indicative of the rapid changes in mainland China. As a *New York Times* journalist wrote, never before had social transformation in China been reflected by people's attitudes towards non-human animals, citing the rising rights awareness in connection with pet dog ownership in urban China.[45] Despite the political, economic, ideological and cultural impediments that tend to downplay the importance of animal-related policies, the increasing societal activism is symptomatic of the existence of some (limited) political openness and the incipient growth of an autonomous society in mainland China.

Political openness

The depth of China's animal welfare crisis highlights the government's ineffectiveness in an important policy area. Elizabeth Economy's recent work on China's environmental mismanagement is thought provoking. She questions the capacity of the Leninist Party-state to make and enforce laws that can address the nation's environmental problems. Yet, she admits that the reforming Leninist state in China is conditionally responsive to societal activism for environmental protection. Such societal activities help fill important gaps that the government cannot or is not willing to fill at the present time. In the animal protection policy area, the same is true about the attitude of government. Despite the fact that the Chinese government is a monolithic whole under strict Party control, steps have been taken in animal-related policy areas largely in response to internal and external pressures.

One political change that was unthinkable in the pre-reform era is the cautious openness of the Chinese political system to external pressures. As part of the efforts to fulfil China's obligations as a signatory of the Convention on International Trade in Endangered Species of Wild Fauna and Flora (CITES), Beijing created within the State Forestry Ministry a Wildlife Conservation Association (CWCA). In 1988, it went on to enact a Wildlife Protection Law. Other policy measures included the banning of use of parts from tigers and rhinos in Chinese traditional medicine. Also in response to domestic and international pressures, the Chinese authorities sat down and met with Jill Robinson, IFAW's China Director, in 1994 on phasing out China's cruel bear farming operation. Two of the worst bear farms were closed in 1995. Two years later, the State Forestry Ministry issued stricter regulations on bear farming requiring farmers to improve conditions on the farms. In 2000, the Chinese authorities officially committed to release 500 bears from a life of torture to Animals Asia Foundation's sanctuary. Today, China has become the focal point of international animal advocacy groups. It is expected that the Chinese authorities, in their public statements, will continue to reject international outcries as unfounded charges. Yet, the heat it feels is likely to motivate Beijing to act in certain policy areas. After all, China's increasing integration in the world economy has made it impossible for Beijing not to take heed of international public opinion.

The reforming Party-state has also in recent years learned to be more open to societal pressures for environmental and animal-related policy change. To a limited extent, the SARS epidemic was China's Chernobyl in that it triggered greater societal participation in discussions on ecological management and China's sustainable development. In May 2003, the Provincial People's Congress of Guangdong held the first ever public hearing on the future of the province's highly controversial wildlife trade. In Beijing, concerned citizens and activists participated in a heated discussion regarding Beijing's draconian dog registration policy adopted in the mid-1990s. As a result of the mounting pressures, the municipal government revised the old regulation and significantly lowered the dog registration fee. The animal advocacy groups are now target-ing the National People's Congress in order to push for anti-cruelty legislation.

What does the government sensitivity to internal and external pressures tell us? Obviously, the Chinese government is experiencing a mind-set change from viewing unofficial activism as dangerous, to be avoided or suppressed at all costs, to seeing it as a 'necessary evil' to be dealt with cautiously. Such a new attitude is sure to invite and encourage societal activism on more sensitive matters in the future. As Elizabeth Economy shows in her book *The River Runs Black*, tolerance of environmental activism in the former Soviet Union opened the floodgate for political activism that eventually led to the demise of the Soviet Empire. No one can predict for sure that what happened in Eastern Europe will be repeated in mainland China. Yet, liberalization of Chinese politics in whatever form is unstoppable. For the animal advocacy groups and individuals, it is important to keep in mind the authoritarian nature of the Leninist Party-state and the limits to its acceptance of societal pressure. As Elizabeth Economy points out, the Chinese government has tolerated criticism largely because such criticism was restrained and did not touch the fundamentals of the Leninist state system.[46]

Societal activism

Scholars and activists who have voiced their views in this evolving debate have done so independently. In other words, they do not publish or speak on behalf of the institutions they are associated with. They have submitted legislative proposals to people's congresses at the provincial and national levels. Their activism during the SARS epidemic period helped stop the government-sanctioned dog culls in many parts of the country. The most vocal activist warned the government of the legal liabilities of encouraging indiscriminate dog killing campaigns.[47] Since the early 1990s, non-governmental environmental groups and animal protection organizations have slowly but steadily increased in number. Despite the continued government imposition of strict requirements on the formation of unofficial groups, the activists have not relaxed their efforts to make an impact.

In China, as in other countries, environmental groups have taken the lead in educating the public, formulating agendas and taking concrete steps. In animal protection, Chinese NGOs and individual activists were the first to act in efforts to protect the Tibetan antelopes. It was only after the initial accomplishments of the volunteers that the government began to get involved in the protection efforts. Likewise, making the vast region from which China's major water systems originate into nature reserves was first proposed by China's environmental activists.[48] The idea was adopted by the government in 2001. In mainland China today, the most vocal supporters of animal welfare legislation are scholars and activists who are speaking on their own initiative.

Autonomous activism has a far-reaching impact on mainland Chinese society. First, the animal protection groups are a good training ground for other similar organizations. It is also a place where critical lobbying skills are developed. In China, where lobbying is little known and discouraged, the rise of interest groups can help connect the government with the society. Secondly, autonomous animal NGOs can develop into a political force. They could 'become enmeshed in broader political movements, providing cover for democracy and human rights activists'.[49] But, more directly, animal advocacy NGOs serve as examples to individuals who intend to organize groups focusing on different policy matters. When autonomous groups multiply in number, the current state–society relations are likely to face greater challenges.

Admittedly, the Leninist state remains formidable in today's reforming China. As Elizabeth Economy writes, the Party-state still maintains a tight control over social groupings. It allows domestic and foreign NGOs to operate only when such groups fill important gaps, bring in much needed foreign funds, serve as an inexpensive supervising mechanism and are silent on political matters.[50] Yet, as long as autonomous activism continues, society as a whole will gain greater influence on public policy-making, thus impacting the monopoly power of the Leninist state on policy matters.

Conclusions

The debate on animal rights and animal welfare is a new phenomenon in the reforming China. On the positive side, China has seen enormous societal changes brought about by rapid economic changes. One indicator of these changes is government's tolerance of society's participation in policy debate. The animal rights and animal welfare debate is one such public discussion initiated by independent-minded scholars and activists. Such initiatives would not have been possible in the pre-reform era.

No intellectual pursuit is value-free. In China, intellectual fervour has always carried normative concerns. The evolving debate on rights and welfare for the animals is no exception. Those who have called for attention to animal rights and welfare are activists who stand for policy change in animal-related issues. As we have shown, the opponents who reject the calls are no less enthusiastic about maintaining the policy status quo.

Importantly, the debate and the increasing societal activism are impacting on the future directions of Chinese politics and Chinese society. Politically, the animal advocacy groups will continue to push for policy change in the area of animal protection. With the increase in the number of such groups and their increasing activism, the Chinese policy-making process is expected to be more open to allow for the friendly participation of the Chinese animal NGOs. In terms of impact on Chinese society, animal advocacy groups and activists represent part of the new societal forces that were nowhere to be found in the pre-reform era. Together with other domestic NGOs, they are contributing to the rise of civil society. Their activism, agenda-setting initiatives and success in facilitating policy change will eventually redefine the state–society relations in mainland China.

Notes

1 Yang, T. (1993) 'The animal rights theory and the eco-centric arguments' (in Chinese), *The Journal of Studies in Dialectics of Nature*, vol 8, available at http://philosophy.cass.cn/facu/yangtongjin/keyanchenggou/03.htm.

2 Qiu, R. (2002) 'It is high time that we discuss the question of rights for animals', *Friends of Nature Reportage*, vol 3, available at www.fon.org.cn/index.php?id=2819.

3 Zhao, N. (2002) 'The essence of the animal rights arguments is anti-humanity' (in Chinese), available at http://shss.sjtu.edu.cn/shc/article021007/dongwuql.htm.

4 Zhao, N. 'The essence of the animal rights arguments is anti-humanity'.

5 Zhao, N. 'The essence of the animal rights arguments is anti-humanity'.

6 Zu, S. (2003) 'The essence of Zhao Nanyuan's arguments is advocacy of cruelty and opposing human morality' (in Chinese), Friends of Nature Reportage, vol 4, available at www.fon.org.cn/index.php?id=3015.

7 Li, G. (2002) 'Chinese and foreign experts gather in Beijing to discuss animal welfare legislation in China' (in Chinese), *People's Daily Online*, available at www.npcnews.com.cn/gb/paper7/17/class000700002/hwz210331.htm.

8 See, for example, Mang, P. (2002) 'Animal welfare: A test of human morality' (in Chinese), *China Youth Daily*, 13 November, p9; Mao, L. (2003) 'Animal welfare legislation in China cannot be postponed any more' (in Chinese), *People's Daily*, 14 January, available at www.people.com.cn/GB/news/6056/20030114/907578.html; Mao, L. (2003) 'Animal welfare should be guaranteed: A call for animal welfare legislation' (in Chinese), *The People's Daily*, 15 January, p14.

9 Zhang, Y. (2002) 'Microwaving a puppy alive: The shocking cruel act of a college student' (in Chinese), *Chengdu Commercial Times*, 21 March, available at http://news.sina.com.cn/s/2002-03-21/0905517109.html.

10 Chao, J. and Song, Y. (2002) 'Another incident of cruelty to animals done by zoo visitors despite prohibition, a brown bear at Heihe Zoo was stabbed' (in Chinese), *Xinhua Network*, available at http://news.sina.com.cn/c/2002-04-26/1004559013.html.

11 Zhao, Y. (2004) 'A live black bear had its four paws chopped off: There was a backstage manipulator behind the bear without paws' (in Chinese), *Zhao Yan Evening News*, 5 November, available at http://gb.chinabroadcast.cn/3821/2004/10/29/301@343223.htm.

12 For information about the scale of China's burgeoning factory farming industry, see also D'Silva, J. (2003) 'The growth of factory farming in China', presentation delivered at the 2nd International Symposium of Asia for Animals, available at www.spca.org.hk/afa/.

13 Interview with former bear farmers, Chengdu, Sichuan, 12 February 2004.

14 Ni, C. (2003) 'Activists claim Chinese zoos abuse animals', Associated Press, 5 January, available at www.buyhard.fsnet.co.uk/animalcruelty.htm#zoos; see also Animals Asia Foundation (2003). 'Emergency help: Starving bears in Yulin Zoo, China', The Official Animals Asia Newsletter, January, p22.

15 Personal communication with Annie Mather, Media Director of Animals Asia Foundation, 27 March 2004.

16 The Epoch Times, 'Households specialized in force watering pigs: A new profession created by the Chinese market' (in Chinese), The Epoch Times, 23 June, available at www.epochtimes.com/gb/4/6/23/n576637.htm.

17 Yi, H., Chiao, Y., Fu, Y., Rissi, M. and Maas, B. (2005) Fun Fur? A Report on the Chinese Fur Industry, Swiss Animal Protection SAP report, London.

18 Guo, G. (2003) 'Bear farming for bile extraction is cruel beyond description' (in Chinese), Sinatech, Guo Geng Column, available at http://tech.sina.com.cn/o/2003-07-25/2305213739.shtml.

19 Li Xiaoxi's letter to Chen Yaobang, Minister of Agriculture, 28 January 1998 (copy by the courtesy of Li Xiaoxi).

20 Cochrane, G. M. and Robinson, J. (2002) Bear Farming in China – Veterinary and Welfare Discussions, Animals Asia Foundation Report, available at www.animalsasia.org/eng/images/cbr/VetCentre/AAF_VetReport.pdf; see also Li, P. J. (2004) 'China's bear farming and long-term solutions', Journal of Applied Animal Welfare Science, vol 7, no 1, pp71–81.

21 Qiao, X. (2004) 'Animal welfare legislation cannot be divorced from China's national conditions' (in Chinese), available at www.people.com.cn/GB/guandian/1036/2515143.html.

22 Wang, Z. (2004) 'There is no need for animal welfare legislation' (in Chinese), an interview with Tsinghua University professor Zhao Nanyuan, China Green Times, 28 May, p2.

23 Li, J. (2004) 'Are you for or against animal welfare?' (in Chinese), The Chinese Readers' News, 28 April, available at http://arts.tom.com/1004/2004/4/28-63573.html.

24 Zhao, N. (2004) 'The strange tales and absurd arguments of "animal welfare" proponents – On Yang Jingtong and Song Wei's views on animal welfare', available at www.blogchina.com/new/display/31484.html.

25 Wang, Z. (2004) 'There is no need for animal welfare legislation' (in Chinese), an interview with Tsinghua University professor Zhao Nanyuan', China Green Times, 28 May, p2.

26 Forestry Ministry of the People's Republic of China (1997) The Tentative Implementation Regulations on the Use and Management of Black Bear Farming Technology (issued 8 May 1997).

27 Ministry of Construction of the People's Republic of China (2004) *Regulations on the Management of Urban Zoological Gardens,* (issued 13 July), available at www.jincao.com/fa/laaw19.114.htm.

28 Mo, J. and Zhou, X. (2004) 'A preliminary study of China's existing animal welfare laws and animal welfare protection' (in Chinese), available at www.riel.whu.edu.cn/show.asp?ID=1772.

29 Mo, J. and Zhou, X. (2004) 'China's current animal welfare conditions and a preliminary exploration of the question of legal protection (in Chinese)', available at www.riel.whu.edu.cn/show.asp?ID=1772.

30 Song, W. and Wang, G. (2003) 'What is the essence of animal welfare (in Chinese)', *People's Daily,* 14 January, available at www.people.com.cn/GB/news/6056/20030114/907573.html.

31 Mao, L. (2003) 'Animal welfare legislation in China cannot be postponed any more' (in Chinese), *People's Daily,* 14 January, available at http://www.people.com.cn/GB/news/6056/20030114/907578.html.

32 Li, X. (2004) 'A proposal on animal welfare legislation', submitted to the National People's Congress, January 2004 (unpublished article and copy by courtesy of Li Xiaoxi).

33 Mang, P. (2001) 'Animal welfare challenges human morality: Animals should be free from fear and distress' (in Chinese), *China Youth Daily,* 13 November, available at http://news.xinhuanet.com/newscenter/2002-11/13/content_627869.htm.

34 Qiao, X. (2004) 'Animal welfare legislation cannot be divorced from China's national conditions' (in Chinese), available at www.people.com.cn/GB/guandian/1036/2515143.html.

35 Hu, J. (2004) 'Should we legislate animal welfare' (in Chinese), *Yangcheng Evening News,* available at www.ycwb.com/gb/content/2004-05/18/content_693002.htm.

36 Zhao, N. (2004) 'The strange tales and absurd arguments of the animal welfare proponents' (in Chinese), available at www.blogchina.com/new/display/31484.html.

37 Personal interview with Song Wei, Houston, Texas, 16 November 2003.

38 Personal interview with Song Wei, Houston, Texas, 16 November 2003.

39 Jie, G. (2003) 'A comment on animal welfare law: A subject of concern to China's legal experts', available at www.xys.org/xys/ebooks/others/science/report/mao3.txt.

40 Jie, G. (2003) 'A comment on anaimal welfare law: A subject of concern to China's legal experts', available at www.xys.org/xys/ebooks/others/science/report/mao3.txt.

41 Jie, G. (2003) 'A comment on animal welfare law: A subject of concern to China's legal experts', available at www.xys.org/xys/ebooks/others/science/report/mao3.txt.

42 Personal interview with Song Wei, Houston, Texas, 16 November 2003.

43 Personal interview with Song Wei, Houston, Texas, 16 November 2003.

44 Personal interview with Song Wei, Houston, Texas, 16 November 2003; see also Mang, P. (1996) 'The zoos: A mirror of human morality' (in Chinese), *China Youth Daily*, 11 June, available at www.fon.org.cn/wenji/no5/p10.htm.

45 Eckholme, E. (2004) 'How's China doing? Yardsticks you never thought of', *New York Times*, 11 April, available at www.nytimes.com/2004/04/11/weekinreview/11eckh.html?position=&ei=5070&en=7f3b27d15741fde2&ex=1105851600&adxnnl=1&oref=login&pagewanted=print&adxnnlx=1105754683-d3af3uZcaIJWEcmjXJy72w.

46 Economy, E. (2004) *The River Runs Black: The Environmental Challenge to China's Future*, Cornell University Press, Ithaca and London, pp156–157.

47 Xu, X. (2003) 'Why should pet dogs be killed to contain SARS?' *Southern Weekend News*, 19 May, available at www.qingdaonews.com/content/2003-05/19/content_1415358.htm.

48 Economy, E. (2004) *The River Runs Black: The Environmental Challenge to China's Future*, especially Chapter 5.

49 Economy, E. (2004) *The River Runs Black: The Environmental Challenge to China's Future*, p242.

50 Economy, E. (2004) *The River Runs Black: The Environmental Challenge to China's Future*, pp129–175.

11
Islamic Philosophy on Animal Rights

Mahfouz Azzam

Al-Minya University, Egypt

Islamic law and animal rights

As an integral part of Islamic history, Islam makes a strong case for the protection of animals. Animal protection is based on the understanding that everything in creation proclaims the Glory of Allah and that amongst His greatest gifts is the creation of animals. It is even arguable that Islam recognized and acknowledged animal rights long before the world as a whole discovered the concept of human rights. Islam requires us to respect the rights of animals in several places in the Holy Qur'an. As long as 14 centuries ago, Islam commanded mankind to be kind and merciful to all animals. The Prophet [Peace Be Upon Him (PBUH)] said: 'Allah is kind and likes everything to be treated with kindness'.

Islamic law is not distinct from religion. In adopting the provisions of the Qur'an as the primary basis for Islamic teachings and jurisprudence, Islam sets out categories of rights as follows:

- rights related to Allah;
- rights related to man;
- rights related to the natural environment, animals, plants etc.

Basic teachings in Islam with reference to the Qur'an and the Sunnah

The following are some of the teachings that define the Islamic view of the relation between animals and humans. Allah says:

> Allah has created every moving (living) creature from water. Of them there are some that creep on their bellies, some that walk on two legs, and some that walk on four. Allah creates what He wills. Verily! Allah is Able to do all things.

[An-Nur: 45]

The reason for creating animals is identified by Allah; to benefit Man and serve him. Allah says:

> And the cattle, He has created them for you; in them there is warmth (warm clothing), and numerous benefits, and of them you eat. And wherein is beauty for you, when you bring them home in the evening, and as you lead them forth to pasture in the morning.
>
> And they carry your loads to lands where you could not reach except with Souls distressed: Truly, your Lord is full of Kindness, Most Merciful. He has created horses, mules and donkeys, for you to ride and as an adornment. And He creates (other) things of which you have no knowledge.
>
> [An-Nahl: 5–8]

The Prophet (PBUH) said, 'Goodness is tied to the forelock of horses up till the Day of Judgment'.

The Prophet (PBUH) also said: 'if a Muslim plants any plant and a human being or an animal eats of it, he will be rewarded as if he had given that much in charity.'

In the Islamic view, animals are the creation of Allah; they must not be harmed, tortured or maltreated, as they are considered partners of man in the universe. As a result, kindness to animals and giving them their rights constitutes an act of worship. A person will be rewarded if he observes this and will be severely punished if he does not. As examples of such punishment, Allah condoned the sins of a prostitute when she gave water to a thirsty dog. On the other hand, a woman was tortured in hell because she imprisoned a cat but failed either to feed it or to let it go free. Torturing animals is prohibited by Islam. He who commits such a sin is cursed by Allah. On one occasion the Prophet (PBUH) passed a donkey that had been branded on its face and said, 'Cursed is he who branded it'.

Islamic requirements for the welfare of animals

Islam requires that humans respect the welfare of both domestic and wild animals in all areas of human activity.

Animals must be provided with appropriate food and water

An authentic hadith relates that 'A woman was tortured in hellfire for denying food and water to a cat'. To be fed, watered and cared for is one of the rights that animals possess in Islam. Unless one's animal grazes in pasture, the owner has the obligation to feed it. If the animal is pastured, the owner is obliged to allow it access to the pasture until its hunger is satisfied.

Animals must be kept clean and healthy

It was related that the Prophet (PBUH) was seen cleaning his horse with his garment. When he was asked about the reason, the Prophet (PBUH) said, 'I was blamed by Allah last night on account of my horses'.

Animals should not be cursed or insulted

Muslims should not curse or swear at an animal. It was related that there was a woman who became annoyed and cursed her animal as she was mounting it. On hearing her, the Prophet (PBUH) ordered her to dismount and to let the animal go free, as a punishment.

Animals should not be overburdened or overworked

People should not overload animals or require them to do work that tires them excessively. The Prophet (PBUH) ordered that an animal should not be used as a mount to carry three persons at the same time. The ancient Egyptians used to sing and talk with their animals while milking them. Subsequently, it has been shown scientifically that doing this relaxes the animals and leads them to produce more milk.

Animals must not be caused harm or be tortured or frightened

Islam forbids separating an animal from its offspring. Moreover, the Prophet (PBUH) forbade frightening a bird and forcing it to leave its nest. Umm Korz said, 'I came to the Prophet, I heard him saying "leave birds in their nests"'.

Using an animal in sports or as a target to be shot at is also forbidden in Islam. The Prophet (PBUH) cursed whoever used a living thing as a target. When he passed by a group of people shooting at a bird for fun, he said: 'Cursed is he who does this'. Islam forbids hunting without good reason; it is forbidden to kill an animal without benefiting from it. It was related that the Prophet (PBUH) said, 'If someone kills a sparrow or other bird, they will complain to Allah at the Day of Judgment, "O, Allah, this person killed me in vain"'. It is forbidden to kill an animal for no benefit, and it is forbidden to stone animals that have been tied up.

Mutilation of animals is also forbidden in Islam. It was related that the Prophet (PBUH) found some people eating parts of camels and sheep that had been cut off from living animals, even though they were forbidden to do so; 'Any part that has been cut off from a live animal by mutilation is to be considered a dead body that it is forbidden to eat'. Similarly, the Prophet (PBUH) cursed those who beat or branded animals on their faces.

Requirements for slaughtering animals

The Prophet (PBUH) said, 'Verily, Allah has enjoined goodness to everything; so when you kill, kill in a good way and when you slaughter, slaughter in a good way. So every one of you should sharpen his knife, and let the animal die peacefully.'

The animal should be given water to drink before being slaughtered and should be taken to the slaughtering location with care and tenderness. It is related that the Prophet (PBUH) addressed a butcher, 'you led the goat tenderly'. The knife should be sharpened well away from the animal's sight. It is related that the Prophet (PBUH) said, 'When one of you slaughters a goat, he has to do it as quickly as possible'. Further requirements are that the person relax the animal, lays it down kindly and mentions the Name of Allah when slaughtering. The slaughtering should be done with a sharp tool. The use of a blunt knife is prohibited. The animal should be slaughtered by cutting the neck or the throat. Skinning of the animal should not be started until the animal is completely dead. It is forbidden to slaughter an animal in front of another animal.

How Muslims apply this philosophy in practice

Earlier Muslim Caliphs showed care and kindness to animals

The Earlier Caliphs used to send out emissaries to train and educate people about the right methods of caring for and being kind to animals. In his message to the governor, `Umar ibn `Abdul-`Aziz ruled that people should not allow horses to be used in any harmful way and forbade people to put heavy wheels on animals. One of the great companions, Abu Ad-Darda`, called his camel after it had died and said: 'My Camel! Complain not to my Lord for I have never overburdened you'.

Prevention of cruelty towards animals

Muslims were the first to establish societies that were founded on the application of Islamic philosophy relating to the treatment of animals. While riding his horse, the Caliph Al-Mu`tasim saw a dog with broken legs dying of thirst. He dismounted from his horse, filled his palms with water and offered it to the dog until the dog was satisfied. He later gathered the princes and leaders and established societies for the safety and caring of animals.

Islamic system of endowments

The application of this philosophy on animals was extended to include the system of endowments, where the revenues of lands and estates were used to help animals. During the Memluke dynasty, there were numerous establishments in place dedicated to protect animals and providing medical support and treatment.

Conclusion and future directions

This overview of the Islamic approach to the rights of animals has shown that Islam was one of the pioneers of animal protection. Islam requires that we are kind and compassionate to animals. It is our responsibility to implement and foster the teachings of rules for the kind treatment for animals in light of the Qur'an and the Sunnah. In order to disseminate understanding and practice relating to the rights of animals, we need to build a positive environment where we can foster a stronger relationship and provide people with educational and scientific facts about animals. In this regard, religious leaders need to be more involved in educating their respective communities on the teaching relating to the protection of animals. It is also necessary to provide greater exposure in the educational system about animal protection and to incorporate programmes that tackle the rights of animals in society.

12
The Ethical Matrix as a Decision-making Tool, with Specific Reference to Animal Sentience

Ben Mepham

University of Nottingham, UK

This chapter has two main objectives. First, it outlines a framework, the ethical matrix, for ethical analysis of technological procedures – for example, in cases in which animals are used in agricultural systems. The framework has been described in several earlier publications so that the brief summary provided here is intended primarily to provide an appropriate context for discussion of the second objective. The latter focuses on an aspect of the framework that relates specifically to the relevance of animal sentience in the process of ethical deliberation. This aspect has not been discussed extensively in earlier publications on the ethical matrix.

The ethical matrix in the decision-making process

The ethical matrix was designed as a tool to facilitate, but not determine, the process of ethical decision-making; and to that end it has been used in various ways, by various groups and in various contexts. But it will be useful here to focus on its potential use by a group of policy-makers seeking to arrive at, and justify to the general public, an ethical decision on a proposed technological innovation affecting animals used in agriculture.

According to John Rawls, the normal outcome of the exercise of human reason within democratic societies is 'a plurality of reasonable yet incompatible doctrines' (Rawls, 1993). Consequently, he considered that achieving consensus on a moral orthodoxy was probably an unrealistic (if not, indeed, a dangerous) objective, and that a sounder aim might be that of devising a social contract that benefits from social cooperation despite the differences of opinion between the contractors. From this perspective, the role of ethical theory in the decision-making process is not to determine the *right* policies but to act as a means of assessing whether specific proposed policies are ethically acceptable. A useful reference point is Karl Popper's characterization of the scientific method as 'the method of bold conjectures and strenuous and severe attempts to refute them'

(Popper, 1979). Analogously, proposed courses of action might be assessed from an ethical perspective by submitting them to 'attempted ethical refutation'.

Typically, differences in ethical evaluation reflect differences in *world view* and are often bound up with cultural, religious and political perspectives. This has wide-ranging consequences because in a world in which increasing globalization of trade seems inevitable, there are likely to be enormous costs if international agreement cannot be reached on how technology should be regulated. After all the debate, there is a need for *closure*, that is, for some mutually agreed course of action. Broadly speaking, ethical judgements on biotechnologies that have political consequences depend on two factors. Take, for example, the case of genetically modified (GM) food crops. In this case, there is a need for:

1   acknowledgement of relevant general ethical principles (such as, 'people should be free to choose the type of food they eat');
2   agreement on scientific facts (e.g. whether or not there is a significant difference between the GM food product and the non-GM product to which it is claimed to correspond).

The common morality and a principled approach

With respect to the first of these factors, an approach I have been developing for several years appeals to the notion of the *common morality* as a starting point for ethical analysis. This builds on the approach proposed by Tom Beauchamp and James Childress, which has achieved wide currency in the field of medical ethics (Beauchamp and Childress, 2001). The approach recognizes *prima facie* duties to respect certain principles, viz. non-maleficence, bene- ficence, autonomy and justice. Thus, in treating patients a doctor is regarded as having ethical duties to:

●   cause no harm (enshrined in the Hippocratic Oath) [non-maleficence];
●   effect a cure (or at least provide palliative treatment) [beneficence];
●   respect patients' autonomy (and not regard them merely as 'cases') [autonomy];
●   treat patients fairly (e.g. without racial or sexual discrimination) [justice].

It must be appreciated that this so-called *principled approach* is not an ethical theory and does not aspire to be a decision-making procedure. But, according to Raanan Gillon, it provides a set of 'substantive moral premises upon which to base reasoning in health care ethics'. Moreover, it: 'Offers a transcultural, trans- national, transreligious, transphilosophical framework for ethical analysis' by allowing differences of emphasis within a scheme of universal applicability (Gillon, 1998). So, although the common morality is unlikely to provide the last word in moral judgement, it would be difficult to conceive of a better starting point for encouraging public deliberation on ethical issues.

In recent years, I have extended the applicability of the Beauchamp and Childress principles in order to assess the ethical impacts of biotechnologies in the fields of agriculture and food technology (e.g. Mepham, 1996, 2000), and thereby provide a means of ethical analysis that might facilitate political decision-making. Despite sharing a common dependence on biological science, the agri-food industry differs substantially from medicine in the pervasive impact of its activities at the production, distribution and consumption stages, so that application of the principles to this different field requires that they be translated into terms appropriate to a wide range of different interest groups.

Specification of principles and interest groups in the ethical matrix

In Figure 12.1, suggested interpretations of the ethical principles as they apply to four such interest groups (treated organisms, producers, consumers and biota) are summarized in the form of an *ethical matrix*. The matrix permits analysis of the ethical impacts of any production system (e.g. application of a biotechnology) from the perspective of the different groups affected by its employment. Effective use of the matrix entails participants in the process (e.g. members of a regulatory committee) imagining themselves as belonging to each specified interest group in turn, thereby facilitating assessment of the overall ethical impacts of introducing the proposed technology. The object here is simply to describe the methodology briefly: rigorous analysis would require much fuller treatment.

In the form of the matrix illustrated in Figure 12.1, the principles of beneficence and non-maleficence are combined as 'respect for well-being', partly because it simplifies the framework, but also because in terms of human stewardship over organisms used in agriculture these two principles are inextricably related: combining them in no way diminishes the importance that attaches to them separately. The, now, three principles may be considered to correspond to three major theories of ethics, viz. utilitarianism (well-being), Kantianism (autonomy) and Rawlsian theory (fairness) (Winkler, 1993).

It is clear that principles employed in medical ethics need to be appropriately specified for each interest group if they are to be effective in this different context. For example, in relation to animals treated in biotechnology, respect for well-being, autonomy and fairness are interpreted as respect for welfare (freedom from pain and stress), freedom of behavioural expression and respect for intrinsic value (i.e. as opposed to 'instrumental value'), respectively (see Figure 12.1). In the case of consumers of food produced by biotechnology, these principles are interpreted as: respect for food safety, consumer choice (e.g. by appropriate labelling) and affordability, respectively. By extending the number of affected groups, a matrix of any desired degree of complexity can be constructed.

RESPECT FOR:	WELLBEING	AUTONOMY	FAIRNESS
TREATED ORGANISM	eg Animal welfare	eg Behavioural freedom	Intrinsic value
PRODUCERS (eg FARMERS)	Adequate income and working conditions	Freedom to adopt or not adopt	Fair treatment in trade and law
CONSUMERS	Availability of safe food; acceptability	Consumer choice (eg labelling)	Universal affordability of food
BIOTA	Protection of the biota	Maintenance of biodiversity	Sustainability of biotic populations

Figure 12.1 *The ethical matrix*

The aims and limitations of the ethical matrix

It is important to appreciate the aims and limitations of the matrix. These may be summarized as follows:

- The factors in each cell of the matrix that are relevant to performing an ethical analysis of the impacts of a technology are of two major types. In some cases scientific evidence is required, for example, relating to productivity or implications for animal welfare. But other cells of the matrix concern values. For example, they are concerned with the degree of acceptability, in the pursuit of economic objectives, of compromising animal welfare or taking risks with human health when appropriate scientific evidence is unavailable.
- The duties described are *prima facie* duties: circumstances will frequently arise when there are conflicts of interest between different duties, so that compromises will have to be made.
- The matrix is in principle ethically neutral, that is, it is an analytical tool. In accordance with Beauchamp and Childress's account, the principles 'are general guides that leave considerable room for judgement in specific cases and that provide substantive guidance for the development of more detailed rules and policies' (Beauchamp and Childress, 1994).

- By contrast, ethical evaluation (or judgement) requires a weighing of the different impacts, so that, for example, an animal rightist might consider any exploitation of animals inadmissible, while someone adopting a utilitarian view might consider that substantial human benefits outweigh minor harms inflicted on animals.
- The matrix records ethical impacts in one set of circumstances (e.g. the prospective introduction of a technology) with another set of circumstances (usually the status quo). Hence, the impacts recorded are relative to a pre-existing condition – which itself might be less ethically acceptable than some other, actual or possible, condition.
- While it might guide individual ethical judgements, the principal aim of the matrix is to facilitate rational decision-making by articulating the ethical dimensions of any issue in a manner that is transparent and broadly comprehensible.
- The matrix aims to provide a means for the expression of the full range of ethical perspectives.

Evidence for the latter claim is provided by the fact that people approving of use of a particular agricultural biotechnology and people opposing its use can both use the ethical matrix to justify their differing opinions, as has been demonstrated in workshops conducted with experts (Mepham and Millar, 2001). This indicates two important points about the matrix: (1) it provides a means of explaining and justifying different ethical positions; (2) it facilitates identification of the areas of agreement and disagreement.

A recent account of the theory underpinning the ethical matrix is provided by Mepham (2005), a publication in which its application to the analysis of a wide range of issues in bioethics is discussed in various chapters.

Intrinsic and instrumental value

Many of the principles specified in the matrix are fairly familiar and easily understood. Satisfactory levels of animal welfare and food safety may not always be readily achieved for various political and economic reasons – but there is little debate about what such terms mean. However, the specification of the principle of *fairness to animals* as 'intrinsic value' might be questioned from both philosophical and practical perspectives. Consequently, the remainder of this chapter examines the validity of the concept.

The term *intrinsic value* is best viewed as an alternative to 'instrumental value'. Some things (e.g. stethoscopes and bicycles) are valuable because of their usefulness and are said to have *instrumental value*. By contrast, *intrinsic value* is assigned where it is possessed irrespective of any usefulness; and most of us share the fundamental belief, stressed by Kant, that all *people* have intrinsic value. But most people sometimes (and others, often) *also* have instrumental value, so that possession of the two types is not mutually exclusive. For example, doctors, taxi drivers and refuse collectors all perform useful tasks, making them of instrumental value. This does not raise an ethical concern if they do their jobs by choice and receive a fair income.

Attributing intrinsic value to farm animals emphasizes that their instrumental value is not the only sort they possess. For example, in the case of dairy cows, in addition to their instrumental value in providing us with milk and dairy products, they are also 'subjects-of-a-life' that we can be said to have a duty to respect. According to Tom Regan: 'These animals have a life of their own, of importance to them apart from their utility to us. They have a biography, not just a biology. They are not only in the world, they have experience of it. They are somebody, not something' (Regan, 1990). In other words, their lives are of intrinsic value to them. With reference to the ethical matrix, given all that we now know about the sentience, sensibilities and even 'personalities' of cows, it would be *unfair* to regard them simply as useful objects.

The importance of animal sentience

Regan's appeal to the way animals experience the world may find widespread intuitive support, to the extent that for many people in western societies it may be said to underpin the common morality. Indeed, recent legislation gives official recognition to the concept. For example, the 1999 Treaty of Amsterdam requires that animal sentience and welfare are recognized in the implementation of EU legislation. Some governments have gone even further: for example, the Swiss Federal Constitution relating to the genetic modification of animals has been amended to take into account 'the dignity and integrity of living beings' (Swiss Ethics Committee on Non-Human Gene Technology, 2001).

Such changes are not just the result of an increased sensitivity to animal welfare: they are also due to increasing recognition of the somewhat arbitrary distinction hitherto drawn between our duties to humans and non-humans. For not only is it now recognized that humans share 98 per cent of their DNA with other higher primates, but medical scientists are also contemplating using organs from pigs (with but minor genetic modification) in human transplant surgery. The evolutionary biologist Richard Dawkins illustrated the genetic continuity between humans and non-humans in a memorable sentence when he wrote: 'But for the accidental extinction of the intermediates linking us to, for example, chimpanzees, we would be united to them by an interlocking chain of interbreeding: a daisy chain of the "I've danced with a man, whose danced with a girl, whose danced with the Prince of Wales" variety' (Dawkins, 1999). It is clear that the moral implications of Darwinism are profound (Rachels, 1991).

However, equating the concept of intrinsic value with animal sentience fails to capture a range of other factors that some people have associated with it. Some philosophers argue that intrinsic value is possessed not only by animals, but also by plants and biosystems (e.g. in the form of species and ecosystems). For example, environmental ethicist Laurence Johnson argues that, because plants and the species to which they belong are both characterized by a persistent state of low entropy, self-regulation via homeostatic control processes, organic unity and self-identity, it would seem to follow that they have an 'interest' in not only surviving but also flourishing (Johnson, 1991). In short, they have intrinsic value. Failing to respect that value might thus be considered unfair.

Indeed, to return to the case of animals, if sentience were considered the sole measure of an animal's intrinsic worth, it would seem to follow that painlessly killing a sleeping animal would be ethically unproblematical.

The question of animal rights

Ascribing intrinsic value to animals may be said to be tantamount to attributing to them rights. But many people find the very concept of animal rights problematical. A right may be defined as a 'justified claim or entitlement, validated by moral principles and rules' (Orlans et al, 1998) – but it might be argued that despite their genetic and physiological similarities with humans, animals cannot have rights because these can only belong to beings who can understand the concept. The problem with that view is that being consistent would mean that those humans who lack this ability (such as babies and senile people) would also fail to qualify to possess rights.

But another interpretation is that rights and duties are *correlative*, so that if we have a *duty* to treat animals well, and not to harm them, it follows that they have a *right* to be so treated. From this perspective, animals, like certain humans, are *moral patients*, owning rights but incapable of exercising responsibilities as fully competent moral agents (Rodd, 1990). Possession of such rights would seem to depend rather crucially on sentience, because although it might seem reasonable to refer to the intrinsic value of non-sentient beings such as plants, few would find it meaningful to refer to the *rights of plants*. Of course, the claim that animals have rights only concerns *basic moral rights*, which exclude those clearly only applicable to humans, such as the rights to vote and to a minimum wage.

However, the concept of animal rights is not universally accepted in philosophical circles, even by those who have demonstrated concern for animals in their writing. For example, Mary Midgley argues that 'the ambiguity of terms like "right" ... does not just express a mistake, but a deep and imperfectly understood connection between law and morality'. (Midgley, 1984)

Why has animals' intrinsic value been ignored?

In view of the persuasive evidence for the close identity between animals and humans, it is reasonable to ask why there has been an almost exclusive concentration on the instrumental value of animals for so long. There seem to be two reasons – religious and legal.

For the 17th century French philosopher René Descartes, mind and matter were totally separate. Believing that only humans possessed souls and conscious minds, he thought of animals as mindless automata that existed solely for human use. The idea that animals were created *for* humans seems to have originated in the dominant western traditions that had their roots in Ancient Greek thought and Judeo–Christian religion. For example, the biblical book of Genesis exhorts mankind to 'have dominion over the fish of the sea, and over the fowl of the air, and over every living thing that moveth upon the earth'. By the 18th century, it was widely believed that God had designed animals for specific human purposes. Thus, it was claimed that 'Apes and parrots have been ordained for man's mirth', and singing birds 'on purpose to entertain and delight mankind', while cattle and sheep were given life 'so as to keep their meat fresh till we have need to eat them' (Thomas, 1983). It is difficult to avoid a wry smile at the presumption that God had provided humanity with the equivalent of well-stocked walking refrigerators!

The second reason has to do with property rights, and can be traced back to the theories enunciated by the 17th century philosopher John Locke. Although, as was commonly believed, all people were created by and belonged to God, Locke considered that humans could acquire property by joining their labour with a commonly owned object in nature. Thus, by felling a tree and constructing from the wood a piece of furniture, people could claim exclusive property ownership of the fruits of their labour. Similarly, if animals were hunted and captured from the state of nature, they became people's personal property, which could legitimately be sold to others for food or other uses. In other words, animals had only instrumental value. As pointed out by lawyer Gary Francione (2000), historical evidence shows that the domestication and ownership of animals were closely related to the development of the very ideas of property and money. The point is made strikingly by the fact that the word *cattle* comes from the same root as the word *capital*, and the two are synonymous in many European countries.

Building on the concept of animals as property, it is not difficult to understand how, following the industrialization of agriculture in the 20th century, animals came to be viewed more and more as 'manufactured, tradable products'. After World War II, the application of industrial practices to agriculture was represented as Taylorism, the process by which complex tasks are dispersed into defined specialist activities in the interests of improved efficiency. This in turn led to factory farming, first identified by Ruth Harrison (Harrison, 1964), and more recently to acceptance of a whole range of interventionist technologies, such as artificial insemination, multiple ovulation embryo transfer and (in the US) the use of bovine somatotrophin (BST) to stimulate milk production in cattle.

Respect for intrinsic value

The ethical matrix provides a means of identifying ethically relevant issues and a framework for addressing them. The focus of this chapter has been on a single cell of the matrix, so that it is appropriate to conclude with a brief survey of the different positions people might take concerning this cell ('respect for the intrinsic value of farm animals') when the animals are exposed to the effects of a novel biotechnology. Because a wide range of views is possible, it will be necessary to limit discussion to the two ends of the spectrum and one intermediate position.

The vegan perspective

From biocentric or ecocentric perspectives, farm animals are moral patients whose interests do not differ in any ethically relevant way from those possessed by people. They are sentient beings who are clearly capable of experiencing pleasure, pain and suffering. Consequently, respecting their intrinsic value entails releasing them from all involuntary association with humans. This view would be most consistent with the adoption of veganism.

However, veganism is not ethically unproblematical, since in a finite world, satisfying the interests of both humans and animals (for food, space, resources, safety etc) is liable to encounter conflicts of interest. Indeed, if the major concern of vegans is the suffering to which animals are subjected in industrial agriculture, it is not obvious that releasing them all back to 'the wild' would improve matters. For most modern breeds of farm animal, the anatomical, physiological and psychological changes brought about through selective breeding programmes mean that they can only survive in protected farm environments; while the 'wild environments' to which some might, in theory, be returned are often few and far between. Adoption of veganism as a personal dietary decision represents a serious ethical commitment, but fulfilling the objectives of veganism on a global scale would seem to entail a lengthy and expensive process of accommodation to a new order.

Non-recognition of animals' intrinsic value

At the other end of the spectrum, from the perspective of a strong anthropocentric world view, animals have only instrumental value in respect of human culture. That is to say, it is mankind that has identified and fashioned whatever is now thought to have value – and this gives humans the licence to exploit natural resources (including animals) fully for human benefit. It is a perspective that echoes those of Locke and Kant discussed above, and would seem to endorse all prospective programmes designed to increase animal productivity through the application of biotechnology. But now, in the 21st century, that position is highly problematical in the light of the arbitrary but rigid distinction made between required ethical duties towards humans, on the one hand, and towards animals, on the other. It ignores the implications of the close genetic identity of humans and many non-human animals and denies or trivializes the significance of animal sentience. For example, philosopher Peter Carruthers summarizes his position as follows: 'Since there is no reason to believe that any animals are capable of thinking about their own thinkings... none of their mental states will be conscious ones. If this account were acceptable, it would follow almost immediately that animals can make no moral claims on us' (Carruthers, 1992).

A notional human–animal contract

A middle way between these two extremes is represented by the concept of a *human–animal contract*. This position considers that animal farming is not, in itself, ruled out, but that many current practices (such as those that involve body mutilations, excessive confinement or pharmacologically-induced productivity enhancement) certainly are. It is undeniable that raising animals for food is an exploitative practice, which takes advantage of the instrumental value of animals. But as noted above, exploiting the instrumental value of other *people* (e.g. as doctors, taxi-drivers or refuse collectors) is not deemed unethical if due respect is also paid to two other factors. First, it is required that their intrinsic value also be respected, and secondly, an unwritten contract must be observed by which their efforts are rewarded by a fair level of monetary payment.

By analogy, within the terms of a notional contract (necessarily *notional* when it involves animals as moral patients), certain forms of animal husbandry might be considered consistent with respect for the animals' intrinsic value if the animals were to fare better under human care than they would in a notional 'wild' state. Veterinary scientist John Webster puts the matter in a way that is concise to the point of bluntness. 'If we elect not to eat animals, they will still get eaten. It is an inescapable fate of all living animals to be consumed, sooner or later, by something else and used largely for fuel' (Webster, 1994). This suggests that, notwithstanding the many ethically indefensible practices that are encompassed by current industrialized animal production systems, redesigning animal husbandry along lines that sought to optimally respect animals' intrinsic value might the 'best–worst option'. In seeking a fair treatment of animals, supporters of this position may regard the philosophical agenda for universal veganism as effectively unachievable.

Perhaps the most prominent form of animal agriculture to explicitly show respect for animals' intrinsic value (though not in those precise terms) is organic farming (Food Ethics Council, 2001). However, the slaughter of animals raised organically is usually no different from those not raised organically, so it is an important question as to whether it is in principle possible to produce meat free of suffering and respectful of the animals' intrinsic value. For, even in an 'ideal' meat production system (involving sufficient staff, free-ranging animals, a quick and painless death etc), farmers would have to square their supposedly humane and respectful treatment of the animals with 'the objectively completely unnecessary slaughter of their charges' (Kaplan, 1998). One response to this claim is based on Webster's (1994) assertion that since the end of life is stressful for many animals in the wild, a humane farming system could at least guarantee a gentle death for those in human care.

Practical ethics

It is important to recognize that the ethical matrix in the form represented in Figure 12.1 encompasses 12 cells, so that whether or not respect for intrinsic value plays a critical role in any particular ethical assessment depends on the weight it is ascribed in comparison with the other eleven issues. But as we are not required to do what we *cannot* do, practical considerations demand that we are realistic about the circumstances we are all in, and do not allow our reasoning to be hijacked by fantasy.

Whatever the position adopted, use of the matrix entails explicit identification of decisions on how, and to what degree, current and proposed practices respect the specified principles. It is suggested that its wider use could enhance the rationality, transparency and rigour of ethical decision-making in the public domain.

References

Beauchamp, T. L. and Childress, J. F. (1994) *Principles of Biomedical Ethics*, 4th edn, Oxford University Press, New York, p38

Beauchamp, T. L. and Childress, J. F. (2001) *Principles of Biomedical Ethics*, 5th edn, Oxford University Press, New York

Carruthers, P. (1992) *The Animals Issue: Moral Theory in Practice*, Cambridge University Press, Cambridge, p193

Dawkins, R. (1999) in Burley, J. (ed) *The Genetic Revolution and Human Rights*, Oxford University Press, Oxford, ppxv–xvi

Food Ethics Council (2001) *Farming Animals for Food: Towards a Moral Menu*, FEC, Southwell

Francione, G. L. (2000) *Introduction to Animal Rights*, Temple University Press, Philadelphia, pp51–54

Gillon, R. (1998) 'Bioethics', overview in Chadwick, R. (ed) *Encyclopedia of Applied Ethics*, vol 1, Academic Press, San Diego, pp305–317

Harrison, R. (1964) *Animal Machines: The New Factory Farming Industry*, Vincent Stuart, London

Johnson, L. E. (1991) *A Morally Deep World*, Cambridge University Press, Cambridge, pp216–217

Kaplan, H. F. (1998) 'Vegetarianism', in Chadwick, R. (ed) *Encyclopedia of Applied Ethics*, vol 4, Academic Press, San Diego, pp451–453

Mepham, B. (1996) 'Ethical analysis of food biotechnologies: An evaluative framework', in Mepham, B. (ed) *Food Ethics*, Routledge, London, pp101–119

Mepham, T. B. (2000) 'The role of food ethics in food policy', *Proceedings of the Nutrition Society*, 59, pp609–618

Mepham, B. (2005) *Bioethics: An Introduction for the Biosciences*, Oxford University Press, Oxford, pp45–66

Mepham, B. and Millar, K. (2001) 'The ethical matrix in practice: Application to the case of bovine somatotrophin', in *Food Safety, Food Quality, Food Ethics*, preprints of the 3rd EURSAFE Congress, Florence, A&Q, University of Milan, pp317–319

Midgley, M. (1984) *Animals and Why They Matter*, University of Georgia Press, Athens, pp62–63

Orlans, F. B., Beauchamp, T. L., Dresser, R., Morton, D. B. and Gluck, J. P. (1998) *The Human Use of Animals*, Oxford University Press, New York, p28

Popper, K. (1979) *Objective Knowledge*, revised edition, Oxford University Press, Oxford, p81

Rachels, J. (1991) *Created from Animals: The Moral Implications of Darwinism*, Oxford University Press, Oxford

Rawls, J. (1993) *Political Liberalism*, Columbia University Press, New York

Regan, T. (1990) 'The rights view', in *Animal–Human Relationships: Some Philosophers' Views*, RSPCA, Horsham, p8

Rodd, R. (1990) *Biology, Ethics and Animals*, Clarendon Press, Oxford, pp241–242

Swiss Ethics Committee on Non-Human Gene Technology (2001) *La Dignité de l'animal*, ECNH, Berne

Thomas, K. (1983) *Man and the Natural World: Changing Attitudes in England, 1500–1800*, Penguin, Harmondsworth, pp19–20

Webster, J. (1994) *Animal Welfare: A Cool Eye towards Eden*, Blackwell, Oxford, p15

Winkler, E. R. (1993) 'From Kantianism to contextualism: The rise and fall of the paradigm theory in bioethics', in Winkler, E. R. and Coombes, J. R. (eds) *Applied Ethics*, Oxford University Press, Cambridge, Mass, pp343–365

PART 3

Implications for Farming and Food Production

13
Ideals and Realities: What Do We Owe to Farm Animals?

John Webster
University of Bristol, UK

The title 'Ideals and realities' was conceived by Compassion in World Farming Trust (CIWF Trust), who organized the conference out of which this book arose, but it is one that I recognize. In my two *Animal Welfare* books (Webster, 1994, 2005), Eden defines the ideal state wherein humans and the other animals can live in perfect harmony. This is an impossible goal: but one to which we should look with a cool eye and one to which we can direct our progress, however halting this may be.

When the European Commission, through the Amsterdam Protocol, formally acknowledged that farm animals are not simple commodities but sentient creatures, it committed all who use farm animals in any way, whether as producers or consumers, to a social contract, albeit one that neither we nor they can properly fulfil. The contract compels them to work and die for us, but equally compels us to respect their right to a reasonable standard of welfare through life and at the point of death. This is only fair. A further problem with the social contract is that it is we, not they, who define what is meant by fair. In this regard, the status of farm animals is similar to that of children. We define the standards according to our perception of their needs. This is becoming an ever more realistic goal, thanks to research pioneered by such as Marian Dawkins (1993) that seeks to discover what matters to animals as they seek to meet their physiological and behavioural needs, and how much these things matter. A proper understanding of the needs of farm animals can help to provide the evidence necessary to establish the moral, scientific and practical principles that should underpin good husbandry. Expressed in the simplest possible form, the aim of good husbandry should be to ensure that the animals stay fit and happy throughout their working lives. New draft UK Animal Welfare legislation proposes that it shall be an offence to predispose animals to suffering whether through defects in management, breeding or both. Management systems that involved veal crates, sow stalls and barren cages for laying hens were all once recognized as 'accepted practice' but each has been, or will be, banned (at least in Europe) on the basis that it may predispose the animals to suffering. However, it is still permissible to breed animals such as broiler chickens and dairy cows that are not 'fit for purpose' because they are unable to sustain fitness throughout their working lives. Under the new legislation it may become an offence to breed the conventional broiler chicken, or indeed the Bulldog or Basset Hound.

I repeat: the responsibility to animals as stakeholders in society is shared by us all. We cannot take the cable car to the high moral ground and, at no personal cost, harangue the farmers as cruel profiteers. Very few are cruel and very few are making a profit. Standards must be set by all who, directly or indirectly, derive any value from the exploitation of animals to suit our ends, whether for food, clothing, sport or companionship. Our responsibilities may be categorized as follows:

- to acknowledge and understand sentience in animals;
- to breed and manage farm animals so as to promote good welfare and avoid suffering throughout their working lives;
- to improve farm animal welfare through an effective system of welfare assurance for farms and others involved in the food chain;
- to increase public demand for real improvements in farm animal welfare through increased understanding of the problems associated with 'accepted agricultural practice' and an increased awareness of the value of each individual farm animal to society.

Sentience, stress and suffering

The welfare of a sentient animal must be defined both by its physical and emotional state. In short, it must be fit and happy. I first proposed the 'Five Freedoms' in 1981 as a structured, comprehensive approach to defining and assessing the elements necessary to meet the physiological and behavioural needs of a sentient animal (Farm Animal Welfare Council, 1993; Webster, 1994). Freedoms 1–3 address fitness, 3–5 address happiness or 'feeling good'. Although these have gained widespread acceptance among those who think about these things, too many animal welfare debates still fail because the protagonists are operating according to different terms of reference. Producers talk fitness, animal welfarists talk happiness. Moreover, the politicians who claim to speak for different societies assign different relative values to fit and happy. For example, the decisions to ban the sow stall in Europe but permit it in Australia and the US were based on a review of exactly the same evidence, but Europe gave greater value to behavioural needs.

It would be unprofitable to attempt to assign absolute values to each of the Five Freedoms. However, I suggest that political decisions will have no value at all unless they are based on a proper understanding of the nature of sentience in animals. My simple definition of sentience is 'feelings that matter'. This requires some explanation. All animals receive sensations and information from the internal and external environment. In response they use the physiological and behavioural resources available to them to act in a way designed to keep them fit and happy. Many of these responses in all animals are reflex or automatic. Sentient animals are those that have evolved mental processes for interpreting sensations and information so that they can choose what action, if any, is most appropriate to their needs. Darwin recognized sentience as an essential feature of evolutionary fitness widely distributed within the animal kingdom. Figure 13.1 provides a simple illustration of how it works. Sentient animals first process information as categories (e.g. food, predator) then interpret this information in an emotional sense: 'Does this make me feel good or bad (or indifferent)?' The strength of this feeling will determine the strength of motivation of the animal to do something appropriate to its physiological and behavioural needs. The strength of motivation to act is a direct measure of how much specific feelings matter to a sentient animal. Some animals will also interpret some information in a cognitive way, that is, they will incorporate reasoned thought into the decision-making process.

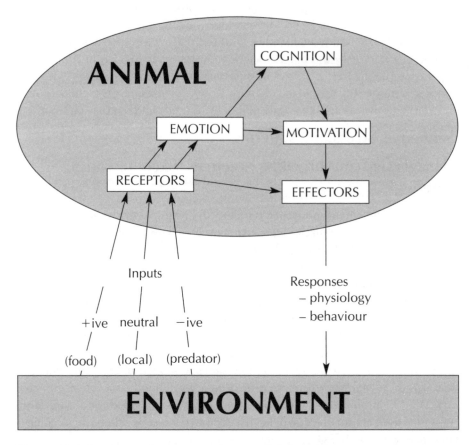

Figure 13.1 *Sentience: An emotional view of the world*

Source: Webster, 2005

When a sentient animal is faced by stress, it will act in a way designed to cope with that stress and then review the consequences. If the actions have been effective it will achieve a sense of security and satisfaction. This makes it feel more confident about its ability to deal with such stresses in the future. However, it may fail to cope, either because the stress is too severe, complex or prolonged, or because it is constrained in such a way that it is prevented from doing what it feels necessary to relieve the stress. In these circumstances its mood will shift progressively to one of anxiety or depression.

It follows from this that stress and suffering are not synonymous. Suffering occurs when an animal learns that is unable to cope with stress. However, the capacity for suffering is an inevitable consequence of the evolution of sentience, that is, all sentient animals have the capacity to suffer. This class certainly includes all the mammals and birds that we farm for food and probably the fish as well.

Sentience and suffering are manifestations of the fact that animals are primarily motivated by their emotions. The other driver of choice in animals, the cognitive or reasoned response, is certainly more developed in humans than in other animals and probably, although not certainly, more developed in primates than other mammals and birds. However, the potential for suffering is primarily determined by the emotional, rather than the reasoned response to stress. We cannot therefore assume that the species most similar to man are those that experience the greatest intensity of suffering. If you have difficulty with this concept, consider the case of a child with Down's syndrome. Such children may lack the cognitive abilities of an educationally normal child but they lack nothing in their capacity to feel joy and pain.

Management and breeding practices 'likely to cause suffering'

My next recommendation for action to improve farm animal welfare is directed specifically at campaigning groups such as CIWF. This recommendation arises directly from the draft Animal Welfare Bill (England and Wales) (available at www.defra.gov.uk), which will impose upon owners a duty of care to ensure the welfare of animals based on existing good practice. In other words, it will no longer be necessary to prove that suffering has occurred. It should be possible to bring a prosecution on the basis that it is an offence to keep or breed animals in a manner that would be considered by a competent and compassionate individual as likely to cause suffering. This new law should, at last, address Ruth Harrison's grim paradox: 'If one person is unkind to an animal it is considered cruelty but where a lot of people are unkind to a lot of animals, especially in the name of commerce, the cruelty is defended, and once large sums of money are involved, will be defended to the last by otherwise intelligent people' (Harrison, 1964).

CIWF has repeatedly challenged existing law by bringing prosecutions against individual companies on the basis of systematic disregard for animal welfare. In the 1980s they prosecuted a white veal unit for rearing calves in extreme confinement; in 2003 they took the UK government to the High Court for breeding broiler chickens in a cruel manner. In both cases they lost on the basis that these things were 'accepted agricultural practice'. However, in the case of veal calves, European Law now recognizes that the CIWF were right all along. When the new Animal Welfare Bill becomes law it will be time to confront the broiler issue once more. Since the international broiler industry is dominated by less than five breeding companies that supply over 80 per cent of the world market, it would not be too difficult to achieve a significant improvement in broiler welfare through a ban on the commercial sale of strains that fail to meet defined standards in relation to leg disorders and cardiac failure. This would have to be subject to strict independent review and enacted sympathetically to allow breeders to change their specifications. Nevertheless I see no difference in principle between existing European Law that requires egg producers to provide a cage to new, improved specifications within ten years and a law that required broiler breeders to produce within ten years a bird to new, improved specifications for lifetime fitness.

Welfare-based quality assurance

Wherever shoppers for food are offered a choice and have a reasonable income, they demand quality. They can set their own standards for qualities such as appearance, taste and price. However, they have to take other things on trust, such as source, food safety and production standards, which, of course, include animal welfare. This has generated a plethora of farm assurance schemes ranging (in the UK) from the 'Little Red Tractor'[1] to organic standards set by the Soil Association and 'Freedom Food' welfare standards set by the RSPCA. The intention is that both consumers and producers should benefit from a system that adds value based on the quality of the production methods. Organic food standards (which include a proper concern for animal welfare) have been conspicuously successful. Standards based strictly on animal welfare have not yet fared so well, with the notable exception of free range egg prod-uction according to the 'Freedom Foods' standards that now make up about half of total egg sales in many UK supermarkets.

The most important question for consumers, and indeed the animals, is 'Do these welfare-assurance schemes deliver what they claim to deliver?' Do they:

● ensure good standards of animal welfare?
● ensure better standards of animal welfare than on non-assured farms?
● address specific welfare problems as they occur?
● incorporate a protocol for regular review and upgrading of standards?

At present, the answer to all these questions is either 'No' or 'Don't know'. Nearly all current standards are based on measures of the resources and records necessary to promote good husbandry. This is good as far as it goes but it fails to address the most important questions: 'Are the animals fit and how do they feel?' At Bristol, my colleagues David Main, Becky Whay and I have developed animal-based protocols for the direct assessment of animal welfare outcomes. These have been used as an independent audit of the RSPCA Freedom Food scheme. To summarize our published and unpublished work very briefly, I can say that the welfare of the free range hens in our study, in general, looked good, but dairy cows had their problems, especially lameness, whether or not the farms were accredited to Freedom Foods or organic standards (see Main et al, 2003; Whay et al, 2003).

One of the main problems with farm assurance schemes is that they can simply become pieces of paper to be filed away between inspections. A scheme for farm animal health and welfare becomes effective only if it is part of a dynamic strategy to ensure and improve standards. This is illustrated in Figure 13.2. The accreditation body sets husbandry and welfare standards acceptable to both producers and consumers/retailers. The sequence of events for the producer is as follows. S/he first carries out a self-assessment of the enterprise to check on compliance with standards and identify any problems. An independent monitor then assesses the unit using a protocol looking mainly at welfare outcomes, such as the amount of lameness that is found in a group of animals or other measurable indications of welfare. The farmer, monitor and veterinary surgeon then address any immediate problems and devise a living strategy for health and welfare. This strategy is reviewed after an appropriate time (e.g. one year, or less if there are problems that need to be resolved quickly). The effectiveness of the strategy then feeds back to the farmer for further self-assessment and to the accreditation body who can benchmark the farm against approved standards and provide real assurance to the public as to what is being done. This sets in motion a virtuous cycle of review, action, improvement and further review.

Any welfare-assurance scheme will, of course, work only if the public is aware of it, values its standards and trusts the assurances that it provides. It is necessary therefore also to set in motion a second virtuous cycle of information transfer between the accreditation authority and the public that sets out clearly the quality standards and provides honest evidence to indicate how well the scheme is working. In this way all stakeholders can benefit: consumers, society and the animals themselves.

Increasing public demand for farm animal welfare

I cannot reiterate too often the message that if we are to achieve improved welfare standards for the farm animals then the lead must be given by the majority who consume these products not the minority who produce them. The drive towards proper respect for animals in society and proper treatment of animals in society should be driven by three engines for change, all operating together:

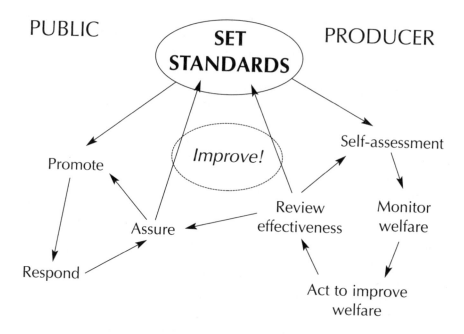

Figure 13.2 *Quality control and quality assurance: The two virtuous cycles*

1 increased international awareness of the nature of animal sentience and the responsibilities that this entails;
2 realistic, practical, step-by-step strategies for improving animal welfare within the context of other, equally valid aspirations of society;
3 a policy of education that will expand the human demand for welfare standards deemed acceptable by the animals themselves.

The first action, increasing awareness, is perhaps the most important of all. Too many people in too many regions of the world are simply not aware of the nature of sentience and suffering in farm animals. Once they are, their attitudes should improve (if only a bit). Animal welfare charities like CIWF, RSPCA and the World Society for the Protection of Animals (WSPA) have demonstrated that they are the most effective media for spreading this awareness. The second action, the development of effective strategies for improving farm animal welfare, depends on continued progress in our understanding of what it takes to keep farm animals fit and happy, and the application and marketing of these principles through the coupled virtuous cycles of quality assurance and quality control (Figure 13.2).

The final key necessary to convert right thought into right action is *education*. It is right to work towards an increased *awareness* of the nature of animal sentience and animal suffering, but it is not enough. All those who are actively involved with animal farming, in any way, need a proper education. This requires a profound understanding of the science, ethics and politics necessary to work towards a fair social contract between humans and animals. I cannot begin to expound on this in a brief chapter. I shall simply outline my view of the rights and responsibilities of the main stakeholders in a social contract that gives proper respect to animals within society (Table 13.1). Consumers have rights to wholesome, affordable food, but this carries the responsibility to demand high standards of animal welfare. It is an actuarial fact (not a moral judgement) that more could be achieved for farm animal welfare by the majority who consume animal products than the small minority (vegans, not ovolactovegetarians) who avoid the issue altogether. Farmers have the responsibility to ensure the highest possible welfare standards for their animals but these standards are determined by what society is prepared to pay. Farmers have the right to receive a fair reward for their efforts, measured both in terms of income and pride in their work. It is in their interests to improve their own quality of life by promoting increased quality rather than quantity of production. Finally, the farm animals, stakeholders according to our terms, have the right to be fit and happy throughout life and unafraid at the point of death. Their contribution to the contract is to work for us and to die at a time of our choosing. If this appears to be unfair, then death itself would appear to be unfair. Few of us die at a time of our own choosing and none of us escape death altogether.

Table 13.1 *The social contract between humans and animals: Rights and responsibilities*

Stakeholder	Rights	Responsibilities
Consumer	Good, affordable food	Demand high-welfare food
Farmer	A fair income and pride in work	Assure the highest possible standards level of animal welfare
Animals	To be fit and happy in life	To work and die at a time of our choosing

Finally, but not in conclusion

I conclude by quoting from the closing chapter from my book *Limping towards Eden*, because it encapsulates my essential message:

And so to bed. This is the end, not of a journey; merely a very long day on a journey that has no end. In A Cool Eye towards Eden (Webster, 1994), I was able to set down guidelines for the understanding of animal welfare based on the study of how it feels to be an animal. I was then able to progress to careful polemic; a constructive approach to the problem of man's dominion over the animals. Much of this could be considered in an abstract and academic sort of way because, at the time, the journey had scarcely begun. Now we are well into our journey and limping a little because the going is hard. It was relatively easy, and very satisfying, to pronounce on what should be done in the interests of animal welfare. It is harder, and more frustrating, to make real progress within a world of messy realities and conflicting objectives. This is therefore a tale of work in progress and work that will still be in progress long after I am gone. As such it would not, I think, be fitting to conclude with a phrase as exalted as that with which I closed the 'Cool Eye', namely Albert Schweizer's assertion that 'Until he extends the circle of his compassion to all living things, man will not himself find peace.' Embarked upon an endless journey, the hopeful traveller needs something more down beat. 'The path of duty lies in what is near.' We may never expect to see our final destination but, for those who are prepared to open their eyes, the immediate horizon is full of promise.

(Webster, 2005)

Note

1   The Little Red Tractor is the mark of Assured Food Standards, a food assurance scheme set up by the National Farmers Union, The Meat and Livestock Commission, the British Retail Consortium and others in the UK food industry.

References

Dawkins, M. S. (1993) *Through Our Eyes Only? The Search for Animal Consciousness*, Freeman, Oxford

Farm Animal Welfare Council (1993) *Second Report on Priorities for Research and Development in Farm Animal Welfare*, DEFRA Publications, London

Harrison, R. (1964) *Animal Machines*, Stuart, London

Main, D. C. J., Whay, H. R., Green, L. E. and Webster, A. J. F. (2003) 'Effect of the RSPCA Freedom Food scheme on dairy cattle welfare', *Veterinary Record*, vol 197, pp227–231

Webster, J. (1994) *Animal Welfare: A Cool Eye towards Eden*, Blackwell Publications, Oxford

Webster, J. (2005) *Animal Welfare: Limping towards Eden*, Blackwell Publications, Oxford

Whay, H. R., Main, D. C. J., Green, L. E. and Webster, A. J. F. (2003) 'Assessment of dairy cattle welfare using animal-based measurements', *Veterinary Record*, vol 153, pp197–202

14
Animal Sentience in US Farming

Michael C. Appleby

The Humane Society of the United States

Introduction

The US agricultural sector is comparable in size with that of the European Union (EU) before the latter enlarged in 2004. For example, in 2001 there were about 250 million laying hens in the US and 300 million in the EU (Fisher and Bowles, 2002). However, while there is increasing discussion of farm animal welfare in the US (Rollin, 2004), there has been relatively little improvement in the treatment of livestock compared to that in Europe. Most of the industry is very intensive. For example, over 99 per cent of laying hens are in battery cages that are very crowded: in 2002 many provided less than $361cm^2$ ($56in^2$) per bird and a programme was launched to increase the minimum allowance initially to this amount (United Egg Producers, 2002). This article will consider attitudes to the sentience of animals in US farming and implications for future changes in farm animal welfare.

Attitudes to sentience

Producers often claim that the welfare of their animals is satisfactory. The National Pork Board (2005a), for example, says that: 'Because the welfare of their animals directly affects their livelihood, pork producers work to ensure their animals are treated humanely. Anything less would be self-defeating.' However, such claims generally disregard sentience. Thus the National Pork Board (2005b) runs the Swine Welfare Assurance Program, which, while it doesn't actually assure swine welfare, is positive in that it does encourage producers to review many of their practices that affect welfare. Yet of the nine care and well-being principles in the Program (Table 14.1), only one, animal observation, even touches upon anything related to sentience, and that only considers inquisitiveness or fearfulness in pigs' responses to humans. There is no mention of suffering in relation to certain housing systems or any other aspect of pig sentience.

It is widely accepted that there are varied approaches to animal welfare, emphasizing physical, mental or natural aspects or a combination of these

Table 14.1 *Care and well-being principles of the Swine Welfare Assurance Program*

1	Herd health and nutrition
2	Caretaker training
3	Animal observation
4	Body condition score
5	Euthanasia
6	Handling and movement
7	Facilities
8	Emergency support
9	Continuing assessment and education

Source: National Pork Board, 2005b

(Duncan and Fraser, 1997; Fraser et al, 1997). Even more than elsewhere, producers in the US tend to emphasize physical aspects of welfare such as health and growth. The general public, by contrast, tends to emphasize both mental aspects, such as suffering, and aspects concerned with naturalness. This is doubtless why advertising campaigns emphasize sentience. For example, the California Milk Advisory Board (2005), which is part of the California Department of Food and Agriculture, advertises Real California Cheese with the slogan 'Great cheese comes from happy cows. Happy cows come from California' and with pictures of scattered cows in lush pastures. In reality, dairy cows in California are kept in large herds, mostly indoors.

The government has not restricted the ability of producers to dictate the terms in this debate: there are no federal laws on how animals should be treated on farms. As such, housing systems such as crates for sows and veal calves and battery cages for laying hens are usual, and practices such as forced moulting of hens and use of recombinant bovine somatotropin (rBST) in dairy cows are prevalent, all of which result in suffering. Interestingly, though, the one federal law protecting farm animals – the Humane Methods of Slaughter Act, dating from 1958 – is contingent on sentience, as it requires that livestock (excluding poultry) be 'rendered insensible to pain' prior to slaughter.

Voluntary programmes are starting to be introduced by mainstream producers and retailers to address public concerns about welfare, but again they tend to be limited and to focus on physical aspects. For example, companies represented by United Egg Producers (2002) have agreed to increase cage size to $430cm^2$ ($67in^2$) per hen by 2008. This is on the grounds that 'Numerous studies have shown that decreasing space allowance to [less than this] significantly reduces hen-housed production and increases mortality'.

Niche markets

Exceptions to these patterns are found among the farms, mostly small, that are developing niche markets on the basis of criteria such as animal welfare and environmental protection. These are being assisted by a number of programmes offering defined standards, such as the National Organic Plan, the pig welfare standards of the Animal Welfare Institute and the Certified Humane label administered by Humane Farm Animal Care. The standards for the last, for example, state that 'Livestock must have … a diet designed to maintain full health and promote a positive state of well-being' (Humane Farm Animal Care, 2003). Such programmes are still a small minority, but the fact that they are increasing offers hope of growing consideration of animal sentience in the future of US farming.

Pressure against change

Nevertheless, there is considerable pressure against change in mainstream US agriculture. This is partly because consolidation and intensification have progressed further than in any other country. Indeed, consolidation was for many years government policy, led by Secretary of Agriculture Ezra Taft Benson's famous injunction to farmers in the 1950s, 'Get big or get out', and his successor Earl Butz's ultimatum in the 1970s, 'Adapt or die' (Berry, 1999). Consolidation is particularly strong in the pork industry. More than 80 per cent of pigs are now raised on farms housing more than 1000 animals. About 65 per cent of pigs are raised in only five states: Iowa (25 per cent), North Carolina, Minnesota, Illinois and Indiana (US Department of Agriculture, 2002). There is massive concentration in vertically integrated companies. Notably, farms owned by one single company – Smithfields – house about 675,000 sows (Anonymous, 1999). In the dairy sector, 58 per cent of cows are in herds of over 200, and 30 per cent in herds of over 1000 (US Department of Agriculture, 2005).

Individual states can pass their own legislation, and there have been isolated instances of legislation favouring animal welfare: Florida banned gestation crates for sows in 2002 and California legislated in 2004 to phase out force feeding of poultry for foie gras production. However, consolidation of agricultural sectors in particular states – and the consequent emphasis on sale of goods outside the producing states – militates against such legislation because there is resistance to any measures that would reduce competitiveness with other states. In addition, this concentration is one of the factors that leads to the public being much less informed about farm animal welfare than in other areas such as Europe (Rollin, 2004): the majority of the public, buying cheese from California, lives thousands of miles from that state and is unaware that the sight of cows on pasture is rare there.

Intensification has also produced many problems for welfare associated with pressure for increased production efficiency. In egg production, most hens are beak trimmed, and forced moulting is usual, involving feed withdrawal for up to 14 days. In dairy production, average yield is considerably higher in the US, at 8600kg of milk per cow, than in the EU, at 5400 (US Department of Agriculture, 2004a). This is affected by a number of factors, including the use of rBST. This is used on 15 per cent of farms overall, but on 54 per cent of the largest farms (those with 500 or more cows) (US Department of Agriculture, 2003).

Pressure for production efficiency in mainstream agriculture will not abate in the foreseeable future, partly because government policy is actively to promote agricultural exports, including animals and animal products. In September 2003 the US Secretary of Agriculture gave introductory comments at a meeting called Future Trends in Animal Agriculture and said in reference to trade: 'We will continue to aggressively pursue opportunities for our producers' (Veneman, 2003). The website of the US Department of Agriculture (2004b) includes a section on marketing operations that includes the following, among other programmes: Emerging Markets Program; Foreign Market Development Cooperator Program; Market Access Program; and Unified Export Strategy. A Task Force Report for the US Department of Agriculture (USDA) in July 2004 recommended creation of a USDA Basic Science Institute, of which the first objective would be 'nurturing American agriculture that is more competitive internationally' (Russo, 2004).

In the period from 2000 to 2002, the US and the EU together accounted for over one-third of the world's agricultural exports, with 19 per cent from the US and 17 per cent from the EU (Kelch and Normile, 2004). In the 12 months to September 2004, exports of live animals by the US were worth over US$450 million and those of red meats and products about US$3.7 billion, both about one-third lower than the year before, primarily because of the impact of mad cow disease. Animal exports totalled US$10.6 billion. Imports of live animals cost US$1.4 billion, and animal imports totalled US$10.4 billion (Table 14.2; Brooks, 2004). The extraordinary fact that exports and imports of many categories of agricultural product are both huge and approximately balanced for a country or region has been described elsewhere as The Great Food Swap (Lucas, 2001). This trade has considerable negative impacts both on the environment and on animal welfare. Transport of live animals internationally is likely to cause even more problems for welfare than that within countries, while movement of animal products around the world carries severe danger of disease transmission.

Finding mechanisms for change is difficult in an industry largely driven by competition, especially as that competition is intensifying with this burgeoning international trade in agricultural produce.

Pressure for change

Yet there is also gathering pressure for change in attitudes to farming methods in relation to animal sentience, animal welfare and other issues such as environmental impact. When people hear about how animals are treated, they show

Table 14.2 *US trade in the 12 months to September 2004, in million dollars*

	Exports	Imports
Live animals	454	1357
Red meats and products	3700	5527
Poultry meats and products	2435	364
Dairy products	1321	2332
Other animal products	2685	772
Total	10595	10352

Source: Brooks, 2004

considerable concern: as in Florida, where the ban on gestation crates for sows was passed by a 55 per cent vote in a referendum (Humane Society of the United States, 2002). A recent poll showed that 62 per cent of US citizens favour passing strict laws concerning the treatment of farm animals (Gallup, 2003). More than 10 per cent of the delegates at the conference on animal sentience in London in 2005, which gave rise to this volume, were from the US. Furthermore, the increasing sales of organic food and food from animals with enhanced welfare in the US have already been noted. The standards being introduced by major retailers are also a reflection of public opinion. A senior executive of one of the major fast food chains has commented that their customers expect them – the restaurant company – to ensure that the animals supplying them with food are properly looked after (England, 2002). That company is following the lead of the McDonald's Corporation (see Chapter 15), which in 2000 started requiring its suppliers to provide laying hens with the same space allowance as in Europe, and not to practice forced moulting. McDonald's buys 2.5 per cent of US eggs. Subsequently the National Council of Chain Restaurants (NCCR) and the Food Marketing Institute (FMI, which represents the major supermarket chains) developed a collaborative programme, producing husbandry guidelines for their suppliers of animal products in 2002. These do not go as far as European legislation, but they are important in acknowledging the importance of animal welfare, and in forming a basis for possible future raising of welfare standards.

Husbandry guidelines continue to proliferate (Mench, 2003), with some substantive and some more cosmetic. The resultant consumer confusion may lead to consolidation, as in the programme of the NCCR and FMI, but also carries the risk of provoking a levelling-down effect of competition. Factors encouraging improvement of welfare are also, of course, countered by continuing competitive pressure for intensification of livestock production, especially as competition is exacerbated by international trade. One programme that offers some hope of regulating this pressure is the development of animal welfare guidelines by the World Organisation for Animal Health (OIÉ, 2005), which will have some influence on the treatment of at least those animals raised for export (see Chapter 23). The OIÉ programme will also at minimum increase the attention paid to farm animal welfare in the US, emphasizing the importance of this issue and providing a basis for possible future improvements. Indeed, increased communication about animal welfare is maintaining the upward trend in international awareness. People concerned for animals hope, with some justification, that these positive effects are accelerating.

References

Anonymous (1999) 'Pork Powerhouses 1999: 50 largest pork producers in the U.S.', *Successful Farming*, vol 97, p15

Berry, W. (1999) 'Nation's destructive farm policy is everyone's concern', *Herald-Leader*, 11 July

Brooks, N. (2004) 'U.S. agricultural trade update', USDA, available at http://usda.mannlib.cornell.edu/reports/erssor/trade/fau-bb/text/2004/fau95.pdf

California Milk Advisory Board (2005) Available at www.realcaliforniacheese.com

Duncan, I. J. H. and Fraser, D. (1997) 'Understanding animal welfare', in Appleby, M. C. and Hughes, B. O. (eds) *Animal Welfare*, CAB International, Wallingford, UK, pp19–31

England, C. (2002) 'Burger King and animal welfare: Why did this company get involved?' in *Proceedings, Canadian Association for Laboratory Animal Science and Alberta Farm Animal Care conference*, 25 June, Edmonton, Canada, p13

Fisher, C. and Bowles, D. (2002) *Hard-Boiled Reality: Animal Welfare-Friendly Egg Production in a Global Market*, Royal Society for the Protection of Animals, Horsham, UK

Fraser, D., Weary, D. M., Pajor, E. A. and Milligan, B. N. (1997) 'A scientific conception of animal welfare that reflects ethical concerns', *Animal Welfare*, vol 6, pp187–205

Gallup (2003) *Public Lukewarm on Animal Rights*, Gallup, Princeton, NJ

Humane Farm Animal Care (2003) *Animal Care Standards: Pigs*, Humane Farm Animal Care, Herndon, VA

Humane Society of the United States (2002) 'Voters protect pigs in Florida, ban cockfighting in Oklahoma', press release, available at www.hsus.org/press_and_publications/press_releases

Kelch, D. and Normile, M. A. (2004) 'European Union adopts significant farm reform', available at www.ers.usda.gov/AmberWaves/September04

Lucas, C. (2001) *Stopping the Great Food Swap*, The Greens, European Parliament

Mench, J. A. (2003) 'Assessing animal welfare at the farm and group level: A United States perspective', *Animal Welfare*, vol 12, pp493–503

National Pork Board (2005a) 'Animal care: Overview', available at www.porkscience.org

National Pork Board (2005b) 'Swine Welfare Assurance Program', available at www.porkboard.org/SWAPHome

OIÉ (World Organisation for Animal Health) (2005) Available at www.oie.int/eng/press/en_050602.htm

Rollin, B. E. (2004) 'The ethical imperative to control pain and suffering in farm animals', in Benson, G. J. and Rollin, B. E. (eds) *The Well-Being of Farm Animals:*

Challenges and Solutions, Blackwell, Ames, USA, pp3–19

Russo, E. (2004) 'A USDA Basic Science Institute?' available at www.biomedcentral.com/news/20041116/02

United Egg Producers (2002) *Animal Husbandry Guidelines for U.S. Egg Laying Flocks*, UEP, Alpharetta, Georgia

US Department of Agriculture (2002) 'National agricultural statistics service: 2002 census of agriculture', available at www.nass.usda.gov/census/census02/volume1/us/index1.htm

US Department of Agriculture (2003) 'Bovine somatotropin', available at www.aphis.usda.gov/vs/ceah/ncahs/nahms/dairy/dairy02/Dairy02BST.pdf

US Department of Agriculture (2004a) 'Foreign agricultural service: Dairy, world markets and trade', available at www.fas.usda.gov/dlp/circular/2004/04-12Dairy/toc.htm

US Department of Agriculture (2004b) 'Marketing operations staff', available at www.fas.usda.gov/mos

US Department of Agriculture (2005) 'National agriculture statistics service: Agricultural statistics 2005', available at www.usda.gov/nass/pubs/agr05/05–ch8.pdf

Veneman, A. (2003) 'Welcome', Comments at Future Trends in Animal Agriculture meeting, Washington, DC, 17 September

15

McDonald's: Progressing Global Standards in Animal Welfare

Keith Kenny

McDonald's, UK

McDonald's takes animal welfare seriously, and within the global food industry, is at the forefront of those working actively to improve welfare standards. This chapter aims to give readers an insight into the approach taken by McDonald's in order to achieve these high standards, some of the challenges we face in this area as an industry and the steps we have taken to overcome them.

McDonald's believes that sharing information, listening to experts and being transparent are essential to raising standards in animal welfare. Our approach is to strive to develop a culture of continuous improvement in the animal welfare practices of our supply base. This, we believe, is the most effective way of improving standards in animal welfare across the industry.

As a company we have already taken significant initiatives; for example, our use of free range eggs (in the UK, Germany, Austria and Switzerland), in establishing the McDonald's Agricultural Assurance Programme (in Europe), in the auditing of slaughter house practice (globally) and in requiring an increased space allowance for caged laying hens (in the US). Such initiatives and our ongoing consultations with animal welfare experts have improved the lives of many of the animals used for our food production. However, we are in no way complacent and we realize that there is still a lot more to be done.

McDonald's supply chain

To set the context for this discussion, McDonald's was founded in the US in 1955 and there are now over 31,000 McDonald's restaurants in 119 countries. McDonald's moved into Europe in 1971 and now we have over 6200 restaurants in 43 countries employing more than 280,000 staff. In the UK alone we have 1250 restaurants and around 75,000 employees.

One of the main reasons we have been able to develop a global restaurant system is the strength and structure of our supply chain. In order to understand McDonald's impact and ability to improve general standards of animal welfare, it is essential to understand the relationship between McDonald's and our supply chain.

The businesses that make up our supply chain are all independent and McDonald's does not own any part of it. We don't breed our own animals – they come from many of the same independent farms that supply the best supermarkets. We don't own any manufacturing facilities, transport networks or abattoirs. The essential point is that our supply chain operates on the basis of partnership with McDonald's, not ownership by McDonald's. Therefore in striving to move towards higher animal welfare standards, it is important to recognize that our suppliers also have their own business priorities and the need to grow their businesses.

How then can McDonald's improve animal welfare standards across a base of independent suppliers? In our experience, the strongest results are achieved when we work with them to provide incentives for the best technologies, welfare and manufacturing practices and efficiencies; as we see it, this is a partnership in which both parties benefit equally. We would argue that this system has not only enabled the growth of McDonald's globally but also enabled us to develop industry-leading standards in our supply chain.

Animal welfare

McDonald's purchases only a small fraction of the world's goods and services. However, we understand the huge benefits we can bring by working with our suppliers to help improve their practices and set an example for other companies. We believe that we have a responsibility to do this.

McDonald's has a comprehensive approach to corporate social responsibility (CSR). Our CSR approach addresses many different areas including the local communities in which our restaurants are located, our people and the environment. A very significant part of this approach is to address the way we work with our suppliers to incorporate socially responsible practices into their operations and to build capabilities for continuous improvement.

We engage with our suppliers on a broad range of issues such as the quality and safety of our products, conservation of natural resources, our suppliers' employment practices and animal welfare. McDonald's cares about the humane treatment of animals. We recognize that our responsibility as a purchaser of food products includes working with our suppliers to ensure good animal handling practices. Our animal welfare programme is an ongoing process of study, consultation and innovative improvement.

Animal welfare council

We recognize the need to consult with the best animal welfare experts to help determine priorities and action steps. To guide our efforts, we established an independent Animal Welfare Council that consists of internationally recognized experts (see Appendix 1 of this chapter). Three of these experts contributed to the conference that gave rise to this book and their contributions are cited in the Annex (p276).

McDonald's animal welfare guiding principles

McDonald's commitment to animal welfare is global and guided by the principles of safety, quality, animal treatment, partnership, leadership, performance management and communication. These principles apply to all the countries in which McDonald's does business and are described below.

Safety

First and foremost, McDonald's is committed to providing its customers with safe food products. Food safety is McDonald's number one priority.

Quality

We believe that treating animals with care and respect is an integral part of an overall quality assurance programme that makes good business sense.

Animal treatment

We support the policy that animals should be free from cruelty, abuse and neglect while embracing the proper treatment of animals and addressing animal welfare issues.

Partnership

We work continuously with our suppliers to audit animal welfare practices, ensuring compliance and continuous improvement.

A good example of how such partnership can be effective is the work that our European supply base is doing in the area of controlled atmosphere stunning (the stunning of meat chickens by gas before slaughter). Animal welfare experts recognize that there are huge potential welfare benefits to this system, compared to conventional electrical stunning of chickens, but more work needs to be done. There are four companies in our supply base that have test systems in place. Under the McDonald's banner and according to our partnering and information sharing philosophy, we have been able to get all these companies together to share technical information and best practice to drive improvements faster. In all other areas these companies are competitors and would not share such commercially sensitive information.

Leadership

We aim to lead our industry, working with our suppliers and industry experts, to advance animal welfare practices and technology.

McDonald's UK took a real leadership position when we asked our egg suppliers to build sufficient free range egg production capacity to supply us with enough free range eggs for our entire breakfast programme (circa 100 million eggs). We also required that only free range eggs are used in the production of all our sauces.

Performance measurement

Acting as a responsible purchaser, we set annual performance objectives to measure our improvement and will ensure our purchasing strategy is aligned with our commitment to animal welfare issues. For example, we have a set of key welfare indicators that our chicken suppliers use to monitor the welfare of birds at the farm level.

Communication

We will communicate our processes, programmes, plans and progress concerning animal welfare.

Implementation of this overall programme is based on a global framework of common goals, policies and guidelines. Within this framework, individual geographic business units have the flexibility to develop programmes and performance measures appropriate to local conditions.

McDonald's Agricultural Assurance Programme

In Europe, the approach we took was to integrate animal welfare into our quality assurance system. We did this around 3–4 years ago via our McDonald's Agricultural Assurance Programme (MAAP). MAAP is our approach to assuring quality in the agricultural supply chain, whilst supporting the development of sustainable agriculture across Europe. This is the set of standards we ask all our suppliers to aspire to in their agricultural methods, from the start of production to the farm gate (from lettuce and flour to beef and eggs). For arable crops this extends from pre-planting, via cultivation methods, to harvest. For food animals it extends from feed mill and breeder animals through to finishing farms for beef. MAAP standards go beyond national and EU legal requirements.

MAAP is a process of continuous improvement, the aim being to include food safety and quality right from the beginning and ensuring that agricultural production is sustainable and ethical. There are seven policies that guide our course towards sustainable agriculture. They determine the present and future development of our primary supply chain and describe the overall direction in the following areas:

- the environment;
- agricultural practices;
- animal welfare;
- animal nutrition;

- animal medication;
- traceability;
- genetics.

These seven policies are aligned with the McDonald's global corporate social responsibility approach mentioned earlier.

The MAAP policy for animal welfare is as follows:

- to ensure that all animals involved or affected by the production of our products are treated humanely throughout their lives, according to their species' specific needs;
- to ensure that suppliers meet or exceed the relevant national and EU legislation;
- to encourage all levels of the supply chain to continuously improve animal welfare through the exploration and implementation of advances in animal welfare science, rearing and husbandry;
- to promote the positive welfare of animals by having regard to and providing for their needs in accordance with the scientifically based Five Freedoms.

McDonald's has been co-sponsor of the work Roland Bonney and his team at the Food Animal Initiative (FAI) are doing in Oxford (UK) since its conception in 2002 (see also Annex p276). We hope that the work the FAI is doing will result in a move to farming practices that are better from an animal welfare standpoint, but are at least as commercially viable as the current ones. The combination of better welfare plus commercial feasibility is the most effective way to get welfare improvements adopted by all sections of the industry.

How effective has MAAP been in raising standards in practice? I think it is important to stress here how difficult it is to exercise influence when you are as high in the supply chain as McDonald's is. Indeed, to even check that compliance is happening is a significant challenge. To help overcome this problem, we work with existing farm assurance schemes to effect change and have our standards and future goals adopted and accepted by these schemes. Most national farm assurance schemes are independently audited by professional auditors. We have a programme of meetings and lobbying with national scheme organizers to discuss our MAAP requirements and future goals in order to get them written into the national schemes. In this way we believe that we are making a significant contribution to driving and supporting progress in agricultural production, including animal welfare, across the farming community.

It is important to note that MAAP is still a work in progress; we measure the level of compliance within our supply base on an annual basis and continually strive to increase both standards and compliance. Raising standards is a never-ending process. The beef supply chain is the area in which we are best known.

Details of the beef standards system are given below in Appendix 2 of this chapter. Similar standards and processes exist for all products that we purchase. In relation to animal welfare, that means dairy, pork and bacon, and chicken and eggs and covers all segments of the supply chain from hatcheries to breeders and catching to transport and abattoir practices.

In summary, our standards and requirements for animal welfare form an integral part of our quality assurance systems. In our agricultural supply base, this takes the form of MAAP. Further up the supply chain we have separate standards covering animal transport and abattoirs. We believe that McDonald's has made a good start and is leading the industry in the area of animal welfare, but we also recognize how much more we have to do.

Appendix 1: McDonald's Animal Welfare Council

Dr Jeff Armstrong

Department Head and Professor, Department of Animal Sciences, Purdue University; Chair, United Egg Producers Welfare Advisory Committee; member, Board of Directors, National Institute of Animal Agriculture.

Dr Temple Grandin

World-renowned expert and advocate for animal welfare; research and practical experience with animal handling and slaughter systems in the US, Canada, Europe, Mexico, Australia and New Zealand; author of over 300 articles; Associate Professor of Animal Science, Colorado State University.

Diane Halverson

Farm Animal Adviser, Animal Welfare Institute (AWI); author of AWI's humane on-farm husbandry standards for pigs, which are followed by a growing number of family farmers who are able to stay in business through a special marketing programme for pork from humane, sustainable farms.

Dr Joy Mench

Professor, Department of Animal Science, and Director, Center for Animal Welfare, University of California at Davis; member, Scientific Advisory Committee of the American Humane Organization, United Egg Producers Welfare Advisory Committee, Federation of Animal Science Societies Animal Care and Use Committee, and Advisory Board of the Scientists Center for Animal Welfare.

Dr Edmond Pajor

Assistant Professor, Department of Animal Sciences, Purdue University; US Regional Representative, International Society of Applied Ethology; member, Journal of Animal Science editorial board, Indiana Commission on Farm Animal Care, and Steering Committee of the Purdue University Center for Food Animal Well-Being.

Dr Janice Swanson

Associate Professor, Animal Science, Kansas State University; member, United Egg Producers Scientific Advisory Committee on Animal Welfare; Chair, KSU Institutional Animal Care and Use Committee; member, Board of Trustees, Scientists Center for Animal Welfare; former Technical Information Specialist, USDA Animal Welfare Information Center

Appendix 2: Case study – beef supply chain

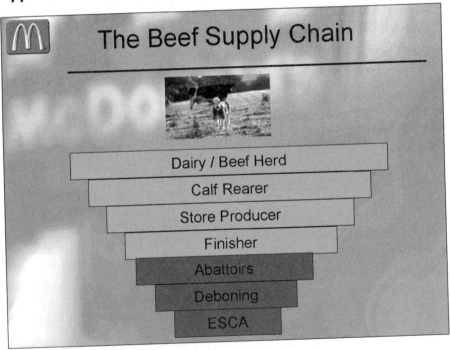

Figure 15.1 *McDonald's beef supply chain*

As set out in the guiding principles, McDonald's believes that treating animals with care and respect is an integral part of an overall quality assurance programme. This holistic approach to quality is explained in more detail below, using the UK beef supply chain as an example.

In the UK, the direct supplier of our beef burgers (beef patties) is a company named ESCA. ESCA has supplied McDonald's pretty much since we started trading in the UK 30 years ago. ESCA operates two production facilities in the UK, supplying us with millions of beef patties each year.

We have extremely exacting requirements of this supplier and their facilities with regard to quality, safety and hygiene standards. These are all detailed in a number of documents and standards, all of which are audited on a regular basis. These audits are not only carried out by McDonald's quality assurance staff, but also by an independent third-party auditor, EFSIS. The beef patties are made to a strict specification, including details of the quality and cuts of beef permitted. All this goes to help ensure consistency and that they all cook properly in our restaurants and taste great.

In the UK the beef is supplied from a number of McDonald's approved de-boning plants, of which there are around 15. All these plants must comply with our Good Manufacturing Practices and Requirements for Beef Plants. They are also audited for compliance against these requirements by ESCA, our beef supplier, as well as by us and by EFSIS, the independent third party auditor.

Going further upstream, the next link in the supply chain is the abattoirs. Here we have about 20 abattoirs supplying the deboning plants. These abattoirs must comply with our Good Manufacturing Practices and Requirements and are audited for compliance against these Requirements by ourselves, our beef supplier ESCA and again by the independent third-party auditor EFSIS.

We also have a number of other standards and requirements covering areas such as hazard analysis critical control point (HACCP), traceability and, because this is the first link in the chain where live animals are being handled, we have the Animal Welfare Guidelines during Transport and Slaughter and the Cattle Welfare Slaughter Protocol. Again all of these are audited by ourselves, ESCA and EFSIS as well as regular self-audits done by the abattoirs themselves.

In summary, we exercise very strict control over the policies and practices in these three links in the supply chain, going much further down the supply chain than is legally required or than is standard practice within the food industry.

As we move down the supply chain, the number of supplying units increases and the resources required to audit and monitor them become bigger too. In addition to this, our influence on these suppliers becomes less and less because the proportion of their business going to McDonald's is smaller with each step. This is why it is important to build long-term relationships with all links in the supply chain. Without this relationship, there is little reason why a slaughter house would want to supply a customer that has much more exacting requirements, spends much more time auditing their factories, and so increases their costs, but only pays the same price for the meat as a customer who doesn't demand all this.

The next step along the supply chain, the farm level, is the biggest jump of all. The 20 or so abattoirs have many thousands of farmers supplying them with cattle. Of these, around 16,500 are approved to contribute to the McDonald's UK supply chain. If you look at this on a European level, the number moves to circa 500,000 farms. To exercise any sort of control over that number of farms without employing an army of auditors is challenging, to say the very least. In Europe the solution that we came up with is the McDonald's Agricultural Assurance Programme, our approach to assuring quality in the agricultural supply chain.

16
Respecting Animal Sentience in Organic Farming

Patrick Holden
Soil Association, UK

Animal welfare consequences of industrial farming

During the 20th century, industrial farming systems have resulted in the exploitation of farm livestock with terrible welfare consequences. This has been made possible by the demand for cheap meat; the low cost of feed and energy; the inappropriate use of new technology; vast-scale, labour-efficient livestock units; and the availability of veterinary medicines, particularly antibiotics, to suppress disease and promote animal growth.

One of the key factors that have enabled this exploitation to take place is public ignorance. The distressing consequences of industrial livestock systems have been mostly hidden from public view. Until recently consumers have been complicit in this arrangement in the sense that they have not wanted to know too much about the story behind the meat and other livestock products they eat.

At the end of the 20th century, a number of food scares, notably concerns about growth promoter residues, pathogens in livestock products, bovine spongiform encephalopathy (BSE) and antibiotic resistance, alerted the public to the human health consequences of intensive livestock systems. In parallel with this, their conscience has been awoken to the vast scale of suffering of the animals involved.

Collectively, this growing awareness and the public's increasing willingness to support radical changes in livestock farming, both through policy instruments and in the marketplace, have created an unprecedented opportunity to move away from industrial livestock farming. However, unless certain fundamental principles are understood, there is a real danger that this opportunity will not be fully realized.

Organic farming standards for 'positive health'

The Soil Association's origins relate to observations made by Sir Albert Howard, an eminent British scientist who came from a livestock farming background in Cheshire. In 1905 he was sent to India by the British Government to teach the peasants how to farm. He quickly realized that he had more to learn from them than to teach. His single most important observation was that health, both in plants and animals, is not merely the absence of disease, but a vital state where the organism is in a dynamic equilibrium with its environment. Applied to livestock, this philosophy requires a radically different management approach if one is to achieve this objective – the husbandry for health principle. The philosophy behind this principle is that farmers need to look after their animals based on the concept that when the husbandry and management are correct, good health and welfare will be the outcome. This concept of positive health, of husbandry for health based on an animal's physical and psychological needs, seems common sense. And yet a vast industry has made its business from ignoring the principles of good husbandry, and instead marketing suppressive 'solutions' which are only necessary because of bad farming.

The Soil Association set about defining standards for livestock production systems based on this 'husbandry for health' principle in the early 1980s. These standards are based on the principle that not only the basic physical needs of farmed animals must be delivered, but that the integrity and autonomy of the animal must be given priority. No other defined farming system gives as much priority to the needs of the animal, although organic farmers recognize that there is still more that could be done.

The Soil Association standards exclude routine drug usage (with the exception of vaccinations where there is evidence of an ongoing threat to animal health that cannot be resolved through husbandry, such as lungworm in cattle). They also prohibit many common mutilations such as tail docking in pigs and de-beaking of laying hens. The standards have often been misunderstood and criticized by conventional vets. These misunderstandings throw into sharp relief the fundamentally different, and, I believe, flawed, mindset of many involved in livestock farming. The very need for these drugs and mutilations demonstrates the unsustainability of any system that requires their usage.

Antibiotics have been massively overused and have actually permitted the continuation of inhumane industrial farming systems by suppressing the inevitable high levels of infection and mortality that would result if they were withdrawn. The same is true of mutilations; the need to beak trim hens or tail dock pigs is an indication that the animal is being kept in such a way that deviant behaviour is likely. It is not, however, that the drug or even the mutilation is an evil in itself. We allow, indeed insist upon, for example, the use of antibiotic treatment if welfare would be compromised were it withheld, and accept, for instance, that lambs' tails must often be docked to prevent fly strike (the worse of two evils). It is the usage of medication or mutilation as a support to the inhumane that is unacceptable.

Soil Association standards require a properly free range lifestyle at modest stocking densities, whenever outside conditions allow; good low-density housing with plentiful bedding when animals need to be indoors; a diet suited to the animals' physiology; extended suckling periods and stable groups.

Organic animal products in the market

These standards are demanding, given this and the requirement for an organically grown diet, and inevitably a higher retail price is needed. Despite this, the growth in consumer demand has been dramatic over the last ten years, albeit from a very low base. Farm gate sales of organic meat have risen from GB£8 million in 1999/2000 to GB£50 million in 2003/04, and the meat sector is still one of the strongest growth areas in the organic market.

This dynamic growth has reached a sufficient scale and market share to raise the question as to whether organic livestock production systems will ever replace intensive livestock farming. This is a question that would have seemed academic and irrelevant just a few years ago and will still be dismissed by many given that non-organic production systems still account for around 98 per cent of the total production market.

In some ways, even the modest success we have had brings some real challenges. The enthusiasm of the multiple retailers to stock organic meat has been a huge boon in growing the numbers of animals benefiting from organic management. At the same time, it has also meant that, as the multiple giants compete with each other, we are facing the same problems as our conventional colleagues of travelling distances, price pressures, and poorer quality products from large scale processors. Our efforts to re-localize the food chain must be redoubled to address these issues, alongside putting pressure on the super-markets to improve their practices.

In addition, there is a threat of lower standards applied by some producers in the organic sector. This applies to products imported from overseas and even, in the case of poultry, products produced within the UK. The result is that the Soil Association lives in a world of competing tensions, where our welfare aspirations can be compromised by those who would abuse consumer trust by watering down standards, thus reducing prices. Our response to this has to be to vehemently defend the highest practical standards, and to take the public with us on these vital issues.

The future of organic livestock systems

Our role, then, is to challenge and change the way farmed animals and fish are kept by striving to develop ever better systems and underpinning these with tough standards and rigorous enforcement. If this means that we limit our 'market share' then so be it. But our success will depend on how successful we are in promoting a welfare agenda to the public. We must also work over time to improve the ecological efficiency of what we do, particularly beyond the farm gate. Our influence, however, should benefit *all* farmed animals; as the 'ceiling' (as Jonathon Porritt recently described Soil Association standards) rises, the rest inevitably have to follow.

We are committed to continuing to influence EU and worldwide standards. An area in which we have a long and successful track record of ensuring that our farmers genuinely deliver the welfare outcomes that society expects from organic systems. This last point is extremely important. Soil Association standards are generally acknowledged to have the highest potential for animal welfare, but ensuring that these standards translate fully into practice is essential. To achieve this we are working with experts such as Bristol University to help us comprehensively audit welfare outcomes.

Public confidence, support and expectation are vital, Consumers are, however, often confused by competing labels, logos and terminologies. So often consumers believe that 'farm fresh' means 'free range', that 'freedom foods' means animals living outside, or even that they are organically reared. Whilst the Soil Association is supportive of any scheme that improves welfare, even if it is simply prohibiting the very worst forms of intensive management, as the 'Little Red Tractor' scheme. However, we do feel that clear and accurate labelling is essential if the consumer is to make an informed choice – let's call a battery egg 'a battery egg', a pig bred in a farrowing crate and reared on a slatted floor, just that.

In addition to the issues already discussed, the Soil Association faces a number of key challenges and dilemmas. The first relates to breeds. Industrial livestock farming has not only resulted in a dramatic reduction of the global gene pool for farmed animals, but so-called 'genetic improvements' have also led directly to violations of animal welfare. It would be no exaggeration to say that some of the most widely used breeds of poultry and pigs and dairy cattle have been so highly bred that they are genetically programmed to give themselves welfare problems; these problems are virtually unavoidable without levels of stockmanship and husbandry which most commercial farms are unable to provide. The Soil Association is currently considering whether we should outlaw the use of some of these breeds in organic livestock systems. At the very least, we must encourage within-breed selection that focuses on much wider parameters than simply productivity.

The second issue is scale. There is a presumption that has informed the development of livestock farming globally that larger flock and herd sizes are inevitable. Yet it is clear that above certain thresholds, both of stocking density and of flock and herd size, animal welfare is compromised. There is also the question of the human and geographical dimensions. For instance, how can milking a 500-cow dairy herd ever be satisfying for a herdsman (it has effectively become a factory job on this scale) and it is also impossible to have an intimate knowledge of this number of animals. There is also the question of herd and flock sizes and their impact on the landscape and soils. Where I farm in west Wales, a 500-cow herd would not only lead to increased erosion, but also result in the creation of a building complex that would look like an industrial unit in one of the most beautiful landscapes in Britain.

Thirdly, we have to be prepared to debate some of the trade-offs that occasionally face us when developing high-welfare systems. For example, (and this is only a theoretical example because we find it difficult to get accurate data from intensive systems) if early piglet mortality from overlying by the sow was found to be increased by, say, 3–5 per cent for outdoor, unrestrained farrowings, how do we balance that against the ability of the sow to fulfil her instincts to nest, move freely and properly attend to her young? Does the risk of occasional fox predation of laying hens mean that we should 'protect' them in barns or battery cages? In my view, we should legitimately take an approach that accepts that an autonomous, fulfilling life may carry some additional risk of mishap.

Lastly, the Soil Association must continue to support those pioneering producers whose endeavours will eventually 'crack' some of the most intractable welfare problems that face both organic and conventional farmers – such as the need to separate dairy animals from their young, and the problem of male calves from dairy breeds.

In conclusion, I believe that this is one of those moments in history where millions of people have a deep thirst for farming systems that reconnect them both with nature and with their inner values. When given sufficient information and the choice to support farming systems that have high integrity and excellent welfare, more and more people are prepared to pay higher prices for this kind of approach. This brings a responsibility on those involved with farming to develop systems that address not only the issue of animal sentience but also human values, scale, sustainable resource use and harmony with the natural environment. A process of change has started and none should underestimate its potential for application on a global scale.

17

The Welfare of Animals Bred for Their Fur in China

Ros Clubb

Care for the Wild International, UK

Introduction

In recognition of persistent welfare problems, several governments in the EU have banned fur farming either fully (e.g. UK) or partially (e.g. The Netherlands), or else have introduced prohibitively expensive husbandry standards (e.g. Sweden).

Research on fur-farmed wild animals, conducted primarily in European farms, has revealed many welfare problems (see Council of Europe, 1999, for a review). These include stereotypic behaviour, self-mutilation, fearfulness, infanticide and reproductive problems. Aspects of husbandry known to affect welfare include cage size and furniture, social grouping and other factors that limit the opportunity to perform natural behaviours.

Nevertheless, the fur industry remains an expanding multi-billion pound business, supplied by fur farms all over the world. The International Fur Trade Federation (IFTF), said to contain practically every fur producer and fur producing country in the world, reported global fur retail sales totalling US$11.7 billion in 2003/2004 (IFTF, 2003, see Figure 17.1). The European Union, now the world's biggest consumer of fur, produced 35.5 million pelts in 2002 and saw retails fur sales of US$4.5 million in 2002/2003 (EFBA/IFTF, 2004, see Figure 17.2). Closer to home in the UK, The British Fur Trade Association turns over an estimated £500 million a year as the world's largest buyers of pelts (IFTF, 2005a), despite the UK government having banned fur farming on humane grounds.

In recent years, fur farming in China has undergone a veritable boom. The country is now the world's biggest fur trade production and processing base. Most Chinese farms have been established in the past ten years and currently house an estimated 1.5 million foxes, an equivalent number of raccoon dogs and unknown numbers of mink and rex rabbits and other species (IFTF, 2005b). China produces around 1 million mink and fox pelts each year, representing 11 per cent of the world's mink and 27 per cent of the world's fox production (EFBA/IFTF, 2004), and a growing number of international fur

Figure 17.1 *Fur sales worldwide*

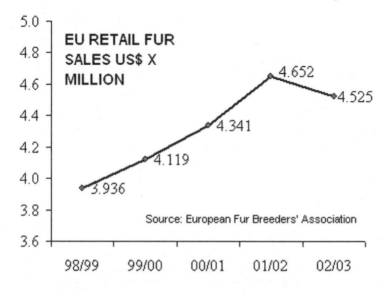

Figure 17.2 *Fur sales in the European Union*

traders, processors and fashion designers have shifted to China. The net volume of fur imports and exports in China for 2003 was US$997.6 million, up 42.5 per cent from 2002 (Renfeng and Qingfen, 2004). More than 95 per cent of fur clothing produced in China is sold to overseas markets, with 80 per cent of fur exports from Hong Kong destined for Europe, the US and Japan.

Given China's rapidly expanding role in the worldwide fur industry, a survey of a sample of Chinese fur farms, markets and slaughter houses was undertaken by Care for the Wild International, Swiss Animal Protection and EAST International in order to assess the welfare of animals farmed for their fur.

Materials and methods

During the course of this survey, investigators visited several sites in China's Hebei Province where animals were reared, slaughtered and sold and where pelts were processed and traded. A focus was placed on foxes – blue/Arctic foxes (*Alopex lagopus*) and silver/red foxes (*Vulpes vulpes*) – but other species were also encountered, including raccoon dogs (*Nyctereutes procyonoides*), an Asian fox-like canid, rex rabbits (*Oryctolagus cuniculus*) and American mink (*Mustela vison*). For the purpose of this paper, results will be limited to foxes and raccoon dogs, for which the most comprehensive data were gathered.

Hebei Province was chosen as the focus of this study as it represents one of the major fur farming areas in China, and it is also a major production and manufacturing base. Many animals reared in adjoining Provinces are also sold and transported to Hebei to be slaughtered and skinned, either in slaughter houses or at wholesale markets.

Sites visited included eight fur farms, two wholesale markets (where farmers bring their animals for sale and large companies come to buy stock) and one major slaughter house. Fur farms were selected according to three main criteria:

1   the primary species – foxes were the main focus of the study and so priority was given to farms with blue or silver foxes;
2   the size – a range of sizes of farms were visited, each housing between 60 and 6000 animals;
3   accessibility to investigators.

Information was gathered at each site through a combination of direct observation, video footage and through interviews with workers. Emphasis was placed on information relating to the animals' husbandry and data indicative of the animals' welfare state. Husbandry factors recorded include details of the housing (cage size and the content), methods of handling the animals and slaughter methods used. Potential welfare indicators included breeding performance (mortality rates, conception rates), self-mutilation (e.g. tail biting), behavioural signs of fear or apathy, and stereotypic behaviour (e.g. pacing in circles). Ongoing uncontrollable aversive stimulation can lead to a behavioural response termed apathy or 'learned helplessness' (Seligman, 1975), which at first glance can appear similar to habituation (Freeman and Manning, 1979). However, the behavioural sign of 'giving up' in the face of uncontrollable aversive conditions is linked to profound physiological effects (Fox, 1984) associated with poor welfare. Stereotypies are repetitive, invariant behaviour patterns that serve no apparent function (Mason, 1991). These behaviours are frequently seen in captive animals, particularly those housed in sterile, restrictive environments (Ödberg, 1987; Dantzer, 1991; Broom and Johnson, 1993) or animals faced with unavoidable fear or frustration (Ödberg, 1987; Mason, 1991; Dantzer, 1991) and as such are used as indicators of poor welfare (Mason, 1991; Broom and Johnson, 1993). In carnivores stereotypies typically take the form of pacing back and forth.

Results

Husbandry

On the fur farms visited, foxes and raccoon dogs were confined in rows of wire mesh cages (3.5 × 4cm mesh) measuring around (L)90 × (W)70 × (H)60cm, although some were far smaller (Figure 17.3). The cages were raised off the ground by 40–50cm, contained no furnishings, nest boxes, and in many cases, no cover. Each cage housed one or two animals. Cages housing breeding females were linked to brick enclosures intended to offer females a degree of seclusion during birth and cub rearing to reduce cub mortality, for example, through infanticide or maternal neglect.

Breeding

Mating takes place from January to April. The majority of farms use artificial insemination, especially to cross-breed blue and silver foxes, whose mating periods do not coincide. Foxes reach sexual maturity after 10–11 months. Breeding animals are used for five to seven years. Farm owners stated that vixens produce average litters of 10–15 cubs a year between May and June. It is assumed that this figure refers to average litter sizes across the two fox species, including cross-breeds, as well as raccoon dogs. Cubs are born in spring and weaned after three months.

Farmers reported breeding difficulties and infanticide, whereby mothers kill their cubs. According to fur farm owners, average cub mortality to weaning is 50 per cent. This means that farmers gain around five to seven cubs per litter.

Handling

Farmers removed foxes from their cage with iron tongs that clamp around the neck and then grab their tail to lift them out of the cage (Figure 17.4). Two

Figure 17.3 *Caged Arctic foxes on a Chinese fur farm*

Source: Swiss Animal Protection/EAST International

Figure 17.4 *Neck tongs used to extract foxes from cages*

Source: Swiss Animal Protection/EAST International

types of tongs were used. One consisted of two pincer-like appendages at the end that could be tightened around the animal's neck. The second comprised a noose at the end of a pole that was placed around the animal's neck and tightened by pulling on a cord. Subsequent handling often involved holding the animals upside down by the hind legs.

Transport

Animals transported from farms to wholesale markets and slaughter houses were often housed in inadequate facilities and sometimes travelled over considerable distances from neighbouring provinces (Figure 17.5). At wholesale markets, foxes and raccoon dogs were observed to be held in mesh cages where they were exposed to many potential stressors, including people walking past, vehicles driving by and animals being slaughtered immediately adjacent to them.

Figure 17.5 *Transportation cage for raccoon dogs*

Source: Swiss Animal Protection/EAST International

Slaughter

Cubs are usually slaughtered after they have undergone their first winter moult. Farmers retain some animals as breeding stock, but most animals are sold at the end of each year. Slaughter occurs adjacent to wholesale markets and in slaughter houses. Workers extracted animals from their cages using a capture pole. Sometimes the animals were held suspended by their necks for some time and carried around, unsupported. Workers grabbed the animal by its hind legs and, using a metal or wooden stick, repeatedly struck the fox or raccoon dog on the head. Alternatively, animals were swung head-first against the ground (Figure 17.6). These actions appeared to be intended to stun the animal. Animals were seen to struggle, convulse and lie trembling or barely moving on the ground. Workers often stood by to watch whether the animal remained more or less immobile. Many, whilst immobile, remained alive. The paws of raccoon dogs were sometimes cut off to facilitate skin removal when they were alive and ineffectively stunned.

Figure 17.6 *Animals were flung head-first against the ground to stun them*

Source: Swiss Animal Protection/EAST International

Skinning began with a knife at the rear of the belly whilst the animal lay on its back or was hung upside down by its hind legs from a hook. In one case, this took place next to a truck that collected the carcasses – for human consumption. Starting from the hind legs, workers then wrenched the animal's skin from its suspended body, until it came off over the head. A significant number of animals were observed to remain fully conscious during the skinning process, writhing and moving around. In these cases, workers sometimes used the handle of the knife to repeatedly beat the animal's head until they became motionless once again. Other workers stepped on the animal's head or neck to strangle it or hold it down (Figure 17.7). Animals that had not been fully stunned or regained consciousness during skinning continued to struggle. Even after their skin had been stripped off, breathing, heartbeat, directional body and eyelid movements were evident for up to five to ten minutes.

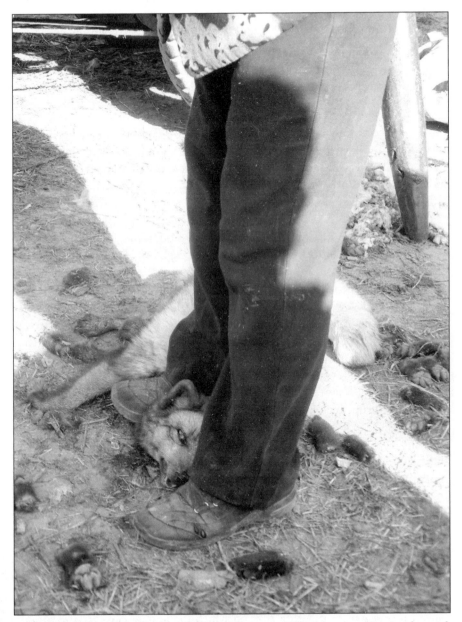

Figure 17.7 *Insufficiently stunned animals were choked by standing on the neck*

Source: Swiss Animal Protection/EAST International

Behaviour

Observations and video footage of foxes confined in Chinese fur farms showed high levels of stereotypic behaviour, including pacing, head twirling, biting, gnawing and digging at the cage floor and wall. Fearfulness, indicated by retreating to the back of the cage, and signs of learned helplessness, indicated by extreme inactivity and unresponsiveness, were seen in animals on all farms visited. Self-mutilation, in the form of self-biting, was also common.

Discussion

This survey of Chinese fur farms in Hebei Province revealed inadequate standards of husbandry, transport and slaughter that failed to come close to *minimum* European standards. Many areas of concern were highlighted, relating to the husbandry of foxes and raccoon dogs, on farms and also in wholesale markets and the slaughter house visited. Data gathered on behaviour and breeding performance indicate unacceptably impaired welfare.

Foxes and raccoon dogs, as well as mink and rabbits, were confined to cramped wire mesh cages. Even in the larger cages, compared to *minimum* EC recommendations, foxes and raccoon dogs had a floor area 20 per cent smaller, a third less volume and 14 per cent (10cm) less cage height (Council of Europe, 1999). In addition to being small, cages were entirely barren of furnishings. No platforms, nest boxes or visual barriers were observed in standard cages. Breeding females were offered a degree of seclusion in the form of a brick enclosure during the birth to reduce cub mortality, but this was not offered to other foxes. Farmed foxes are known to suffer from extreme fear (Wiepkema, 1994; Nimon and Broom, 1998; European Commission, 2001), which is exacerbated by close proximity to humans, frequent and rough handling, inability to withdraw and crowded housing near other foxes. According to Council of Europe recommendations, foxes should be supplied with year-round nest boxes. Fear has been linked to physiological stress, the development of abnormal behaviours, infanticide in nursing mothers and – not surprisingly – poor welfare. All are widespread on Chinese fur farms, as are signs of self-mutilation. In addition to excessive fear, research has identified the barrenness of cages and impaired reproduction as major problems associated with fox farming. Their presence too, has therefore been linked with poor welfare in this species. In recognition of these factors, several European countries have banned or severely restricted fox farming. EC recommendations state that 'Foxes must be able to conceal themselves from people and from animals in other cages or enclosures. They must also be able to rest and to observe their surroundings. Each weaned animal shall have available: a. secluded area; b. either an elevated platform or a nest box with a roof on which the animal can rest and observe the cage door or enclosure entrance.'

The reported infant mortality rate of 50 per cent is exceptionally high, even for foxes on farms. In Sweden an estimated 15–30 per cent of fox cubs die before weaning and in Finland, the fur trade magazine *Turkistalous* mentions an estimated 30 per cent mortality in 1990 (FPA, 1995). A Norwegian study 'Den Norske Pelsdyrkontroll' (1999), referred to by the European Commission (2001) in its report 'The Welfare of Animals kept for Fur Production', describes cub mortality levels of 16.8 per cent for silver foxes and 22 per cent for red foxes.

The general handling of animals observed was inappropriately forceful and rough. Neck tongs were routinely used to remove foxes and raccoon dogs from cages. EC recommendations state that 'The routine use of neck tongs for catching foxes shall be avoided'. Animals were often suspended by the hind legs without support and carried around, treatment that is likely to cause stress to the animal. Animals were loaded into cages using this method for transport to market or slaughter houses for trading and killing. Welfare problems associated with transporting domestic or wild animals are numerous (Maas, 2000); a fact acknowledged by the international fur industry (IFTF, 2005c). Yet, in China, animals are frequently transported to markets, where they are slaughtered, over considerable distances and under appalling conditions.

Slaughter practices used on animals farmed for fur in China involved extremely rough handling and stunning or attempts to stun the animals with repeated blows to the head or by being flung head first against the ground. Following this treatment animals were often left next to each other or piled on top of each other. Some animals may have been dead, others stunned. Clearly injured, many were seen convulsing, trembling or trying to crawl away. Workers made no attempts to ensure that animals were dead before skinning. In other cases animals regained consciousness as their skin was being removed and remained so for five to ten minutes after they had been completely skinned, showing breathing, heart beat, and directional body and eyelid movements.

The evidence that animals feel pain and seek to avoid it is overwhelming (Bateson, 1991 and 1992; Smith and Boyd, 1991; Short and Poznak, 1992). Recent experimental research on several mammalian species (including man) has confirmed that the pain thresholds for thermal stimuli and pressure are approximately the same for all species examined (Ley et al, 1989; Chambers et al, 1993). The treatment of animals farmed for their fur in China during slaughter is therefore likely to cause extreme levels of pain. Regulations and scientific discussions of killing methods for animals held in fur farms generally refer to methods such as gassing, lethal injection and electrocution (e.g. Nimon and Broom, 1998; Council of Europe, 1999; Nimon and Broom, 1998; European Commission, 2001). None anticipated having to address recommendations on animals being clubbed, choked or skinned to death. Regulations and technical discussions of slaughter practices that take at least some account of what science has to say on these matters emphasize the importance of minimizing pain and distress and inducing immediate unconsciousness (see Box 17.1). The slaughter methods fur-bearing animals are subjected to in China fail to meet, or come close to meeting, any of these provisions.

Box 17.1 Regulations and technical discussions of slaughter practices

Article 22 of the Council of Europe Standing Committee of the European Convention for the Protection of Animals Kept for Farming Purposes (T-AP)'s 1999 recommendation concerning fur animals states that:

1. Killing shall be done by a competent person without causing undue agitation, pain or other forms of distress. The method chosen shall either:
   a. cause immediate loss of consciousness and death, or
   b. rapidly induce deep general anaesthesia culminating in death, or
   c. cause the death of an animal which is anaesthetized or effectively stunned without any aversive influence on the animal.

Appendix F lists the principal methods that can, when used correctly, meet these requirements and that should be applied when permitted under domestic law and in accordance with domestic law.

2. The person responsible for the killing shall ensure that for each animal the requirements under paragraph 1 above are fulfilled, and that the animal is dead before further procedures are carried out.
3. Killing shall be done so as to cause the least possible disturbance to the other animals.

Conclusions

This survey shows that China's colossal fur industry routinely subjects animals to housing, husbandry, transport and slaughter practices that are unacceptable from a veterinary, animal welfare and moral point of view.

With fur production, processing and retailing of fur available on international markets increasingly shifting to China, which is part of the IFTF, the issues raised by this study have become something that should concern us all. China is the world's biggest exporter of fur garments; the European Union is the world's biggest consumer of fur. A random market survey of boutiques and department stores in Switzerland and London uncovered fur garments labelled 'Made in China' among top fashion brands. In the Treaty of Amsterdam, EU member states endorse 'improved protection and respect for the welfare of animals as sentient beings'. Yet, housing conditions, husbandry, transport and slaughter practices in China fall radically short of EU and UK animal welfare regulations.

Based on the findings of this study, Care for the Wild International is appealing to fashion designers, retailers and consumers to avoid fur and use non-violent materials instead. EU member states and the European Parliament are being urged to ban the import of fur and fur products from China and we are asking the Chinese government to urgently introduce and enforce effective legislation prohibiting the inhumane practices that have been highlighted.

References

Bateson, P. (1991) 'Assessment of pain in animals', *Animal Behaviour*, vol 42, pp827–839

Bateson, P. (1992) 'Do animals feel pain?' *New Scientist*, vol 34, no 1818, pp30–33

Brambell, F. W. R. (1965) *Report on the Technical Committee to Enquire into the Welfare of Livestock Kept under Intensive Conditions*, HMSO, London

Broom, D. M. and Johnson, K. G. (1993) *Stress and Animal Welfare*, Chapman and Hall, London

Carlstead, K. (1996) 'Effects of captivity on behaviour of wild mammals', in Kleiman, D. G., Allen, M. E., Thompson, K. V. and Lumpkin, S. (eds) *Wild Mammals in Captivity*, The University of Chicago Press, Chicago, pp317–333

Carlstead, K. (1998) 'Determining the causes of stereotypic behaviours in zoo carnivores: Toward appropriate enrichment strategies', in Shepherdson, D. J., Mellen, J. D. and Hutchins, M. (eds) *Second Nature: Environmental Enrichment for Captive Animals*, Smithsonian Institution Press, Washington, pp172–183

Chambers, J. P., Livingston, A., Waterman, A. E. and Goodship, A. E. (1993) 'Analgesic effects of detomidine in thoroughbred horses with chronic tendon injury', *Research in Veterinary Science*, vol 54, pp52–56

Council of Europe (1999) 'Standing committee of the European Convention for the protection of animals kept for farming purposes (T-AP)', in *Recommendation Concerning Fur Animals*, Strasbourg, 24–27 November, adopted by the Standing Committee on 22 June 1999

Dantzer, R. (1991) 'Stress, stereotypies and welfare', *Behavioural Processes*, vol 25, pp95–102

European Commission (2001) 'The welfare of animals kept for fur production', *Report of the Scientific Committee on Animal Health and Animal Welfare*, adopted on 12–13 December 2001, Commission of the European Communities, Brussels, Belgium

EFBA/IFTF, European Fur Breeders' Association/International Fur Trade Federation (2004) 'The socio-economic impact of European fur farming', EFBA, IFTF, www.iftf.com

FAWC, Farm Animal Welfare Council (1989) *Farm Animal Welfare Council Disapproves of Mink and Fox Farming*, Press notice, 4 April, FAWC, Tolworth

Fox, M. W. (1984) *Husbandry, Behaviour and Veterinary Practice*, (viewpoints of a critic), University Park Press, Baltimore

FPA, Federation for the Protection of Animals (1995) 'Fur farming in Finland – an animal welfare angle', *Animalia*

Fraser, A. F. and Broom, D. M. (1990) *Farm Animal Behaviour and Welfare*, Balliere Tindall, London

Freeman, B. M. and Manning, A. C. C. (1979) 'Stressor effects of handling in the immature fowl', *Research in Veterinary Science*, vol 26, pp223–226

IFTF (2003) 'Demand for fur on the increase as sales continue to rise', Press release, International Fur Trade Federation website, 22 May, available at www.iftf.com

IFTF (2005a) 'Labelling', International Fur Trade Federation website, available at www.iftf.com

IFTF (2005b) International Fur Trade Federation website, available at www.iftf.com

IFTF (2005c) 'Farming', International Fur Trade Federation website, available at www.iftf.com/farming/farming1.asp

Jeppesen, L. L. and Pedersen, V. (1991) 'Effects of whole-year nest boxes on cortisol, circulating leukocytes, exploration and agonistic behavior in silver foxes', *Behavioural Processes*, vol 25, pp171–177

Jeppesen, L. L. and Pedersen, V. (1992) 'Correlation between levels of cortisol, behaviour and nest box use in silver fox vixens', *Norwegian Journal of Agricultural Sciences*, supplement 9, pp505–511

Ley, S. J., Livingston, A. and Waterman, A. E. (1989) 'The effect of chronic clinical pain on thermal and mechanical thresholds in sheep', *Pain*, vol 39, pp353–357

Maas, B. (2000) *Prepared and Shipped: A Multidisciplinary Review of the Effects of Capture, Handling, Housing and Transport on Morbidity and Mortality*, RSPCA, Horsham, UK

Mason, G. J. (1991) 'Stereotypies: A critical review', *Animal Behaviour*, vol 41, pp1015–1037

McKenna, C. (1998) 'Fashion victims: An inquiry into the welfare of animals on fur farms', *Report for the World Society for the Protection of Animals*

Morton, D. B. and Griffiths, P. H. M. (1985) 'Guidelines on the recognition of pain, distress and discomfort in experimental animals and an hypothesis for assessment', *Veterinary Record*, vol 116, pp431–436

Nimon, A. J. and Broom, D. M. (1998) *Report on the Welfare of Farmed Mink and Foxes in Relation to Housing and Management*, Cambridge University, Animal Welfare Information Centre, Cambridge

Ödberg, F. O. (1987) 'Behavioural responses to stress in farm animals', in Wiepkema, P. R. and Van Adrichem, P. W. M. (eds) *Biology of Stress in Farm Animals: An Integrative Approach*, Martinus Nijhoff, Dordrecht, pp135–149

Renfeng, Z. and Qingfen, D. (2004) 'Domestic fur demand increases', *China Business Weekly*, 20 January

Rovainen, C. M. and Yan, Q. (1985) 'Sensory responses of dorsal cells in the lamprey brain', *Journal of Comparative Physiology A*, vol 156, pp181–183

Seligman, M. (1975) *Helplessness*, W H Freeman, San Francisco

Short, G. E. and Poznak, A. (eds) (1992) *Animal Pain*, Churchill, Livingstone, New York

Smith, J. and Boyd, K. (1991) *Lives in the Balance*, Oxford University Press, Oxford

Verheijen, F. J. and Buwalda, R. J. A. (1988) 'Doen pijn en angst gehaakte en gedrilde karper lidjen', *Report of the Department of Comparative Physiology*, University of Utrecht

Wiepkema, P. R. (1994) 'Advice regarding the husbandry of fur animals – mink and foxes – in The Netherlands', *Study for the Dutch Government* (unpublished report)

18

The Implications of Agricultural Globalization in India

Vandana Shiva

Research Foundation for Science, Technology
and Ecology, India

Economic globalization is in effect the globalization of violent forms of agriculture that threaten human health, ecosystems and the welfare of animals. The globalization of agriculture is primarily an economic project to increase corporate control over our food systems and corporate profits from the food chain. This has major cultural and ecological implications.

At the consumption level, agricultural globalization pushes consumption towards meat-intensive diets. At the production level it pushes fish and meat production towards resource-intensive systems with a large footprint. As societies become industrialized they eat more meat and saturated fats. This shift is referred to as a 'nutrition transition'. The nutrition transition suggests shifts from highly diverse diets to the monoculture of a meat-intensive, processed food-intensive, western style diet associated with chronic and degenerative diseases (Popkin, 1998). This transition is not a naturally inevitable phenomenon. It is induced by corporate subsidies, corporate advertising and corporate profits. Agri-business corporations gain; people, the planet and animals lose.

The technological myth that 'intensive' factory farming is more efficient allows inefficient production with high ecological externalities to destroy forests, water, coasts and plant and animal biodiversity. Such resource-intensive production also destroys local livelihoods and leaves communities more vulnerable to both economic and ecological insecurity.

Globalization and the promotion of meat exports

Globalization is transforming India from a culture where the sacred cow was worshipped to an economy where cows are slaughtered for export. The promotion of meat consumption is causing major cultural and ecological dislocations. First, animals such as buffalo and cattle are not just meat in the rural economy. They are sources of renewable energy and renewable soil fertility. When animals are killed for meat, sustainable agriculture gives way to chemical and fossil fuel-based non-sustainable agriculture. Secondly, intensive livestock production creates huge demand for intensive animal feed. The destruction of the Amazon for soya cultivation is driven by the globalization of intensive meat production.

The primary cause for the rapid erosion of the numbers of traditional livestock is India's trade liberalization policies. Under the prevailing climate of economic liberation, many government initiatives and legislation, such as the New Livestock Policy, have been implemented with the target of increasing meat exports. The livestock policy paper is disrespectful of the Indian culture of reverence for farm animals. These cultural beliefs are viewed as a block to promoting meat production.

At a time when beef consumption is going down in western countries, India's livestock policy is trying to convert a predominantly vegetarian society into a beef eating culture. In the US, beef consumption per capita per year has declined from 58.6kg in 1976 to 43.2kg in 2002 (FAO, 2004). Cultural attitudes have been the most significant reason for maintaining vegetarian diets for the large majority in India. The livestock policy would like to undermine these conservation policies to promote a meat culture.

As stated in Section 2.10 of the Indian government's Policy on Meat Production:

> The beef production in India is purely an adjunct to milk and draught power production. The animals slaughtered are the old and the infirm and the sterile and are in all cases malnourished. There is no organized marketing and no grading system and beef prices are at a level which makes feeding uneconomic. There is no instance of feedlots or even individual animals being raised for meat. Religious sentiments (particularly in the northern and western parts of India) against cattle slaughter seem to spill over also on buffaloes and prevent the utilization of a large number of surplus male calves.
>
> (GOI, 1996)

The policy then recommends government interventions to stimulate meat production even though this will totally undermine the basis of sustainable agriculture (Section 3.10).

The Ministry of Agriculture has given 100 per cent grants and tax incentives to encourage the setting up of slaughter houses. According to a 1996 Union Ministry of Environment report, at least 32,000 illegal slaughter houses have established themselves in the last five years, compared to only 3600 licensed abattoirs legally established. The government affirms that this is simply an estimate, in reality the number is bound to be much greater.

The total quantity of meat exports from India (meat of buffalo, cattle, sheep and goats) increased from 9580 tonnes in 1976 to 360,638 tonnes in 2003, a 38-fold increase in just under 30 years. Buffalo meat exports account for a large proportion (around 88 per cent) of the total, while cattle meat exports have risen to nearly 25,000 tonnes a year and sheep meat exports have increased 6.5 times in the period (FAO, 2004).

With regard to cattle, the disappearance of the hardy indigenous, well-adapted breeds, serves only to cripple the livelihoods of the rural communities that depend on them. The use of cross-breeds adversely affects small farmers as these cross-breeds can only provide high milk outputs at higher levels of nutrition, unlike the indigenous breeds that have high energy conversion and use scarce fodder and feed resources efficiently.

The promotion of increased meat production for export is leading to the erosion of our genetic livestock diversity and depletion of our cattle wealth. Large populations of indigenous livestock species are disappearing due to the increased slaughter rate for export. Furthermore, the emphasis on commercial dairying with the eventual aim to export is threatening the existence of India's indigenous breeds due to the cross-breeding with exotic species.

Impact of meat exports on animal diversity and the rural economy

In the last four decades there has been a significant decline of the number of traditional livestock available per person in India, particularly the indigenous breeds known for their hardiness, milk production and draught power (Table 18.1). The decline in livestock is primarily due to illegal slaughtering of cattle and buffalo for meat export.

Table 18.1 *Decline in number of animals per 1000 persons in India*

Number of animals per 1000 people and percentage decrease since 1961			
Species	1961	1991	2003	decrease since 1961
Buffalo	113.2	95.2	90.7	20%
Cattle	388.1	235.7	175.9	55%
Sheep	88.9	57.6	58.0	35%
Goats	134.5	132.3	112.7	16%

Source: FAO, 2004

The Food and Agriculture Organization (FAO) in 1996 confirmed that 'the diversity of domestic animal breeds is dwindling rapidly. Each variety that is lost takes with it irreplaceable genetic traits – traits that may hold the key to resisting disease or to productivity and survival under adverse conditions.' For example, some of the declining indigenous breeds today are Pangunur, Red Kandhari, Vechur, Bhangnari, Dhenani, Lohani, Rojhan, Bengal, Chittagong Red, Napalese hill, Kachah, Siri, Tarai, Lulu and Sinhala. The dramatic decline in livestock population in India has reached grave proportions. If measures to arrest this trend are not taken now, most of us will witness the extinction of traditional livestock within our lifetime, and with it the foundation of sustainable agriculture will disappear.

Undermining Rio

The policies of meat export promoted under trade liberalization and the diminishing numbers of traditional livestock unequivocally portray a complete lack of commitment made in Agenda 21 to sustainable utilization and management of animal genetic resources.

The role of animals in tropical farming systems is not fully appreciated, since animal husbandry models come from industrialized countries where grazing livestock are increasingly kept separate from crop production and are maintained only for the dairy industry. As a result, indigenous breeds maintained for animal energy and draught power or for organic inputs to maintain soil fertility have been displaced.

Recognizing the erosion of animal genetic resources, Agenda 21 states the need for conservation and utilization of animal genetic resources for agriculture. Chapter 6, para 76 of Agenda 21 states:

> Some local animal breeds have unique attributes for adoption, disease resistance and specific uses, which in addition to their socio-cultural value should be preserved. These local breeds are threatened by extinction as a result of the introduction of exotic breeds and of change in livestock production systems.
>
> Rebuilding animal and crop diversity is an important policy aspect of sustainable agriculture.

Chapter 14.65 of Agenda 21 calls for conservation and sustainable utilization of the existing diversity of animal breeds for future requirements. But since India's ratification of the General Agreement on Tariffs and Trade (GATT) and the implementation of World Bank recipes of structural adjustment, India's new economic political climate has hastened the rate of depletion of our animal wealth and the extinction of our animal diversity.

The compulsion to non-sustainability

A serious consequence of the declining animal wealth is the undermining of the foundation of sustainable agriculture and the destruction of the rural economy and rural livelihoods. This will adversely affect the landless, the Dalits and women. Women provide nearly 90 per cent of all labour for livestock management. Of 70 million households that depend on livestock for their livelihoods, two-thirds are small and marginal farmers and landless labourers. Cattle meat exports are leading to the escalating costs of purchasing livestock, which are adversely impacting on the small farmer community. Reduced amounts of dung for manure, for cooking fuel and for fuelling biogas plants further reinforce the trend towards unsustainable agriculture systems and rural economies. Consequently, farmers become increasingly dependent on imported non-renewable fossil fuels for fertilizers and energy.

While the export of cattle is justified on the basis of earning foreign exchange, the destruction of the cattle wealth of the country is actually leading to economic destruction and a drain of foreign exchange through increased imports of fertilizers, fossil fuel, tractors and trucks to replace the energy and fertility that cattle give freely to the rural economy. The poor pay the highest price. As they are pushed into non-sustainable, high-input industrial agriculture, farmers can no longer survive. More than 40,000 farmers have committed suicide due to high debts caused by high-cost industrial farming since trade liberalization policies were imposed on India (Shiva 1997, 1999, 2003; Shiva and Jalees, 2004; Christian Aid, 2004). The death of animals translates into the death of small and marginal farmers.

The case of Al-Kabeer slaughter house

At the national level, while animal exports are earning the country 10 million Rupees (Rs), the destruction of animal wealth is costing the country Rs150 million.

Examining the dung economy reveals the unsustainable nature of our reliance on imported fossil fuels. A buffalo produces around 12kg of wet dung every day; this converts to 6kg of dry dung. An average Indian family of five members needs 12kg of dung cakes every day as cooking fuel, which translates into a pair of buffaloes. The 182,400 buffaloes that Al-Kabeer slaughter house kills every year can satisfy the fuel needs of 91,200 families in India.

The depletion of cattle and buffaloes leads to the decline in availability of dung. The government therefore has to supply kerosene or liquefied petroleum gas (LPG). The transport cost of this runs into tens of millions of rupees, which means that poor people pay vastly higher fuel costs, which they cannot afford to do. The import of LPG and kerosene increases every year. Kerosene costing Rs5475 million was imported in 1987–1988. By 1992–1993 this increased to Rs20,090 million (US$460 million) – an increase of almost four times in five years. So the 91,200 families whose fuel requirements have been forcefully altered by the killing of 182,400 buffaloes a year in Al-Kabeer will now spend Rs131 million (US$3 million) on buying fuel. This fuel has now to be imported by the government using foreign exchange.

The return from this gigantic amount of capital, which the state gets, is as follows:

> If animals were not slaughtered in the state of Andhra Pradesh, we would get 1,918,562 tonnes of farmyard manure from of their dung and urine every year. This farmyard manure could cultivate 388,712 hectares (ha). In 1991, the average food grain produced per hectare was 1.382 tonnes. Therefore, the food grain produced would be 530,000 tonnes.

If the animals were allowed to live out their natural lives instead of being slaughtered by Al-Kabeer slaughter house, they would save foreign exchange worth over Rs9102 million (US$209 million) for the state of Andhra Pradesh. The calculation based on data from Andhra Pradesh goes as follows. The annual availability of major nutrients in the farmyard manure of 1,924,000 buffaloes and 570,000 sheep works out as:

- 11,172 tonnes of nitrogen, which at the current price of Rs20.97 per kilogramme at unsubsidized rates, adds up to Rs234.3 million (US$5.4 million);
- 2164 tonnes of phosphorus, which at the current price of Rs21.25 per kilogramme at unsubsidized rates, adds up to Rs46 million (US$1 million);
- 10,069 tonnes of potash, which at the current price of Rs8.33 per kilogramme at unsubsidized rates, adds up to Rs83.9 million (US$1.9 million).

The value of nitrogen + phosphorus + potash = RS364.2 million (US$8.37 million).

All these items are now imported. Thus Andhra Pradesh saves foreign exchange worth $US8.37 million per year from the first lot of animals that are going to be killed. Taking into account their average remaining life span of five years, they will save foreign exchange worth US$41.9 million.

Following the same argument, if all the animals that are going to be killed during (say) five years of Al-Kabeer's operation lived out their natural lives, then they would be able to save foreign exchange worth Rs9102.5 million. This means that against a projected earning of Rs200 million (US$4.6 million) by Al-Kabeer through the killings, the state could actually save over Rs9100 million (US$209 million) in foreign exchange by not killing the animals.

Export compassion, not cows

Movements have grown throughout India against meat exports and slaughter houses. The residents of Narela brought a case in the Tis Hazari Court of Delhi against the Government's plan to move the local slaughter house from Idgah in the Narela area of Delhi.

The judgment passed in the court of Shri C.K Chaturdevi, Sub Judge, Delhi, 23 March 1992 favoured the petitioners. It made an in-depth study of the legal relationship between animal and humans that reprimanded the governing authorities and cautioned society against the destruction and disastrous consequences of the activities of vested interests. The judgment laid stress on preservation and protection of the cattle of the nation from the economic, social, moral, ecological and environmental points of view.

An excerpt from the judgment is as follows:

> This fundamental duty in the constitution to have compassion for all living creatures, thus determines the legal relation between Indian Citizens and animals on Indian soil, whether small ones or large ones. This gives legal status to view of ancient sages down the generations to cultivate a way of life to live in harmony with nature. Since animals are dumb and helpless and unable to exercise their rights, their rights have been expressed in terms of duties of citizens towards them.
>
> Their place in the constitutional Law of the land, is thus a fountain head of total rule of law for the protection of animals and provides not only against their ill treatment, but from it also springs a right to life in harmony with human beings.

If this enforceable obligation of the State is understood, certain results will follow. First, the Indian State cannot export live animals for killing, and secondly, it cannot become a party to the killing of animals by sanctioning exports of dead animals after slaughter. Avoidance of such killing of animals would help preserve the Indian Cultural Heritage, by which we proudly claim India as the land of Gandhi, Buddha and Mahavir. India can only export a message of compassion towards all living creatures of the world, as a beacon to preserve ecology, which is the true and common Dharma for all civilizations. This is in keeping with the culture of living in harmony with nature by showing respect to all life, and that is the *Vasudhaiv Kutumbakam* (the whole world is one family) referred to by our Minister of the Environment at the Conference at Rio in June 1992.

Globalization and the promotion of industrial shrimp farming

Commercial shrimp farming has been actively encouraged in India since the beginning of the 1990s as part of export-oriented globalization policies. Both the Indian government, including the state governments, and international aid agencies such as the World Bank subsidize the production of shrimp for exports. These subsidies, which take the form of soft loans, tax holidays or the tariff relaxation of imports, are made available to the corporations that enter this industry because of the high profit earning potential. In their rush to garner profits, the governments have also become parties to violations of national land and environmental laws.

Globalization, now as never before in history, is providing immense opportunities for the elites of the world to unite, transcending national loyalties and boundaries, while inflicting tremendous hardship on the under-privileged and poor. The key players involved with prawn aquaculture are transnational corporations (TNCs) the World Bank, the Asian Development

Bank and the northern and southern elites, who are creating policies and systems of trade favourable to meet their needs through trade liberalization and globalization.

After having created an economic climate favourable to trade through their Structural Adjustment Programmes (SAP), the World bank and the International Monetary Fund (IMF) as well as other international funding agencies are helping industrial aquaculture expand by giving loans for this purpose to both the central government and the state governments directly. While the World Bank loan to India is for improved fish culture, shrimp aquaculture forms a substantial component. The expansion of this industry is justified on the grounds that it will benefit the poor by providing them with better nutrition, more employment opportunities and higher incomes; another justification is that it makes use of land that is unfit for any other agricultural or forestry purposes. The lure of earning foreign exchange is also a key factor.

The ministries of agriculture, both at the central and the state level are responsible for the development and promotion of aquaculture. Land ceiling laws are undergoing changes in various states to allow individuals and corporations to acquire large tracts of land for aquaculture. In fact, some states such as Orissa and Karnataka have changed their land acts to allow the construction of huge aquafarms on agriculture and forest/mangrove lands. In other places, state governments help aquafarm owners by declaring such land as wasteland, and then leasing it or selling it to the industry.

Communities all along the coast, who have been shrimp farming for centuries – catching shrimp along with other fish, or intercropping them with paddy during the appropriate seasons, and who helped maintain India's position as the top producer of shrimp in the world – are today being marginalized by the industry. As the technology involved in large-scale shrimp production destroys both the marine and the coastal environment, their fish and shrimp catches have critically declined. Those involved in agriculture have had their lands destroyed through salinity. Another factor that has upset the ecological and economic balance of the fragile coastline is the increasing influx of non-local populations as a result of the increase in the aquaculture industry. This has created social, legal and other problems all along the coast.

World Bank's promotion of aquaculture

The World Bank became involved with aquaculture in the 1970s when it began providing loans to governments in Asia and Latin America for the development of shrimp ponds. The Bank financed development projects in Indonesia, the Philippines, Thailand and Bangladesh. By the 1980s, the Bank broadened its support to include China, India, Brazil, Columbia and Venezuela. The aim of the investments in prawn aquaculture was to set up a base for processing and products for the market, which meant an emphasis had to be placed on infrastructure in the form of roads and refrigeration units, so that industrial shrimp production could expand by the 1980s. In 1992, the Bank invested $1.685 billon in agriculture and fisheries, of which India received $425 million for shrimp and fish culture.

The government is providing the aquaculture industry with technical assistance for transfer of knowledge and production, with financial assistance coming from various overseas agencies such as the European Commission (EC). Import–export policies have been changed to stress 'freedom' for trade, substantially eliminating the need for licensing, quantitative restrictions and other regulating controls. The government has further set up the Marine Products Export Development Authority (MPEDA) for assisting the industry and for overseeing the development of both the industry as well as its trade.

Subsidies for exports

MPEDA offers the following subsidies to support the industry:

- subsidy for new farm development, assistance of 25 per cent of capital investment of Rs30,000 per hectare, up to a maximum risk of Rs150,000 (US$3450);
- subsidy for establishment of medium-scale shrimp hatcheries of 30 million eggs/year capacity and above; assistance of 25 per cent up to a maximum of Rs500,000 (US$11,500) can be made available to private parties/individuals;
- subsidy for feed and eggs, assistance at 25 per cent up to Rs3000/ha (US$69/ha) for feed, and up to Rs450/ha (US$10.4/ha) for eggs;
- subsidy for establishment of a broodstock bank; assistance of 25 per cent of capital cost subject to a maximum of Rs150,000 (US$3,450);
- in addition, shrimp farmers are allowed to import shrimp feed at concessional rates of customs duty.

MPEDA has also established two hatcheries of its own: one each in Orissa and Andhra Pradesh. The Ministry of Agriculture is setting up five hatcheries with help from the United Nations Development Programme (UNDP).

Apart from government support, financial assistance for the aquaculture industry has been provided by several public financial institutions such as the National Bank for Agriculture and Rural Development (NABARD), Industrial Credit and Investment Corporation of India (ICICI), Shipping Credit and Investment Corporation of India (SCICI), and Industrial Development Bank of India (IDBI). In addition to the direct subsidies, export-driven industrial aquaculture is also based on ecological and social subsidies in the form of environmental destruction and destruction of livelihoods.

The ecological and the economic impacts of 'the Blue Revolution' indicate that aquaculture projects have actually aggravated the poverty of fishing and farming families. In addition, the aquaculture industry exists at the expense of marine fisheries and does not enhance overall fish production when diverse species, diverse producers and diverse consumers are fully taken into account.

Environmental impact

Industrial shrimp aquaculture captures shrimp from the mangroves and the sea to stock at high density in artificially created ponds on the coast. Pregnant shrimp caught in the sea have their eyes pulled out to force them to spawn in captivity.

The first impact of shrimp farming on land and forests in the coastal region is when the land is bulldozed and excavated for making the gigantic farms. Mangrove destruction is a major impact of prawn farming.

The destruction of coastal vegetation destroys the buffer zone against destructive wind and water action, increasing cyclone and flood vulnerability. The recently released Millennium Ecosystem Report has shown that 1 acre (0.40 hectares) of shrimp farm has an ecological footprint of 200 acres (80 hectares); whereas an intact mangrove provides ecosystem services of $1000/ha, shrimp farming promoted by mangrove destruction provides only about $100/ha (Millennium Ecosystem Assessment Synthesis Report, 2005).

The large-scale pumping of sea and groundwater into the fish farms is another serious environmental impact of shrimp farming. The massive extractions of fresh water from underground aquifers for salinity control in the ponds pose a serious threat to the salinity control of the coastal ecosystems. Emptied aquifers are subject to salt water intrusion. Seepage from the tanks also increases salinization of groundwater. In the village of Kurru in Nellore district, there was no drinking water available for the 600 fisherfolk due to salinization of the drinking water.

As groundwater salinity increases, paddy fields are destroyed. Shrimp farms flush their effluents and wastes directly into the sea and into neighbouring mangrove and agricultural lands. The wastewater from the ponds carries pollution in the form of excess lime, organic wastes, pesticides, chemicals and disease micro organisms. The waste stifles the growth of aquatic organisms and causes water quality to deteriorate. Intensive coastal fish farming has also been linked to 'red tides', an explosive growth of toxic algae that can kill fish and fatally poison people who eat contaminated seafood. Another reason for depletion of marine shrimp is the capture of juvenile shrimp from the mangroves for hatcheries. This prevents the renewal of the wild shrimp at sea. The aquaculture industry thus exists at the expense of existing marine fisheries, which have supported traditional fishing communities over centuries. (Shiva and Karir, 1995)

Social impact

The enclosure of the beaches for pumps and powerhouses has pushed fishing communities, called 'pattapu raja', the kings of the coastline, off their ancestral homes. The depletion of marine fish due to the environmental impact of fish farming has destroyed their resource base. Not only are fishermen displaced, local communities can no longer consume fish. Since intensive farms are export oriented, they do not supply local markets. The cost of fish locally has risen worldwide as a result of commercial fisheries. The destruction of clean groundwater immediately translates into increased work burden for women. Women say they are working 4–6 hours extra per day to collect fuel and water as a result of the environmental destruction caused by shrimp farms. As the shrimp farms render the fertile coastal region a salinated wasteland, there is destruction of agricultural livelihoods and food production. Very soon there will be a famine in the rice bowls of Andhra and Tamil Nadu.

When these social and ecological costs are internalized, intensive prawn farming emerges as a highly wasteful and inefficient technology for ecological and equitable utilization of land, water and fish resources. Shrimp farms embody an assumption of the dispensability of coastal ecosystems and the fishermen and farmers they support. A National Environmental Engineering Research Institute (NEERI) Report submitted the following estimation of the social and ecological costs of aquaculture to the Supreme Court of India.

The ecological destruction caused by industrial aquaculture is two to four times higher than revenues earned from exports. In addition, even though industrial aquaculture is presented as a substitute to marine fisheries, industrial aquaculture actually depends on marine resources both for stocking fish ponds and for feed. It actually consumes more fish resources than it produces.

As Dr John Kurien has pointed out, in 1988 global shrimp aquaculture consumed 180,000 tonnes of fishmeal derived from an equivalent of 900,000 tonnes wet-weight of fish. It is further estimated that by the year 2000 about 570,000 tonnes of cultured (farmed) fish will be produced in Asia. The feed requirement for this will be of the order of 1.1 million tonnes of feed. This is equivalent of a staggering 5.5 million tonnes of wet-weight fish, nearly double the total marine fish harvested in India today. Fishmeal provides the crucial link between industrial aquaculture and industrial fisheries, since the fish used for fishmeal is harvested from the sea by trawlers using purse seine nets, which totally deplete marine stocks. This falsifies the often used argument by agencies like the World Bank that promotion of aquaculture is like moving from hunting and gathering to settled agriculture in fisheries and will reduce the pressure on marine resources (Shiva, 1996). The ecological footprint of farmed shrimp is thus at least 10–15 times larger than the value of the shrimp on global markets.

Lessons from the tsunami

Gaia could not have picked a more appropriate time and place to send us a message of her hidden powers, and the message that we are Indians and Indonesians, Sri Lankans and Swedes, Thais and Maldivians only secondarily – we are first and foremost citizens and children of the Earth, sharing a common fate and a common desire to help and heal. The Christmas and New Year holidays bring the entire world to Asia's beaches. The earthquake-induced tsunami on 26 December 2004 in the Indian Ocean became a global tragedy because it impacted not just on Asians, but on visitors from across the world who had come to holiday on Asia's sunny beaches. And while the immediate tragedy faced by millions has to be our first response, there are long-term lessons the tsunami brings to us. We need to listen to Gaia.

The first lesson is about development in coastal regions. Over the past years of market-driven globalization, respect for the fragility and vulnerability of coastal ecosystems has been sacrificed for hotels and holiday resorts, shrimp farms and refineries. Mangroves and coral reefs have been relentlessly destroyed, taking away the protective barriers in the face of storms, cyclones, hurricanes and tsunamis. India is the only country in the world to have brought about the Coastal Regulation Zone Notification (CRZN) system to protect the coast. The Notification, which came about on 19 February 1991, initially directed that the beaches have to be kept clear of all activities for at least 500m.

However, through sustained pressure from the tourism and shrimp farming lobby, the distance was reduced first to 200m and finally to nothing. That was when the case was taken before the Supreme Court, which through a land-mark judgment on 18 April 1996, reinstated the original position of 500m and directed the formulation of Coastal Zone Management Plans.

When we carried out a study of the Orissa cyclone in 1999, which killed 30,000 people, we found that the destruction was much more severe where the mangroves had been cut down for shrimp farms and an oil refinery. The people's movement against industrial shrimp farming led to a Supreme Court order to shut down the farms within 500m of the coastline in accordance with the CRZN. As the order of Justice Kuldip Singh and Saghir Ahmed stated:

> Before parting with this judgment, we may notice the 'Dollar'-based
> argument advanced before us. It was contended before us by the
> learned counsel appearing for the shrimp aquaculture industry that the
> industry has achieved singular distinction by earning maximum foreign
> exchange in the country. Almost 100 per cent of the produce is
> exported to America, Europe and Japan and as such the industry has a
> large potential to earn 'Dollars'. That may be so, but the raised
> production of shrimp is much less than the wild-caught production.
> The report shows that world production of shrimp from 1982 to 1993
> is as follows:

Table 18.2 *World production of shrimp (thousands of tonnes)*

Year	Farm raised	Wild caught	Total
1982	84	1652	1786
1983	143	1683	1626
1984	174	1733	1907
1985	213	1908	2121
1986	309	1909	2218
1987	551	1733	2264
1988	604	1914	2918
1989	611	1832	2443
1990	633	2168	2801
1991	690	2118	2808
1992	721	2191	2912
1993	610	2100	2710

It is obvious from the figures quoted above that farm-raised production of shrimp is of very small quantity as compared to wild caught. Even if some of the shrimp culture farms which are polluting the environment are closed, the production of shrimp by environmentally friendly techniques would not be affected and there may not be any loss to the economy specially in view of the finding given by NEERI that the damage caused to ecology and economics by the aquaculture farming is higher than the earnings from the sale of coastal aquaculture produce. That may be the reason for the European and American countries for not permitting their seacoasts to be exploited for shrimp culture farming. The UN report shows that 80 per cent of the farm cultures of shrimp comes from the developing countries of Asia.

However, instead of obeying the order, the shrimp industry tried to undo the ecological laws for protection of coastal zones by influencing government to exempt the shrimp industry from environmental laws. This subversion of environmental laws to protect coastal zones by the shrimp industry has definitely had a role in increasing the destruction caused by the tsunami. Every hectare of shrimp farm has an ecological footprint of 100ha in terms of destruction of mangroves and land and sea destroyed by pollution. Every dollar generated by exports of shrimps leaves behind ten dollars of ecological and economic destruction at the local level.

Nagapattinam, the worst impacted zone by the tsunami, was also the worst impacted by industrial shrimp farms. The indigenous tribes of Andaman and Nicobar, the Onges, the Jarawas, the Sentinelese and the Shompen, who live with a light ecological footprint, had the lowest casualties even though in the

Indian subcontinent they were closest to the epicentre of the earthquake. The Government of Kerala, observing that the tsunami left less destruction in regions protected by mangroves than in barren and exposed beaches has started a Rs350 million project for insulating Kerala's coasts against tidal surges with mangroves (Das, 2005). The research carried out by us for sustainable rehabilitation of the tsunami areas has confirmed that wherever mangroves survived, people survived (Shiva and Jalees, 2005).

The tsunami reminds us that we are not mere consumers in a marketplace driven by profits. We are fragile interconnected beings inhabiting a fragile planet. This is the message of responsibility and duty to the earth and all people. The tsunami reminds us that we are all interconnected through the earth. We are earth beings – compassion, not money, is the currency of our oneness. Above all it brings a message of humility: that in the face of nature's fury we are powerless. The tsunami calls on us to give up arrogance and to recognize our fragility. In the tsunami, it was not just the waves of the sea that collided with the coast. Two world views collided. One was the world view of free markets and corporate globalization, useless and helpless in dealing with the environmental disasters it has contributed to. The other was the world view of earth democracy in which people reach across the world as one humanity to rebuild lives and prepare for an uncertain future on a fragile planet, living with full awareness of our environmental vulnerabilities and responsibilities and our ecological interconnectedness. The most important long-term response that we can make to the tsunami is to reduce the ecological footprint on our fragile planet, and reduce our ecological vulnerabilities. Ecological resilience, not economic growth, will be the real measure of human survival in these uncertain times. And ecological resilience is born of reverence for all species and protection of biodiversity. In caring for the earth family, we secure our own future.

References

Christian Aid (2004) *The Damage Done: Aid, Death and Dogma*, Christian Aid, London

Das, M. K. (2005) 'After the disaster, Kerala's green drive', Indian Express, 3rd January, available at
www.indianexpress.com/archive_full_story.php?content_id=62000

FAO (2004) FAOSTAT agricultural statistical database of the UN Food and Agriculture Organization, available at http://faostat.fao.org/faostat/

Government of India (1996) New Livestock Policy, Ministry of Agriculture, Government of India, New Delhi

Millennium Ecosystem Assessment Synthesis Report (2005), 23 March 2005, p48

Popkin, B. M. (1998) 'Urbanization, lifestyle changes and the nutrition transition', *World Development*, vol 27, p11

Shiva, V. (1996) *Globalization of Agriculture and the Growth of Food Security*, Report of the International Conference on Globalization, Food Security and Sustainable Agriculture, July 1996, New Delhi

Shiva, V. (1997, 1999, 2003) *Seeds of Suicide*, Research Foundation for Science,

Technology and Ecology, New Delhi
Shiva, V. and Jalees, K. (2004) *Farmers Suicide*, Research Foundation for Science, Technology and Ecology, New Delhi
Shiva, V. and Jalees, K. (2005) *Report on Tsunami*, Research Foundation for Science, Technology and Ecology, New Delhi
Shiva, V. and Karir, G. (1995) *Chemmeenkettu: Towards Sustainable Aquaculture*, Research Foundation for Science, Technology and Ecology, New Delhi

19

Sustainable Development and Animal Welfare: The Neglected Dimension

Kate Rawles

St Martin's College, Cumbria, UK

Sustainable development – two problems

The idea that societies need to develop in ways that are sustainable is – in theory at least – almost universally endorsed. Since the concept first came to prominence at the 1992 United Nations' Conference on Environment and Development – better known as the Rio Conference or Earth Summit – 'sustainable development' has become a guiding policy principle across the world. But the language and concept of sustainable development is definitely a double-edged sword.

It *can* be extremely constructive. For example, it has shown us that poverty and environmental degradation are not separate, competing, concerns, but profoundly interrelated. And it confronts us with the imperative need for humans to learn to live within the carrying capacity of our planet. But there are downsides. I want to focus on two of these. The first is that sustainable development is sometimes used – or misused – to mean economic growth that can continue indefinitely. More generally, it can be used – or misused – in a very uncritical way in relation to western, industrialized paradigms of development. In other words, sustainable development can be a euphemism for business as usual. The second problem is that it has systematically neglected animal welfare. I want to argue that these two issues are, in various ways, interconnected – and that both need to be addressed if sustainable development is to be a constructive and worthwhile goal.

The sustainability triangle

I will begin with the second of these two problems, and by raising a question. In the vast body of sustainable development theory and policy, why has concern with animal welfare been so consistently neglected? Part of the answer relates to the way the main aims of sustainable development are characterized. Sustainable development – and this is one of its strengths – embraces a range of different goals. These are often summarized in various versions of the 'sustainability triangle', with social justice, economic development and environmental protection (or similar) in each of the corners. (See Figure 19.1)

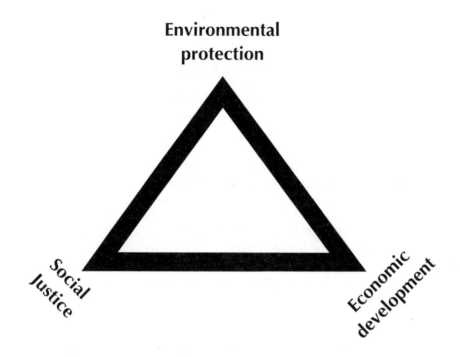

Figure 19.1 *The sustainability triangle*

None of these corners readily encompass animal welfare concerns. Social justice typically refers to justice within human societies rather than to justice across species. Economic development is pursued primarily as a means to enhancing *human* quality of life. The environmental protection corner is probably the best candidate, but even here, animal welfare does not really fit. The primary focus of environmental protection is with species, habitats, ecosystems etc, in other words, with ecological 'collectives' of various kinds. By contrast, the primary focus of animal welfare is with individuals. Moreover, whereas the environmental movement is typically concerned with looking after natural or semi-natural habitats, systems and processes, animal welfare is concerned with all sentient animals, including domesticated ones (Rawles, 1997). So, if the goals of sustainable development are characterized in the form of this kind of triangle, animal welfare will almost inevitably be neglected. It is not naturally included under the social justice or economic development corners. And, while environmental protection seems the most likely candidate, environmental movements and animal welfare movements in fact have a very different focus.

Animal welfare as 'unscientific'

Worse than this, there can be downright resistance to including animal welfare as part of the environmental agenda. This is another part of the answer to our question. Worrying about the treatment of individual domestic animals can be seen as suspect. It is irrelevant from a species conservation perspective. It may be branded sentimental. And of course there is a long legacy of scepticism within (some) scientific communities about animals even *having* subjective mental states. This scepticism is much less prevalent now, but in the past it has tended to support the view that concern with animal welfare – which after all assumes that animals can experience not only subjective mental states but particular kinds of mental states, including unpleasant ones – must be both anthropomorphic and unscientific. Given that many of the different elements within the environmental movement draw authority from science, being associated with animal welfare might, in the past at least, have been resisted for fear of a loss of credibility.

I think there may still be a similar worry from a sustainable development perspective. Sustainable development is strongly associated with environmental issues and is (rightly) informed by science and scientific approaches in a range of ways. It, too, draws a deal of credibility from its links with scientific methods and evidence. Indeed, it is sometimes presented as exclusively concerned with the scientific, rational, objective and value-free project of establishing the earth's limits, and then figuring out how we can live within them. Presenting it in this way can appear to make the need for sustainable development a simple logical deduction from certain facts about the world, and therefore indisputable. From this perspective, an ethical concern with how we treat individual domestic animals is not only (allegedly!) irrelevant but might be seen as weakening the apparently value-free, hard-nosed, objective credibility of sustainable development, when presented in this way.

Animal welfare – threatening to business as usual

So far, then, I've suggested that the sustainability triangle, and the fear of being perceived as 'unscientific', may explain why concern with animal welfare has been neglected within the sustainable development agenda. A final part of the answer is that animal welfare can be perceived as threatening to business as usual. This is particularly true of business within the agri-industry sector, a sector with turnovers in the billions and one that is still expanding. The Worldwatch Institute, for example, says that:

> Global meat production has increased more than fivefold since 1950, and factory farming is the fastest growing method of animal

production worldwide. Industrial systems are responsible for 74 per cent of the world's total poultry products, 50 per cent of pork production, 43 per cent of the beef, and 68 per cent of the eggs.

(Worldwatch Institute, 2004)

Industrial farming systems are very big business. They are also, of course, a main focus of animal welfare concerns, and not just in the sense that there may be particular cases of poor husbandry. Beyond a certain point, the industrialization and intensification of animal husbandry systems is, arguably, *inherently* incompatible with good welfare for the animals reared within them. Taking animal welfare seriously, therefore, amounts to a significant challenge to this form of agri-business.

In general, then, given the way that sustainable development is often characterized, the relative exclusion of animal welfare from the sustainability agenda actually has a certain sort of logic, and can certainly be understood. There is an additional dimension to this logic if sustainable development is understood as business as usual or as economic growth that can be continued indefinitely. In this case, animal welfare concerns are not only different from the main concerns of sustainable development, but threatening to them.

Business as usual – profoundly inadequate

I began this chapter with the suggestion that two downsides to the concept of sustainable development are the neglect of animal welfare and the possibility of presenting sustainable development merely as a euphemism for business as usual. That concern for animal welfare can be seen as a threat to business as usual indicates where the two problems intersect – and how they might be solved. Absolutely central to this resolution is the recognition that sustainable development *cannot* be about business as usual. Economic growth cannot continue indefinitely. It is inevitably constrained by ecological limits such as the earth's finite capacity to provide the resources that fuel economic growth, and to absorb the pollution that resource consumption generates. Moreover, the business as usual model is underpinned by a particular way of understanding the concepts of 'development', 'progress' and 'success' that is highly problematic. These concepts, as they are currently understood in the industrialized worlds, support ways of life that are environmentally destructive and that cannot be enjoyed by everyone – in other words, ways of life that are environmentally and socially *un*sustainable. So these concepts in conjunction with a bit of technological efficiency cannot lead us to sustainability.

The situation can be summarized like this. First, highly industrialized, consumer-based societies and lifestyles – held to be developed, successful and progressive – have an enormous negative impact on the environment. This manifests as a range of environmental problems, including species extinction, climate change, other forms of pollution and so on. Secondly, these lifestyles are currently enjoyed only by a minority of the world's human population. Thirdly, the majority who don't have this lifestyle would, on the whole, like it. And fourthly, this section of the population is increasing in number. So we have a minority living a privileged, and damaging, way of life, and a majority aspiring to it. But if everyone on earth were to live in 'middle class comfort' then, by 2020, we would need three planet earths (WWF, 2004).

One-planet choices and rethinking our values

The stark choices that this summary presents us with also makes clear why sustainable development is not, fundamentally, a value-free, scientific challenge to do with establishing the earth's limits and harnessing efficient technology to allow us to live within them. Sustainable development is fundamentally about our social values. Consider the choices. We could continue as we are, a route that seems certain to lead to environmental collapse. We could endeavour to restrict 'development' to a minority of the human population. Even leaving ethical concerns aside, this route seems certain to lead to social collapse, or at least to the exacerbation of social instability and violent protest. Or, we could try to redefine 'development', 'success' and 'progress' in ways that, when put into practice, would offer quality of life for all, compatible with protecting our environment. This third option means rethinking what we currently *mean* by 'quality of life' as well as by 'success', 'progress' and 'development'. In other words, *accepting the challenge of sustainable development means rethinking our values*. In particular, it means critically reassessing the values and priorities that underpin modern, industrialized societies and lifestyles.

This is not an anti-modern, back-to-the-caves point of view. There are, of course, many wonderful things about modern industrialized societies and ways of living. However, there are also some major insanities. Conjure, here, your own most powerful images of waste, pollution, human degradation, excessive consumption, human poverty and environmental damage. One in five people, currently, suffer malnutrition and about the same number – more than one billion people – do not have access to clean drinking water. The phenomena of conspicuous consumption, junk food and obesity 'epidemics' exist in conjunction with this. The lives of the economically privileged global minority are far from invariably richly fulfilled. I think it was Peter Singer who wrote that we are destroying the planet ... for beef burgers. Taken literally, of course, this is too simplistic. But, as a metaphor for the most problematic aspects of industrialized societies, it is extremely telling.

Sustainable development and ethically decent societies

So, a central challenge of sustainable development is fundamentally a values-based one. It is about reassessing and rethinking the values that underpin western, industrialized notions of development, progress and success. And it is about articulating our vision, or visions, of an ethically decent society. As a minimum, this must be one in which *all* people, rather than just a minority, are enabled to achieve a basic quality of life; and one in which the non-human world is respected and looked after. Part of this respect and looking after involves acknowledging that the resources we take from our planet are not infinite and need to be used wisely – sustainably. But part of respect involves going beyond this to acknowledge that the living world is not just a set of resources for the benefit of one species. Of course we are bound to use the environment, animals and people as resources in many and various ways. We cannot avoid this. But seeing the environment *purely* as a set of resources – the resource view – fails, at a theoretical level, to acknowledge the value that other forms of life and living systems have in their own right. More importantly, the resource view fails in practice, in that it underpins the exploitation of people, the environment and animals. This is where we reconnect with animal welfare. The idea of an ethically decent society is simply not compatible with a society that systematically treats sentient animals in its care *merely as things*. The resource view in this context is encapsulated in this often-quoted claim from *Farmer and Stockbreeder* (1982):

> The modern layer, is after all, only a very efficient converting machine, changing the raw material – feedingstuffs – into the finished product – the egg – less, of course, maintenance requirements.

It is this attitude that has led to the animal welfare atrocities associated with many intensive agricultural systems. And it is this same attitude that lies at the heart of the problem with the business as usual approach to sustainability and, arguably, at the heart of the problem with modern industrialized societies – the tendency to see the world and everything in it primarily as a set of resources to service economic development, and the inappropriate prioritization of economic development *above* social justice and *above* environmental protection.

Conclusions

In sum, there are many points that could be made about the ways in which industrialized, intensive husbandry systems, a key source of animal welfare issues and concerns, are in fact also unsustainable. Examples would include their reliance on very high rates of energy consumption, low human employment, high rates of pollution and so on. This in itself provides a powerful argument against them. But I've chosen to focus here on the deeper links between sustainable development and animal welfare. Three main conclusions, I believe, follow.

First, I have argued that the sustainability triangle will not naturally accommodate animal welfare concerns. My suggestion is that, rather than trying to force such accommodation, we turn the triangle into a diamond, with animal welfare as the fourth corner (see Figure 19.3). In my view, sustainable development

Figure 19.2 *The battery cage for egg production*

understood and promoted in a form that explicitly acknowledges the importance of animal welfare would be a richer and more adequate concept in both theory and practice.

Secondly, I have argued that sustainable development is badly misrepresented when it is understood as giving priority to the economic corner of the triangle – or diamond – and when it supports, rather than challenges, the dominant understandings of 'development', 'progress' and 'success'. These concepts, and the general prioritization of economic over other concerns, have contributed in no small way to the social and environmentally unsustainable status quo. Acknowledging this reveals that the real challenge of sustainable development is about rethinking the values and priorities that underpin modern industrialized societies, and about developing our visions of what an ethically decent society would involve.

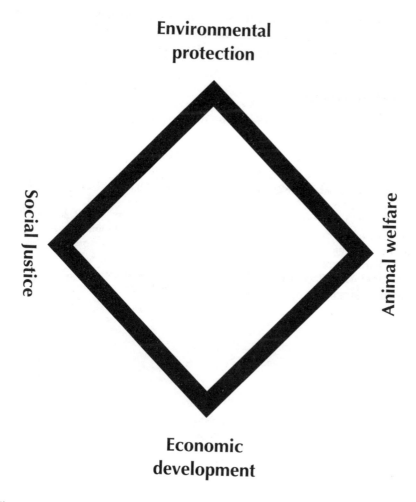

Figure 19.3 *The sustainability diamond*

Thirdly, I have suggested that such visions must include a rejection of an exclusively resource-based approach to the environment, people *and* animals – and that this brings animal welfare into the heart of the sustainability agenda at its best. Respect for sentient animals is neither sentimental nor unscientific. Rather, respect for sentient animals reflects compassion that is rooted in a scientifically informed understanding of how other animals actually experience the world – including the worlds that we impose on them. We should not be sheepish about being compassionate. Compassion for others, and resistance to using others – human or non-human – merely as resources, is a fundamental value that underpins sustainable development in its fullest, most constructive sense. In my view, this is the only sense of sustainable development worth fighting for. Translating this understanding into real practical change is undoubtedly amongst the most important and urgent challenges we face.

Acknowledgements

Thanks to Martin Chester for the design of the sustainability diamond.

References

Farmer and Stockbreeder (1982) quoted in Singer, P. (1990) *Animal Liberation*, 2nd edn, Thorsons, London

Rawles, K. (1997) 'Conservation and animal welfare', in Chappell, T. D. J. (ed) *The Philosophy of the Environment*, Edinburgh University Press, Edinburgh

Worldwatch Institute (2004) *State of the World, Progress Towards a Sustainable Society*, Earthscan, London, p73

WWF (2004) *Living Planet Report*, WWF–International, www.panda.org/news_facts/publications/key_publications/living_planet_report/index.cfm

PART 4

Animal Sentience in International Policy

20
Outlawed in Europe: Animal Protection Progress in the European Union

David B. Wilkins

International Coalition for Farm Animal Welfare (ICFAW) and World Society for the Protection of Animals (WSPA)

Today a great depth of scientific knowledge exists about animals and their welfare. However, it is vital that we translate this wealth of knowledge and expert opinion into action that will improve the welfare of animals in practice and not sit back and expect that it will just happen. This is particularly important in livestock production where commercial, socio-economic and political considerations are often considered as having precedence over animal welfare.

The Council of Europe

Over the last 30–40 years in Europe, great strides have been taken to introduce legislation that in some instances has, or will, dramatically improve the welfare of many intensively reared animals. Some countries, Sweden is a good example, already possessed, or were in the process of introducing, high standards of farm animal welfare, but the majority would only bring about change when forced to by legislation. The story of how such legislation was achieved is fascinating and demonstrates how many factors played a part in this achievement.

The first steps towards giving animals protection through legislation were taken in the Council of Europe – not to be confused with the European Union. The Council of Europe was founded in 1949 and it now has 46 member countries, including all 25 that make up the EU. The primary aims of this august body are to defend human rights, parliamentary democracy and the rule of law. It also promotes local democracy, education, culture and environmental protection. To achieve these aims a series of Conventions have been agreed and these include five concerned with the welfare of animals. In 1968 a Convention on the protection of animals during international transport was published. This was followed in 1976 by one on animals kept for farming purposes, in 1979 by one on slaughter, in 1986 by one on animals used for scientific purposes and finally in 1987 one on pet animals.

This was the start of the European debate on animal welfare legislation at government level. Unfortunately, Council of Europe Conventions do have some disadvantages. These are:

- all decisions have to be unanimous;
- no member country is obliged to sign and ratify any of the Conventions;
- those countries who have ratified are not obliged to put the provisions into legislation but can use codes of practice or educational programmes.

Nevertheless, these Conventions have had a considerable influence, and whilst their importance in some areas is not as great as before, particularly because the EU now has 25 member states, they can still have an impact.

European Union law

Which brings me to the European Union. This began its life as the European Economic Community (EEC), or Common Market, when the Treaty of Rome was signed in 1957 by six countries: France, Germany, Italy, The Netherlands, Belgium and Luxembourg. By 1995 a further nine countries had joined (the UK in 1974). In 2004 ten new member states (most from Eastern Europe) joined and therefore the total membership of the EU is now 25 countries, representing some 450 million people.

The original Treaty of Rome had an important influence on this story because it was drawn up as a means to ensure that trade between the member states could be carried out without interference and on a so-called level playing field. Animals were simply referred to as agricultural products and had less protection than sugar beet. There was some concern about farm animal welfare because in 1974 the EEC agreed a Directive that required that food animals should be stunned before slaughter. Then, in 1977, the EEC took the Council of Europe's Convention on the protection of animals during international transport and converted it into a Directive, which meant that the rules contained therein became obligatory for all member states to implement. However, the provisions only applied to animals being transported from one member state to another or to a third country.

The chances of any further EEC legislation to protect animals seemed remote because the Treaty of Rome provided no legal base for any such laws to be proposed. However, in 1979 there were two very significant events. First, the European Parliament became an elected body rather than the members being appointed by the various governments. This establishment of a democratic institution meant that the members were now directly representing the wishes of the people.

At that time the influence of the Parliament was not great, although, under the Treaty, it was required to give an opinion on all legislation going through the system. The decision-making process of the European Institutions is unique.

The Council of Ministers may make the final decision in all farm animal legislation but the Parliament's opinion and the amendments that it puts forward to any draft legislation have become increasingly influential. In most national parliaments voting usually takes place on political party lines. In the European Parliament there may be some political voting but on some issues such as farm animal protection, many members of the European Parliament (MEPs) will vote according to their opinion and not follow party instructions. This is very encouraging for animal welfare.

The second significant event was the decision by the leading animal welfare organizations in the then nine countries of the EEC (led by the RSPCA in the UK) to come together and establish a lobbying office in Brussels. Thus, in 1980 the Eurogroup For Animal Welfare was formed. Animal welfare had arrived in the heart of Europe. Animal welfare concerns put forward by Eurogroup and other animal welfare organizations – particularly Compassion in World Farming (CIWF) – were sympathetically received by MEPs and also by the Commission, at least by some of the veterinarians. It is important to point out here that it is the Commission, and only the Commission, that can draft legislation. It is vital, therefore, for any lobbyist to establish contact with those Commission officials who are responsible for any of the animal welfare issues, whether these be farm animals, wildlife or animals used in research.

It is also important to point out that in 1980 the veterinary section of the Commission was only concerned with animal health and not with welfare. Member states were mostly hostile to the inclusion of animal welfare in EU law and considered that animal welfare should be dealt with through national legislation.

The next significant date was 1986, when several important events occurred:

- The Parliament, by a very large majority, produced a comprehensive report on farm animal welfare policy. This followed extensive lobbying and campaigning by the animal welfare movement. This report demanded action by the Commission. Action followed. A veterinarian was appointed to be in charge of animal welfare, and legislation was promised on pigs and calves.
- The Treaty was modified by the Single European Act, which required borders and border checks between member states to be removed by 1 January 1993. It also introduced majority voting in the Council of Ministers. No longer could one member state block legislation, at least in most areas.
- A Directive laying down minimum standards for hens kept in battery cages was agreed by the Council. It was then referred to the European Court of Justice by some member states who argued that legislation on animal protection was not possible under the Treaty. The Court's verdict in 1988 said that the Commission was entitled to draw up minimum standards for the rearing of farm animals as this would help to prevent unfair competition. The gate was open!

- The use of animals for scientific purposes was regulated by a Directive based on the Council of Europe's Convention. This was agreed in 1986 but because of the lack of a proper legal basis it was confined to those animals used in the development and testing of products. Again, the reason was to prevent unfair competition.

Directives on minimum standards for the protection of calves and pigs were agreed in 1991 and also a new Directive on the transport of live animals. This had to apply to the transport of all animals in all circumstances and not just on international transport. Under campaigning pressure from the animal welfare movement, led by Eurogroup, member states could not agree on transport times, feeding and watering intervals and stocking densities for farm animals. The arrival of three new member states in 1995 helped to break the deadlock. Sweden, Finland and Austria were all willing to apply strict rules governing animal transport, so the eventual compromise in 1995 was not all we wanted but it was better than we expected.

The 1991 Directives on pigs and calves were disappointing in that calf crates and pregnant sow stalls were allowed to continue. But in each case a review was mandatory after five years to be preceded by a report from the recently established Commission's Scientific Advisory Committee. These reports severely criticized intensive methods of rearing calves and pigs, and as a consequence the revised Directives proposed by the Commission contained a phasing out period for calf crates (after 2007) and pregnant sow stalls (after 2012).

There is no doubt that over the last 20 years there has been an increasing amount of scientific evidence that criticizes many of the most intensive livestock production systems but also provides a great deal of information about those systems that do provide for good animal welfare. It is to the European Commission's credit that it has set in place procedures for gathering in that evidence. The scientific investigations now come under the recently formed European Food Safety Agency. The setting up of the EFSA is a recognition that animal health, food safety and animal welfare are interdependent.

The year 1993 saw a new and comprehensive Directive on the slaughter and killing of food animals and then, in 1998, a long-overdue General Farm Animal Welfare Directive based on the Council of Europe's Convention was adopted.

The future of animal welfare legislation

I have referred on several occasions to the Treaty not containing a proper legal basis for drafting animal welfare legislation. The Treaty was modified dramatically in Maastricht in 1992. The concept of the European Union was introduced and co-decision (involving the Council and the Parliament) was established as a procedure in certain legislative areas. New areas of Community competence were also introduced, including consumer protection, education, culture and health, but not animal welfare, in spite of a well organized campaign by all the major animal welfare organizations based on the CIWF demand for a recognition of the sentience of animals. Member states agreed to introduce a Declaration on animal welfare but, whilst being a small step forward, it had no practical significance. Campaigners continued and intensified their activities, knowing that another Treaty change was due in 1997. At Amsterdam the co-decision procedure was extended to include all environmental decisions. Most importantly for us, the member states agreed (and this has to be unanimous) to a Protocol on Animal Welfare. A Protocol is part of the Treaty and therefore it is mandatory on member states and the European Institutions to apply the provisions of the Protocol. It reads as follows:

The High Contracting Parties,

DESIRING to ensure improved protection and respect for the welfare of animals as sentient beings, HAVE AGREED upon the following provision which shall be annexed to the Treaty establishing the European Community.

In formulating and implementing the Community's agricultural, transport, internal market and research policies, the Community and the Member States shall pay full regard to the welfare requirements of animals, while respecting the legislative and administrative provisions and customs of the Member States relating in particular to religious rites, cultural traditions and regional heritage.

This was a major step forward, but it still does not make animal welfare a basic principle of the European Community, unlike, for example, protecting the environment or conserving wildlife and habitats. There were hopes that this would be achieved when the new Constitution was being drafted, but to no avail. If the new Constitution does come into force (there is some doubt that this will happen) then one of the changes will mean that agriculture decisions will be decided by co-decision. In theory, at least, this should mean that there is a greater likelihood of better animal welfare standards.

Another example of the problem caused by the lack of a legal basis was the 1999 Directive on zoo animals. Originally intended to be legislation that laid down the conditions under which zoo animals are kept, it was eventually passed under that part of the Treaty concerned with conservation. As a consequence, zoos have to be inspected, licensed and to have conservation programmes in place. Standards for keeping animals are only in an annex and these are only voluntary.

Given the legislative background, it is remarkable that so much progress in animal welfare has been made in the last few years. This has been due to a well organized and knowledgeable animal welfare movement; increasing public awareness and concern about the way animals are reared, transported, slaughtered and used in research; positive political responses to this public concern; support from the retail food industry and scientific evidence.

What has become apparent in recent years has been the international implications of the farm animal welfare improvements brought about in the EU through legislation. The most obvious example is the 1999 Directive on minimum standards for the protection of laying hens. This replaced the 1988 Directive and laid down standards for all egg laying production systems. Most importantly for all animal welfarists, it proposed the phasing out of the iniquitous battery cage system by 2012. It is inevitable that the new animal welfare standards contained in this Directive will lead to higher production costs for EU egg producers. This, coupled with an almost certain requirement under a revised agriculture agreement soon to be agreed by the World Trade Organization for the EU to remove the tariffs that raise the cost of imports, may mean that the influx of cheap eggs and egg products from countries like India and Brazil (which still use battery cages) will endanger the EU egg production industry. The solution to this problem is still not clear, and it may be repeated in other parts of the EU livestock production industry that have good animal welfare standards.

The animal welfare movement and EU public opinion will not allow our hard won animal welfare gains to be sacrificed on the altar of international trade rules. A possible way forward might have been found in the initiative of the Office International des Épizooties (OIÉ), or the World Animal Health Organisation, when it decided in 2002 to embark on the difficult task of formulating standards of animal welfare in addition to its already complicated process of developing international animal health standards. The International Coalition for Farm Animal Welfare (ICFAW) was formed to provide the OIÉ with an internationally based animal welfare body that it can consult during its decision-making process.

In Europe we have made considerable progress in improving animal welfare through legislation, but there is much still to be done. Future progress may not be easy in the EU with the new scenario of 25 member states. By the end of 2005 the Commission is due to publish a proposal for standards for the rearing of poultry for meat (broilers) and it will be interesting to see how good these will be in animal welfare terms.

On the international stage, where most developing countries believe animal welfare to be another protectionist measure invented by the EU, it will be important for organizations such as WSPA to counter such a belief. The future is a challenge and the outcome uncertain, but I am convinced that events such as the conference out of which this book arose can only improve the knowledge and understanding of the needs of animals and our responsibilities towards them.

21
Why China is Waking Up to Animal Welfare

Paul Littlefair
RSPCA International

In June 2004, China Central Television's current affairs series *News Probe* broad-cast a documentary entitled simply *Animal Welfare* (CCTV1, 2004). This groundbreaking programme examined abandoned animals, livestock prod-uction, animal disease and global trade, and concluded rhetorically: 'For Chinese society today, isn't the need for animal protection legislation a matter of utmost urgency?'

Until very recently, 'animal welfare' was a wholly novel concept to most mainland Chinese. Given that the state media make such broadcasts only with direction from the highest levels, what has led them to address this issue now? This chapter explores some of the factors that have combined in the past decade to raise the profile of animal welfare among government officials, academics and the wider public. It takes as its starting point the legal status of non-human animals, then goes on to examine issues surrounding China's wildlife, livestock, research animals and companion animals. It provides examples of how cruel treatment of animals in many cases has served to alert the government to the need for change, and highlights some of the more significant and encouraging developments that appear to indicate that China is, indeed, waking up to animal welfare.

Wildlife as a resource

At present there is no legislation in place for the protection of domestic or captive animals in China, and no definition of their status other than as possess-ions. The legal status of wild animals is indicated by the Wildlife Protection Law of 1988, which serves to 'protect, develop and rationally use wildlife resources'.[1] The concept of 'rational use' encapsulates official policy – and to some extent public opinion – towards not only wildlife, but all animal species.

The success of China's giant panda captive breeding programme is well docu-mented, but many other species face a quite different fate. The growing exploit-ation of wildlife as food, medicine, leather, fur and other products has undoubtedly brought great economic benefit, often to the most impoverished parts of the country, but it has had a disastrous impact on China's environment.[2] Since the mid-1990s, reflecting a trend of increasingly conspicuous consumption, the trade in wild animals has expanded to the point where they are being used in greater numbers and in a greater variety of ways than ever before. Species that previously may only have been found on the tables of specialized southern restaurants have now become available in many cities across the entire country. This demand has fuelled an explosion in the trafficking of wildlife, internally and through cross-border trade, in particular with China's Southeast Asian neighbours.[3]

The 'rational use' policy encourages exploitation as long as it can be sustained. Indeed, state conservation projects involving the captive breeding of endangered species such as the Chinese or Yangtze alligator, for example, are shaped by this legal framework. The status of this 'precious fauna resource'[4] is markedly different from that of China's 'national treasure', the giant panda. The artificial breeding of over 10,000 alligators since 1981 (People's Daily, 2001) has enabled the authorities to sanction the sale of alligator meat – not a traditional food – and leather. In an environment where animals are seen increasingly as sources of income, new methods of deriving profit from wildlife abound. In the 1980s, for instance, production of bear bile extracted for medicinal use from farmed bears[5] soon far outstripped demand. Bear bile tonics, shampoos and other imaginative new products were then developed to stimulate the market and reduce the stockpile.

While reports of such 'development' of animals as a resource paint a pessimistic picture, there has been a public reaction within China itself to some of the most extreme excesses. Arguments against unreasonable use of wildlife surface repeatedly in the media, and three public opinion surveys[6] carried out among urban Chinese indicate a growing distaste for both the misuse and abuse of animals.

There have also been welfare-orientated developments in the field of wildlife protection and conservation. The Beijing Raptor Rescue Centre[7] was established in 2002 as China's first specialized rehabilitation facility operating to international standards. China's zoos have long been the target of criticism for their poor infrastructure, animal performances and, most recently, the feeding of live prey to carnivores. The China Wildlife Conservation Association, responsible for zoo animals, has grown more responsive to demands for welfare improvements, recently agreeing a voluntary ban on using livestock as live prey.[8] At the same time, Beijing Zoo, Shanghai Zoo and others have begun substantial rebuilding programmes with improved enclosures and the introduction of enrichment programmes.

Threats to public health

Since economic reforms began in 1979, the country has striven to improve virtually all aspects of its regulatory institutions, including those governing food production. A number of food quality scandals have surfaced recently,[9] seriously shaking public confidence in food safety and bringing production methods and practices under increasing scrutiny. The forced watering of livestock prior to slaughter,[10] for example, involves inserting a tube into the mouth of the animal and siphoning water into its stomach, often to saturation point, to increase carcass weight. This widespread illegal practice has been repeatedly attacked in the state media, albeit not usually on the grounds of cruelty but rather on those of public hygiene (from contaminated water) and trading standards.

The recent outbreaks of severe acute respiratory syndrome (SARS) and avian influenza have highlighted the connection between animal health and welfare and public health. When, in the spring of 2003, SARS was first traced to so-called 'wet' markets in Guangdong province, the authorities were forced to consider the risks of allowing wild-caught animals, farmed wild animals and domestic animals to be sold and slaughtered on the same site. While international criticism over China's handling of the outbreak led to the dismissal of key officials from the public health agencies, the animal management and welfare lessons of the crisis were not lost on the government. In summer 2003, the provincial authorities ordered a temporary closing down of the wet markets. Although the ban was lifted, fears remain that the custom of slaughtering livestock at market will have to be addressed if the country is to avoid further outbreaks of SARS or other potentially fatal zoonoses.

Competing in a global market

Other animal diseases, such as foot and mouth, while posing no substantial threat to human health, have adversely affected China's ability to trade internationally. Since 2002, in view of shortcomings in China's disease control measures and the use of certain proscribed substances in husbandry and food processing, the EU has banned the importation of some Chinese animal products, arousing government fears of potential damage to the country's economy (China Daily, 2002). China's accession to the World Trade Organization in 2001 has also brought a realization of the increasing power of consumers in other countries to make choices in their food purchasing on the basis of animal welfare considerations. Such external pressures have convinced some officials of the significance of welfare at all stages of production, from rearing to transport to slaughter. In November 2005 China's *Meat Hygiene* journal, under the Ministry of Commerce's Department of Market Operation Regulation, in conjunction with CIWF Trust and the RSPCA, held a three-day International Forum on Pig Welfare and Meat Quality in Beijing. This landmark event brought together leading foreign and Chinese specialists and local pork producers, and addressed the impact that current production methods have on welfare, quality and competitiveness. The forum concluded with the establishment of an international committee aimed at strengthening cooperation between foreign farm animal welfare academics and organizations, and the Chinese authorities.

Leading international manufacturers of food processing equipment[11] have moved into the Chinese market, establishing joint ventures with local producers and setting new standards for modern slaughter lines in the country. The motivation for such improvements on the Chinese side has been mainly economic, but evidence from government trade journals[12] suggests that welfare *per se* may be a factor for some individual officials and even some producers. Veterinary colleges, too, have begun to recognize the international status of animal welfare science. Northeast Agricultural University in Harbin, among others, has in recent years increased the animal behaviour and welfare component in its veterinary teaching.[13]

Other factors indicate China's potential to develop higher welfare production systems in the near future. With a well established capacity to produce fruit and vegetables to international organic standards (China Daily, 2005), it is reasonable to assume that, given the incentive of lucrative export opportunities in the EU and elsewhere, Chinese farmers could develop the high-welfare production of meat, eggs and milk. Moreover, just as in some developed countries the concerns of consumers about the worst aspects of intensive farming have led to welfare gains, it seems fair to argue that Chinese consumers could exercise a similar influence in their own market. This is especially likely as the urban population is at once the driving force behind economic development and the most receptive to animal welfare concepts. But this awareness could spread beyond the cities – as a leading Chinese proponent of higher farm animal welfare puts it: 'Which average person in China doesn't care what kind of meat they are buying?'[14]

The pressure to compete internationally in other areas has already begun to influence China's regulatory systems. The past decade has seen the country emerge as a leading exporter of animals bred for specific research purposes, for which the standards of care and accommodation are necessarily high so as to ensure consistency and quality. China has also sought to achieve compatibility with international norms in its own animal testing and to establish Good Laboratory Practice (People's Daily, 2004a). Against this background, in December 2004, the first regulations to specifically address research animal welfare were passed by the Beijing authorities (People's Daily, 2004b). While the provisions are limited in scope and apply only to the capital, their inclusion at least acknowledges that a duty of care is owed to laboratory animals. National regulations currently being drafted are expected to contain similar articles (People's Daily, 2004c).

The companion animal boom

Ownership of companion animals, for decades regarded as a bourgeois indulgence and a public health nuisance, has risen dramatically in recent years.

Historically, dogs have been specifically bred for food in some regions and in certain periods.[15] The management of dogs in urban areas is the responsibility of the Public Security Bureau, a fact that reflects the official view of dogs as a threat to order.

As living standards have steadily risen, greater affluence and other social factors have stimulated the demand for pets. Since the early 1980s, as China's 'one child only' policy has seen a generation of youngsters grow up alone, pets have often been acquired as surrogate siblings. At the same time many urban families that traditionally lived as 'three generations under one roof' soon began to be able to afford separate housing. Many elderly Chinese now live in couples or alone and clearly welcome the companionship of pets.

As the dog population grew, registration fees were set by local governments, until recently at levels well beyond the means of most citizens, presumably as a disincentive to ownership. Other constraints applied, such as on the size of dogs permitted and on the public places and times they could be walked.[16] These restrictions did little to deter people from acquiring dogs, but did force many who could not afford to register their pets to keep them hidden. As the authorities recognize that high fees lead to low uptake and a failure to truly manage the dog population, they are gradually cutting fees and so reducing the proportion of unregistered animals.[17] Some major cities have no restrictions in place on the keeping of dogs.[18]

As dog and cat numbers rise, some cities have seen a sharp increase in abandonment. Although individual animal lovers rescue strays, the establishment of shelters is possible only outside built-up areas. In 2000, the International Fund for Animal Welfare (IFAW) and the RSPCA jointly funded the construction of China's first purpose-built rescue and rehoming facility, the Beijing Human and Animal Environmental Education Centre (BHAEEC), on the outskirts of the city.

Reports in the Chinese media[19] put the current pet dog population at 150 million, with average annual growth in the cities of ten per cent.[20] Annual spending by Beijing owners on their dogs is 500 million yuan (over £34 million) and the pet economy could be worth £1bn within a few years. It is particularly worth noting that, from the government's standpoint, the economic potential that may be realized by this commercial expansion may outweigh any lingering ideological antipathy that exists towards pet keeping. Not only that, it may eventually prove to be that the companion animal boom is decisive in raising awareness of animals' needs and welfare among urban Chinese and leading the country towards anti-cruelty legislation.

Reactions to cruelty

Since the late 1990s, as China's legal framework has been strengthened, there have been frequent clashes on a wide range of social issues between the authorities and a public growing in confidence in their rights as citizens, and often complaining of unfair treatment at the hands of officials. Indeed, academics are apt to suggest that a strengthening of the rule of law is central to the development of 'democracy with Chinese characteristics'. In line with this general trend, Chinese have become more vocal in their opposition to traditional 'catch-and-kill' campaigns, in which dogs are often beaten to death on the streets by local police and security departments. Such campaigns have been a feature of city life for decades, often sparked by a single incidence of rabies or a dog bite, or simply the official perception that the dog population has become unmanageable. In October 2004, for instance, in the city of Cixi, Zhejiang province, an estimated 40,000 dogs were reportedly killed in less than a week.[21]

A number of high-profile incidents of animal cruelty have captured public attention, serving to expose the lack of legal protection for captive animals. In February 2002 at Beijing Zoo, Liu Haiyang, a student at the prestigious Tsinghua University, poured sulphuric acid and caustic soda onto brown and black bears in their enclosures (People's Daily, 2002). Five animals suffered severe burns, and the zoo authorities called in expert veterinarians to provide intensive treatment.[22] In the weeks that followed, daily media reports described the bears' recovery as the authorities pondered how best to deal with the offender. It soon emerged that, as captive bears are not covered by China's wildlife law and no law exists to prevent deliberate cruelty, the prosecution's case rested on the charge of 'damage to state property'. A significant section of the public responded with outrage, not only at the plight of the bears, but also at the legal loophole and the lenient handling of the perpetrator. The incident brought calls for the introduction of anti-cruelty legislation to the attention of the whole nation.

The government has been sensitive, too, to criticism in the foreign media over particular incidents involving the treatment of animals. Between 1998 and 2002, for example, the international press covered a range of issues from the dog killing campaigns[23] to the feeding of live prey to carnivores in wildlife parks and zoos.[24] China is aware of damage to its international image, as Chinese embassies around the world are periodically inundated with letters of protest.[25]

A national debate on animal welfare

In the author's encounters with Chinese of various educational backgrounds, typical questions raised include: 'Why should we consider the welfare of animals when the welfare of humans is by no means guaranteed?' The government, too, has until recently been cautious in accepting animal welfare as a legitimate area for public debate, not least because of the uneasy links with animal rights and the implications for human rights.

In China, even a single television programme may be a subtle signal that change is afoot. The documentary *Animal Welfare*, in common with most state media output, was unequivocal. It made a very clear and unbalanced case for the introduction of animal protection legislation. The arguments against such a move, voiced quite forcefully by academics and journalists in a number of essays,[26] news articles and online debates in recent years, include the assertion that animal welfare is alien to Chinese culture, 'not applicable to conditions in China', and impossible to realize in a developing country.

None of the cultural, moral, or economic arguments opposing animal welfare were aired in any depth throughout the CCTV documentary, which was screened nationally several times in 2004, and followed by other similar coverage.[27] It would appear that the authorities have accepted the principle that animal welfare has a place in Chinese social and economic development, and the public is being prepared for moves in this direction.

An emerging animal welfare community

Other changes in Chinese society have stimulated the development of a fledgling animal welfare community. University students, historically at the forefront of change in China, have shown a growing interest in the environment, the protection of habitat and other wildlife issues. Activism in this area has been able to flourish and a wave of volunteering, outreach education and other community activity has followed.

Recent reforms have created limited opportunities for the formation of NGOs, allowing a number of animal protection groups to emerge and gain formal recognition. To conform to China's current policy priorities, they generally organize themselves under the broader umbrella of environmental protection and are attached to a 'GONGO' ('government organized NGO'), a local government department or relevant professional association. Once established, however, these organizations have often been successful in gaining the overt support of local authorities, in particular by providing education on responsible pet ownership or through other community projects.[28] Internet access has enabled many Chinese concerned about animals to interact and in some cases networks are being formed between small, informal animal clubs[29] that currently lack the status of officially recognized NGOs.

In the city of Wenzhou, Zhejiang province, the environmental NGO, Green Eyes, has been rescuing injured wild animals for several years. In 2004, the city government's forestry bureau gave Green Eyes volunteers a mandate to legally carry out this work on the bureau's behalf and, significantly, to patrol local markets and confiscate illegally traded species.[30] Such cooperation between China's usually conservative bureaucracy and voluntary organizations is still rare, but as animal welfare groups grow in capacity and lobbying ability, this trend looks likely to strengthen.

Increasingly, Chinese officials are attending international conferences on welfare. The March 2003 Manila Inter-government Conference,[31] aimed at working towards a UN Convention on animal welfare, was addressed by a representative from the Chinese Academy of Sciences, who gave an overview of welfare in China.

International animal protection organizations have also played a role in raising the profile of welfare in China. Since 1994, the Beijing office of IFAW has collaborated with government departments and NGOs on a range of projects from companion animal rehoming to wildlife rehabilitation and the protection of endangered species. Animals Asia Foundation has had remarkable success in negotiating with the authorities for the closure of China's bear farms and the rehabilitation of almost 200 bears rescued from the worst farms. The RSPCA has promoted welfare through the funding of companion animal and wildlife rescue projects and through sustained support for a number of key academics at the forefront of this field. Most recently it has launched a project with the Jane Goodall Institute's 'Roots & Shoots' programme to train Chinese environmental educators in animal welfare concepts. Other foreign organizations working from outside the country have had an impact, for example, through exposing some of the most extreme incidents of cruelty.

Moving towards legislation

In 2000, the law faculty of the University of Science and Technology of China in Hefei became the first department to offer an elective course in comparative animal welfare legislation.[32] Law academics have since begun the process of drafting a tentative animal welfare law. Mainland China has also been influenced by progress among its Asian neighbours, at different stages of development, in the field of legislation protecting domestic animals. Although enforcement varies considerably across the region, India,[33] South Korea,[34] the Philippines[35] and most recently Taiwan[36] at least have anti-cruelty provisions on the statute.

Almost certainly as a result of the Beijing Zoo incident and other reports of animal abuse, in May 2004, Beijing city government apparently considered including a welfare provision in new local animal sanitation regulations (Beijing Review, 2004). The proposed clauses were eventually dropped, reportedly as officials felt that China currently lacks a *national* legal framework to accommodate such a radical provision. Beijing's 'near-miss' in legislating against animal abuse is a promising indicator that some sections of Chinese society are ready for laws that tackle at least deliberate cruelty.

The Games as a catalyst

After Beijing was awarded the 2008 Olympic Games, the city government embarked on a programme of rebuilding and rejuvenation under the slogan 'Green Olympics'. Improved provision for animals is very much seen as intrinsic to the city's facelift. Along with a relaxation of the dog control regulations, the city's '5Rs Green Lifestyle' campaign, for instance, includes 'Rescue wildlife and protect the natural environment',[37] and a new wildlife rescue centre is due to be completed by 2008 (Beijing Organizing Committee, 2004).

As the Games approach, the government is naturally eager to show China in its best light, and the timely introduction of a basic animal protection law may serve to enhance its international image. That China will introduce legislation that departs from the 'rational use' tradition is unlikely, and the view of animals as a resource is likely to remain the dominant paradigm. It may be possible, however, in the light of the public reaction to animal abuse cases and the government's desire for progress in this direction, to legislate against the worst cases of obvious, deliberate cruelty. Such a law would be enforceable if it did not interfere with economic activity or reasonable daily necessity, such as traditional methods of slaughter of food animals.[38]

There remain huge barriers to legislating for the humane treatment of all animals across the country. The biggest challenge is posed by the scale of the task. Around half the world's pigs live in China,[39] for instance, and the drive towards increasingly intensive farming may prove disastrous in welfare terms. Away from the rapidly developing urban and coastal areas lie vast, mainly rural provinces where animal welfare appears rather abstract and impracticable.

On the other hand, the strongest driving factor for advances in animal welfare remains the country's rapid growth in virtually every area of economic, social and cultural activity. The designation of Beijing as an Olympic city has, for many Chinese, brought a long-awaited sense that the world has recognized both China's progress and its potential. The urge to leave old practices and ways of thinking behind and to embrace new technology and concepts will be central to any legislative moves in the direction of improved animal welfare. The government will naturally seek to avoid pitching such laws too far ahead of what is practicable and acceptable to the public. Once the state has decided on a policy direction, however, China's political system to a great extent enables it to bring about huge change very swiftly. If the government is truly convinced of the necessity for animal welfare to play a part in the country's future, then we can expect to see real progress in the coming years.

Notes

1   *Wildlife Protection Law of the People's Republic of China*, Article 1.1 (author's translation).

2   Peter Li, assistant professor, University of Houston-Downtown, has produced an accessible summary of the status of wildlife in *Politics and China's Wildlife Crisis*; related publications at www.uhd.edu/academic/colleges/humanities/sos/Peter_Li_Publications.htm.

3   Examples at www.traffic.org/25/network9/ASEAN/articles/index_1.html.

4   'Yangtze Alligator Nature Reserve', China Biodiversity Conservation Foundation (www.cbcf.org.cn/english/zrbhq/hd_yangzie.html).

5   Animals Asia Foundation's website gives details of this trade and their work to rehabilitate bears (www.animalsasia.org).

6   The *Public Opinion Survey on Animal Welfare*, carried out for IFAW in Beijing and Shanghai in 1998, showed that while 37 per cent of respondents indicated they had eaten wild animals, under 3 per cent admitted to having eaten endangered species. Two surveys taken in 2002–2003 entitled *Animal Welfare Consciousness of Chinese College Students*, carried out by Peter Li, Zu Shuxian and Peifeng Su, show increasing intolerance for a range of cruel acts towards wild and domestic animals (www.uhd.edu/academic/colleges/ humanities/sos/Peter_Li_Publications.htm).

7   Funded by International Fund for Animal Welfare (IFAW) and set up on the campus of Beijing Normal University, the BRRC has received training support from foreign experts and handles over 300 birds annually. The centre has also received grants from the RSPCA for a vehicle and diagnostic veterinary equipment.

8   In the 1990s some Chinese wildlife parks built arenas specifically designed for live shows involving the feeding – before paying audiences – of live pigs and calves to lions and tigers. At a meeting of 22 zoo directors in March 2005, after a campaign led by Mang Ping and supported by the RSPCA, an informal agreement was signed to discontinue the practice for larger livestock species (reported 13 March 2005, www.thebeijingnews.com). In safari-style wildlife parks, however, it may still be possible for visitors to buy live poultry, and reportedly even goats, to be thrown from tour buses as they pass through the carnivore enclosures.

9   In 2004 a widely sold baby milk formula was exposed as having virtually none of the nutrients claimed by the manufacturer, but only after use of the product led to the death of a dozen babies and the ill health of hundreds more in Anhui province. At the March 2005 National People's Congress, food safety was high on the agenda, and most recently the 2008 Beijing Olympics Food Safety Committee was established (*Beijing Review*, 8 September 2005).

10   Mang Ping (2002) 'Animal welfare is a test of human morality', *China Youth Daily*, 13 November 2002. Forced watering has been reported for cattle, pigs and poultry.

11   For example, MPS Group (formerly Stork) exported poultry slaughter equipment to China in the 1980s and has since expanded its business to cattle and pigs.

12   *Animal Health* (*dongwu baojian zhuankan*) and *Meat Hygiene* (*roupin weisheng*) journals now regularly publish animal welfare items.

13   Dr Bao Jun, vice principal, and Dr Cui Weiguo, assistant professor, of Northeast China Agricultural University.

14   Mang Ping, assistant professor, Central Institute of Socialism, in the CCTV documentary 'Animal Welfare'.

15   The traditional 'six domestic animals' (*liuchu*) are pig, ox, goat, horse, fowl and dog.

16   Typically there are restrictions in built-up urban areas on the height and/or weight of dogs. Certain breeds are forbidden and walking is allowed only between dusk and 8am.

17   In October 2003, following an encouraging period of genuine consultation between the Beijing city government and local animal protection NGOs, the authorities agreed to drastic reforms of the dog control regulations, reducing the annual registration fee from 5000 yuan to 1000 yuan (£68). Public Security Bureau estimates put Beijing's registered dog population at only ten per cent of the total. See *China Daily Website*, 7 May 2004, www.chinadaily.com.cn/english/doc/2004-05/07/content_328639.htm.

18   For example, at the time of writing, Nanjing, Jiangsu province

19   Following statistics quoted in 'Pets contribute to China's economy', Xinhua News Agency, 14 February 2005.

20   Growth may continue rapidly as many Chinese view neutering as cruel (over 40 per cent of respondents to the *Animal Welfare Consciousness of Chinese College Students* survey, see note 6).

21   Photographs and a description of this incident provided by an anonymous local source and publicized through the news forum of the Asian Animal Protection Network (www.aapn.org).

22   Two bears were euthanized immediately, one died later and the remaining two recovered satisfactorily.

23   For example, in Fuzhou, Fujian province (UK's *Mail on Sunday*, 20 December 1998); in Changsha, Hunan province (UK's *Daily Mirror*, 26 October 2002).

24   For example, 'Feeding time at the zoo (Chinese style)', UK's *Daily Mail*, 22 July 1999; 'Killing time at cruelty park', Hong Kong's *Sunday Morning Post*, 28 November 1999; 'I'll have mine rare', Thailand's *Bangkok Post*, 22 April 2002.

25   In a 1999 conversation with the author, an official at the Chinese embassy in the UK described the increase in such complaints as 'enormous' whenever the press covered animal suffering in China.

26   'The crucial question around the animal rights argument is anti-humanity' by Zhao Nanyuan, provided to the author by Professor Zu Shuxian. Other debate took place in an online discussion (http://cul.sina.com.cn/s/2004-05-09/55722.html) translated by Animals Asia Foundation. Peter Li's *The Evolving Animal Rights and Welfare Debate in China: Political and Social Impact Analysis* provides a comprehensive summary of recent discussion.

27   For example, Liu Guoxin, (2004) 'An overview of animal welfare law around the world', *China Green Times*, 10 November 2004.

28   In 2003, after three years of operation, BHAEEC received an award

from the city government in recognition of its animal rehoming and education work.

29 In east China, for example, there is a web-based network of cat protection societies.

30 Personal interview between the author and Fang Minghe of Green Eyes, Wenzhou, March 2005.

31 Jointly sponsored by WSPA and the RSPCA.

32 In its first year, the course, established by Dr Song Wei, attracted over one hundred undergraduates. Dr Song went on to develop China's first textbook on animal welfare law, *Kindness to Living Creatures (shandai shengling)*, in 2001.

33 *Prevention of Cruelty to Animals Act*, 1960.

34 *Animal Protection Act*, 1991.

35 *Animal Welfare Act*, 1998.

36 *Animal Protection Law*, 1998.

37 Beijing city government's '5Rs Green Lifestyle' campaign slogan: 'Reduce waste and pollution; Re-evaluate our consumption and make greener choices; Reuse products; Recycle waste; Rescue wildlife and protect the natural environment'.

38 Most Chinese buy and kill poultry themselves, for instance

39 In 2002 over 450 million (www.thepigsite.com/FeaturedArticle/Default.asp?AREA=Markets&Display=858).

References

Beijing Organizing Committee for Games of the XXIX Olympiad (2004) 'Ecological conservation and construction', section 4, available at http://en.beijing-2008.org/22/49/article211614922.shtml

Beijing Review (2004) 'Being humane to animals', *Beijing Review*, May 2004, available at www.bjreview.com.cn/200426/Forum.htm

CCTV1 (2004) *News Probe: Animal Welfare*, first broadcast 30 June 2004

China Daily (2002) 'EU's ban on meat "runs counter to rules"', *China Daily*, 28 January 2002, available at www.china.org.cn/english/2002/Jan/25989.htm

China Daily (2005) 'Organic food booms in provinces', *China Daily Website*, 22 February 2005, available at www.chinadaily.com.cn/english/doc/2005-02/22/content_418309.htm

People's Daily (2001) 'Wild Yangtze alligator population in China diminishes', *People's Daily Online*, 13 September 2001, available at http://english.people.com.cn/english/200109/13/eng20010913_80216.html

People's Daily (2002) 'College student pours sulfuric acid on bears in zoo', *People's Daily Online*, 25 February 2002, available at http://english.people.com.cn/200202/25/eng20020225_90929.html (details of the Liu Haiyang incident are covered by Dr Song Wei, University of Science and Technology of China, at www.animallaw.info/nonus/articles/arcncs1.htm; further information provided by Jackson Zee, International Fund for Animal Welfare)

People's Daily (2004a) 'China GLP standard safety evaluation center to be set up', *People's Daily Online*, 6 August 2004, available at

http://english.people.com.cn/200408/06/eng20040806_152090.html
People's Daily (2004b) 'Beijing deliberates draft regulation on animal welfare',
  People's Daily Online, 25 October 2004, available at
  http://english.people.com.cn/200410/25/eng20041025_161485.html
People's Daily (2004c) 'China revising regulations on laboratory animals', *People's
  Daily Online*, 27 May 2004, available at
  http://english.people.com.cn/200405/27/eng20040527_144581.html

22

Animal Welfare and Economic Development: A Financial Institution Perspective

Oliver Ryan

International Finance Corporation – World Bank Group

The International Finance Corporation (IFC) is a member of the World Bank Group (WBG), which consists of IFC, the International Bank of Reconstruction and Development (IBRD) and the Multilateral Investment Guarantee Agency (MIGA). In brief – IFC lends to private enterprise, while the IBRD lends to Governments. IFC is the largest private sector investor in emerging markets today. It is AAA rated with a portfolio of US$17 billion in 140 countries. IFC promotes sustainable private sector development in emerging countries to help reduce poverty and improve people's lives. IFC does this through:

- financing private sector ventures in partnership with private investors;
- providing loans, equity and partial guarantees in developing member countries;
- mobilizing capital and loans from other sources;
- providing technical assistance in partnership with donors;
- operating on commercial terms without subsidies.

The WBG/IFC is funded by member countries and is responsible to the World Bank Board, which represents these countries. These countries have their unique development agenda, including the development agenda for livestock.

IFC funding of agri-business projects

The IFC Agribusiness Department (CAG) is responsible for funding agri-business projects. Included in CAG's portfolio and its future investment strategy are livestock and aquaculture projects. CAG has a portfolio of around US$300 million in livestock. Projects focus on integrated pig and poultry sectors (with some beef processing) in countries that have a competitive advantage in livestock production (Brazil/Ukraine) and in countries with a livestock development agenda (Russia/China). However, the portfolio is spread across other countries including Lebanon, Ecuador, Mexico, Korea, Russia, Bosnia and Turkey. In addition IFC has investments in shrimp aquaculture in Madagascar, Honduras, Belize and Venezuela. The companies involved have significant turnovers (up to US$2.5 billion in annual sales) and are usually market leaders. Production is largely for local markets but can be for export. Projects are usually large (capital expenditure of US$20–300 million). Investments are usually in capacity/capability expansion but can involve rehabilitation of privatized, ex-state-owned operations. A large number of stakeholders are involved (e.g. up to 20,000 staff can be directly employed in production, processing and distribution, and up to 10,000 farmers supplying an operation with livestock). These people are often living on around US$1000 per annum.

The animal production systems within these operations can be company owned and/or contract and can utilize either intensive or extensive livestock production systems. Very often, pig and poultry projects have controlled environmental housing with automatic feeding and watering systems, but not always. Veterinarians are an integral part of operations and generally there is a good understanding of good practice in livestock management and disease control. Some operations have older facilities or practices posing specific management challenges. In all cases environmental and social programmes within a project must comply with WBG guidelines. Commitment to food safety and quality (such as the use of HACCP[1] and ISO programmes for risk assessment and control) within companies is variable, as is commitment to animal welfare. Some companies have animal welfare standards, with external audits being required by European clients.

While the WBG has detailed policies and guidelines for environmental and social issues, it does not have any policy or guideline for animal welfare. A major reason for this is that the International Bank of Reconstruction and Development (IBRD) arm of the WBG, which funds large Government-sponsored livestock projects, is more often focusing on small-scale livestock development or projects in regions impacted by harsh climates. Animal welfare issues within IBRD projects are therefore more likely to be drought in sub-Saharan Africa, snow drifts in Mongolia or predator threats to village animals. The welfare initiatives are therefore more indirect, often being through initiatives such as good management practices, animal health programmes or, in the case of Mongolia, stock reduction. Thus, the projects and clients that IBRD and IFC support can be vastly different – with extremely different animal welfare issues. Since IFC is the arm of the WBG that is involved in funding private sector livestock projects, IFC is the organization that is equipped to address animal welfare issues in commercial projects.

Although IFC is often the only source of long-term finance, so essential in agri-business in emerging markets, IFC has several competitive advantages as a financial institution. No other development finance institution has as much experience in creating and administering environmental and social safeguards.

We have invested more than any other development finance institution in sustainability research, sustainability training and capacity for working with private sector clients on building sustainable businesses. We have a history of investing in carbon emission trading, biodiversity and other environmental fields unmatched by any other private sector development institution. Our track record on corporate governance and HIV/AIDS sets the benchmark. We have broad-based partnerships with the UN, FAO, foundations, civil society and NGOs. These partnerships have now been extended to the Equator Principles – which embody the acceptance of IFC social and environmental standards – in selected projects by over 20 international banks under a single social and environmental policy framework. This consortium of banks is responsible for 80 per cent of project finance in emerging markets. However, until now, neither IBRD, IFC nor the consortium of Equator banks have addressed animal welfare directly.

Within its sustainability agenda, IFC is seeking ways to assist its livestock and aquaculture clients. One of the emerging issues for these clients is animal welfare. While there have been considerable changes in developed countries in recent years in animal welfare issues, it is expected that eventually these changes will come to the less developed countries. IFC believes that since a strong business case can be made to improve animal welfare then it has an opportunity to engage with clients and act as a primary agent for change.

IFC recognizes that it cannot establish itself as an authority on animal welfare. IFC therefore decided to be guided in addressing animal welfare issues through its alliance with the Office International des Épizooties (OIÉ). OIÉ, IBRD and IFC have common global membership and recognize that these members have different cultural, scientific, religious and political backgrounds that need to be considered. Also, recognizing that IFC does not have the internal resources, or expertise, to develop the necessary roadmap for animal welfare, we employed International Animal Welfare Consultants (IAWC Limited), to provide the necessary credibility and required insights into how we might approach animal welfare issues.

Stakeholder liaison

IAWC Limited approached a number of key international agri-business and animal welfare NGO stakeholders to ascertain their perspectives, and concerns with regard to animal welfare and IFC investments in livestock. Seventeen such stakeholders responded and shared various perspectives as follows:

- Existing animal welfare policies of NGOs were founded on the philosophy that the use of animals in livestock farming contributes to the well-being of humans and that with this use comes a responsibility to treat animals with compassion and care. Animal welfare was seen as separate from, but linked to, animal health, human health and prosperity, and the environment. While the right of humans to use animals for food was challenged, this was a minority stance amongst the stakeholders. However, in recognizing that any improvements in animal welfare are steps in the right direction, these organizations also reflect some of the philosophies of animal welfare and animal protection groups. Only one stakeholder interviewed represented an animal rights position, the remainder preferring to address animal welfare.

- The Five Freedoms reflecting the needs of animals (freedom from hunger, thirst and malnutrition; freedom from fear and distress; freedom from physical and thermal discomfort; freedom from pain, injury and disease; and freedom to express normal patterns of behaviour) were taken as a central tenet for ensuring and enhancing animal welfare by most participants. While there was opposition to intensive farming, confinement itself was not always the major issue, but rather the needs of animals *per se*.
- Whilst accepting the place of animal use in human society, some stakeholders were opposed to all forms of farming that caused animal suffering or distress, or deprived them of the opportunity for natural behaviour. There was particular opposition to intensive or 'factory farming' systems of production, which some saw as being wasteful of resources, something they believed emerging markets could ill-afford.
- Standards of animal welfare have to be based on sound science, research and education, with emphasis being given to the welfare outcome for the animal, rather than the prescriptive standards. Animal welfare principles were seen as universal and there was an urgent need to assist communities in emerging markets with support for animal welfare.

The stakeholders were asked for suggestions as to how IFC might develop animal welfare principles. Those who responded suggested that animal welfare principles should be based on the Five Freedoms, and that these should be used in deciding which projects IFC should fund. These principles should be practical and realistic and have a degree of international consensus. They should be based on strong scientific standards and allow for continuous evolution and improvements in performance and evolve from being purely prescriptive to becoming more outcome based.

The stakeholders suggested that IFC should work cooperatively with other groups, such as the OIÉ, and where possible should use guidelines already developed to support its animal welfare principles. The stakeholders also recognized that:

- Moves towards improving animal welfare should be made incrementally, recognizing the ability of businesses and emerging markets to accommodate them. Thus, improvements cannot, and will not, be made immediately.

- A verification system should be implemented to provide a significant measure of animal welfare, and therefore provide official recognition for the production methods used. The verification system should be based on key welfare indicators, rather than inspection audits.
- IFC needs to deal with the many paradoxes that exist when addressing various farming systems in emerging markets. Animal welfare principles need to demonstrate cognizance of the issues of poverty, communities, environment, business sustainability and globalization, while addressing the reality of demand for food production and compromises to animal welfare.
- IFC should work through various agents, especially farmers and retailers who can effect changes in animal welfare; however, it should be recognized that this may pose different challenges in emerging markets compared to the US and EU who can afford to discriminate.
- The driver of animal production systems in emerging markets is more likely to be concerns for bio-security and food safety, and this approach may, or may not, have positive outcomes for animal welfare.
- Education is an important contributor to addressing animal welfare. NGOs, the scientific community and the veterinary profession are important in shaping both consumer expectations and public pressure.
- Legislation and public policy is a strong force on animal welfare standards. Ultimately, it is society that decides what use of animals is acceptable. The increasing isolation of urban populations from rural life in many developed countries, changing perceptions of the correct way to treat animals, public opinion, regional/cultural differences and the leadership roles of some countries in animal welfare all impact this.
- A major force of change is helping people to change, rather than imposing external standards. It was suggested that most people in most countries care about animal welfare, and although there are cultural variations, the humane treatment of animals is never viewed as inappropriate. People from outside the emerging markets must be prepared to work with livestock industries and effect change through demonstrating the advantages and costs, and accept that practices evolve over time. It is not helpful to merely tell people what to do – nor is it for outsiders to say how things should be done.
- Economics has been a major constraint on improving animal welfare, especially the way it has driven the development of intensive systems such as caged egg-laying hens. Whilst the cost of production does not contribute greatly to the overall price of food to the consumer, it significantly impacts producer margins, so mechanisms are required to ensure equitable distribution of the costs of improving animal welfare. Initiatives should also acknowledge the need for transition and not force reform on industries in emerging markets.

Guiding principles

Since animal welfare is an issue that comprises both ethical and business dimensions, it was necessary for IFC to establish a set of driving principles that would enable it to integrate its animal welfare initiative with its mandate to promote sustainable private sector development that addresses economic, environmental and social outcomes. Working with IAWC, IFC determined these to be as follows:

- Since intensive livestock farming can have a major positive impact on the economic viability of poor rural communities, use of animals for food and wealth creation is acceptable, provided that this is undertaken in a humane and responsible manner.
- While animal welfare is an important issue, it has to be seen within the context of other social and economic issues. Economic development may not be positively correlated with improvements in animal welfare.
- Animal welfare is a multifaceted issue and there are many different and complex views about how animals should be used or treated. IFC respects the right of people to hold and express those views.
- IFC respects the rights of different communities and cultures with regard to animal welfare and recognizes the importance of engagement with local communities who have experience and beliefs about how animals should be treated.
- Although intensive farming of animals is currently accepted in principle, many systems pose animal welfare challenges, and it is essential that clients accept their responsibilities for animal care.
- IFC will approach projects with an 'its better to engage than not engage' philosophy and promote animal welfare to its clients with an 'incremental improvement' approach.
- IFC will become increasingly selective in its assessment of livestock investments where they do not contribute to improving the standard of animal welfare.
- The basic needs of animals, encapsulated in the Five Freedoms, form the basis of welfare standards and principles for good practice.
- Guidelines should be based on sound science and practical experience utilizing accepted national/international guidelines.
- IFC will support standards that focus on animal welfare outcomes, rather than being unduly prescriptive with regard to inputs.
- IFC is committed to being guided by the animal welfare initiatives of the OIÉ, and will continue to liaise closely with key international organizations, including the FAO, the World Veterinary Association (WVA), industry organizations and international animal welfare NGOs.
- While IFC is committed to improving animal welfare good practice, it recognizes that there are important economic, practical and cultural

aspects affecting change. IFC proposes to concentrate on achieving improvements through demonstrating business case scenarios for change that are practical and achievable.

IFC commitment to good practice in animal welfare

AWC Limited presented a roadmap to IFC in mid-2004. The report addressed the issues raised by the above stakeholders. It presented a Folio of Good Practice derived from codes of welfare published in Australia, Canada, New Zealand, the US, the UK and the European Union that could be used as reference material for IFC to develop client/species-specific folios along with animal welfare success stories that assist with the development of the business case. It also addressed how IFC might develop standards, monitoring and compliance within its projects. This has resulted in a commitment by IFC to developing good practice in animal welfare amongst its client projects. IFC will do this by:

- producing a Primer on animal welfare that will outline IFC's commitment to the issues and how IFC proposes to engage with clients and stakeholders;
- producing a Good Practice Note to be used by clients as a more substantial introduction as to why they should address animal welfare. This will advise clients of the Five Freedoms and raise awareness of the importance of delivering acceptable animal welfare standards to improve business sustainability. The document will follow the format used by IFC for subjects such as AIDS/HIV and child labour and focus heavily on the business case;
- undertaking a review of client animal welfare practices and developing the business case for addressing these;
- informing clients of animal welfare principles developed for global application by the OIÉ and other organizations;
- drawing its clients' attention to obligatory animal welfare standards developed by national governments;
- liaising with food distribution companies/retailers who impose animal welfare standards on client companies to promote understanding of these requirements and assist with compliance;
- providing clients with good practice guidelines produced by Governments, organizations, industry bodies and individual companies;
- providing clients with business case material and developing business cases that can be shared by client companies;
- addressing the balance that must be achieved between animal welfare objectives and human economic development needs.

The challenge

IFC does not underestimate the challenge of impacting change in animal welfare in many of its projects, nor the time it will take. While clients who supply British supermarkets fully understand the issues of animal welfare and have standards and audits imposed upon them, there are many current and future clients who have not reached that awareness. The IFC philosophy is that it is better to engage these clients and make a difference, rather than not engage at all. This philosophy is well proven with environmental and social issues and we are confident that the same will apply to animal welfare. However, a prerequisite of achieving transformation is that the sponsor must be willing to make the change. The clients we are seeking are those willing to embrace WBG social and environmental guidelines, to change how financial statements are audited and to improve their corporate governance. Our best clients are those who seek to reach international standards in all areas of business. These will be the sustainable operations of the future. These are the clients that will understand the business case for improving animal welfare.

However, there will be many forces (both positive and negative) impacting our ability to effect change. In addition there are many paradoxes in economic development that impact efforts to influence change in animal welfare, and which need to be understood and considered. The following is a small sample of the issues that IFC faces when addressing livestock production projects and animal welfare:

- IFC has been urged by some NGOs not to engage in livestock projects. However, it is often shareholder Government policy to develop the livestock industry, as is the case in China and Russia today. The major reason for this is that rural communities country's poorest contain the people. Governments believe that developing local livestock and grain production will raise the price of locally produced grain, to the benefit of peasant farmers, and also help drive the development of a local livestock economy, which in turn reduces the risk of social instability and enhances food security. While Governments support the development of livestock production, our approach will be one of selective engagement, and addressing animal welfare issues on a project by project basis.
- 'Intensification' of livestock production systems has been blamed for many of the negative animal welfare practices. Intensification of animal production systems in developing countries is not only driven by efficiencies achieved from genetics, modern technology and economies of scale, but also by the realization that more intensive systems can enhance the environment (and project sustainability), by setting standards not possible in backyard production. A move to more intensive systems may, or may not, result in lower animal welfare standards. It is IFC's intent to assist with the promotion of appropriate systems, and the development of guidelines within systems, that will positively impact animal welfare.

- Disease has a major impact on the sustainability of livestock production systems. The bio-security status of small-scale livestock production in countries such as China and Vietnam is a major constraint to sustainable development of the industry. The growing concern that bio-security is compromising livestock development has received special international attention since avian influenza (AI) has impacted the Asian poultry industry. Controlling any disease is a positive animal welfare initiative and in many developing countries is the primary one. AI is receiving particular attention because it is also transmissible to humans. International demand to tighten disease control is therefore increasing, and the need to enhance bio-security may drive a move to more intensive systems in these countries, resulting in a shift in animal welfare challenges.

- When a disease such as AI is mentioned, the methods used to destroy diseased and 'at risk' birds rise to the top of the welfare agenda. The IBRD plays a role in working with stakeholders such as the World Health Organization (WHO), the World Organisation for Animal Health (OIÉ), the UN's Food and Agriculture Organization (FAO) and shareholder Governments to establish policy and procedures that in turn impact IFC clients. It will be IFC's role to incorporate these requirements into its animal welfare guidelines.

- It has been argued that intensification of livestock production drives out small-scale producers. If it does, it may be because small-scale production in its current form is not sustainable, perhaps for economic reasons or on the grounds of inadequate bio-security, traceability or food safety. However, small-scale production can have the advantage of low labour costs and such systems can be incorporated into larger business models. An example of this is an IFC project in China, which relies totally on small-scale village farmers to produce one million pigs under contract. However, the challenge to control disease and ensure product quality in these models is enormous. If they are to be sustainable in the long term, changes to these production systems constantly need to be addressed, along with any impact (positive and negative) on animal welfare. However, while the ability to impact a wide range of animal welfare issues does exist in small village farms, the primary welfare issue on these farms, in the medium term, will be disease control.

- A concern expressed by stakeholders who responded to IAWC Limited was that development of animal welfare standards in developing countries would only reflect the best of systems employed by developed countries. However, this could be a significant positive development. Livestock production systems across developing countries have sub-standard disease control, housing, transport and slaughter methods, and highlight the absence of standards or correctional motivation. A more positive approach may be to suggest that standards that are developed in the west can be adapted and adopted by developing countries. IFC sees this as being an area where we may be able to benchmark and promote positive change.

- The force of global trade initiatives also influences animal welfare. While free trade is being proposed as a viable model, many countries are imposing quotas and tariffs to protect their own industries. This is resulting in the movement to increased livestock production in countries as diverse as Russia, Ecuador and Egypt. While there is a paradox in protecting local industries when proposing a level global playing field, legislation in developing countries is likely to require that local animal welfare standards be no more stringent than those of its trading partners. That will also make it more difficult to 'go beyond' what is practised in the west.

In summary, IFC supports the positive initiatives being made by the animal welfare community. Although IFC is a development bank, and not an animal welfare organization, we believe that by engaging clients through the business case we can assist in improving animal welfare in developing countries. The challenges posed by animal welfare issues in many of these countries cannot be underestimated. Governments do not have the necessary regulatory frameworks. Societies view animal welfare issues differently. There are market constraints to setting lofty standards and our clients may not have perfect systems. However, we believe that it is better to engage and promote change, rather than not engage at all, and that by taking a proactive approach we will make a difference.

Note

1   Hazard Analysis and Critical Control Points

Reference

Bayvel, A. C. D., Mellor, D. J., Milne, J. B. and Fisher, M. W. (2004) *Technical Assistance Report Prepared for IFC*, IAWC Limited, Wellington, New Zealand

23

The International Animal Welfare Role of the Office International des Épizooties: The World Organisation for Animal Health

A. C. David Bayvel

Permanent Animal Welfare Working Group, Office International des Épizooties

The Office International des Épizooties (OIÉ) is a Paris-based, inter-governmental organization, with 167 member countries, established in 1924. In drawing up its strategic plan for the period 2001–2005, animal welfare and food safety were identified as two areas for future OIÉ involvement and these were formally accepted as strategic initiatives at the 2001 OIÉ General Assembly meeting. An international expert group was established to provide specific recommendations on the nature and scope of the OIÉ animal welfare role. The expert group's recommendations were reviewed and adopted as Resolution No. X1V at the May 2002 OIÉ General Assembly meeting. A permanent international working group was established and met for the first time in October 2002.

This chapter gives an overview of animal welfare as an international trade policy issue and provides an update on progress, to date, in developing an OIÉ animal welfare mission statement, supporting guiding principles and policies, and an agreed modus operandi. Priority areas for OIÉ involvement have been identified and emphasis placed on the importance of making use of all available expertise and resources, including those from academia, the research community, industry, animal welfare organizations and other relevant stakeholders.

With its 75-year history of achievement as a science-based international animal health organization with an established infrastructure and international recognition, the OIÉ is well placed to play a key international leadership role in animal welfare.

Public policy in relation to animal health and welfare

Over the last 50 years, there have been dramatic increases in agricultural productivity due to general advances in agricultural and veterinary science; specific improvements in genetics, nutrition, disease control and prophylaxis; plus the impact of agriculture support programmes. There has also been an inexorable and substantial move to more intensive systems of production, especially in the more densely populated nations of Europe, Asia and North America and particularly with pigs, poultry and beef cattle. More extensive systems of production continue to be practised in Africa, Australia, New Zealand and South America, for grazing species, and there is a strong public perception that more extensive management systems are synonymous with better welfare.

Seminal texts by authors including Ruth Harrison, Peter Singer, Tom Regan, Bernard Rollin, John Webster and others, plus the UK's Brambell Committee report (cited in Appleby and Hughes, 1997); the concept of the Five Freedoms; and the influence of behavioural science have all had a significant impact, particularly in Europe and North America, on the attitudes to animal welfare of scientists, of the public at large and, through them, of politicians. Welfare aspects of animal agriculture and associated consumer preference behaviour have also attracted increasing attention from some agricultural economists (McInerney, 1998; Harper, 1998) and agricultural ethicists.

In their paper 'Animal welfare and product quality', Jago et al (2000) emphasize the importance of science-based animal welfare standards and the value of the Five Freedoms by stating:

> Most concepts of animal welfare include avoidance of undue suffering,
> optimizing animal health and vigour and are aimed at achieving
> practices and environmental conditions which are fair and reasonable
> for the animal. Although the concept of animal welfare is widely
> regarded as being important, currently there is no single definition of
> animal welfare that has met with universal approval. People's beliefs
> and understanding of what is meant by 'welfare' and what is optimal
> or sub optimal welfare will vary, depending on such factors as their
> cultural, scientific, religious and political backgrounds.

According to Kellert (1988), the attitudes people have towards animals can be classified into nine categories including naturalistic, ecologistic, humanistic, moralistic, scientific, aesthetic, utilitarian, dominionistic and negative and that differences exist between countries in the predominant attitude. Despite these differing attitudes towards animals, there is a biological basis for evaluating animal health and welfare, and widespread acceptance that decisions about animal welfare should be based on good scientific evidence.

The Council of Europe has played a key role in developing standards for Europe, and these are taken note of internationally. These standards are based on both scientific evidence and practical experience and also emphasize the importance of the relationship between animal health and animal welfare. There is an unfortunate tendency to underestimate the importance of animal health in relation to animal welfare. The prevention and control of disease in all species makes a major contribution to animal welfare, and veterinarians, in general, and the OIÉ, in particular, play a vital role in this regard.

It is helpful to have basic guidelines or rules to refer to when making decisions that may impact on an animal's welfare. Probably the most widely utilized set of guidelines is the Five Freedoms (Farm Animal Welfare Council, 2001). These state that for an animal's welfare not to be compromised it must have: freedom from thirst, hunger and malnutrition; freedom from discomfort; freedom from pain, injury and disease; freedom to express normal behaviour; and, finally, freedom from fear and distress. Sometimes slight modifications are made to these basic freedoms (e.g. fear is sometimes omitted from the final freedom), however, they generally serve as a set of goals towards which animal owners and handlers should strive. The Five Freedoms have been used by many legislators and frequently appear as the basis upon which animal welfare codes and practices have been established.

As guidelines, the Five Freedoms provide a most useful paradigm. They should, however, not be taken as absolute requirements and, increasingly, they are seen to have important limitations by forward-looking animal welfare science thinkers (Mellor, 2003).

Adams (2001), in reviewing the publication *Livestock to 2020: The New Food Revolution* (Delgado, 1999), emphasizes the opportunity for veterinarians 'to act locally but think globally' about animal welfare. This joint publication of the International Food Policy Research Institute in Washington, the Food and Agriculture Organization of the United Nations (FAO) and the International Livestock Research Institute in Nairobi provides detailed information on the dramatic increase in the world's consumption of food derived from animals over the last 30 years.

Expanding human populations, urbanization and income growth are expected to continue, and even accelerate, the trend and Adams (2001) asks 'is it time to rejuvenate the science of animal husbandry to ensure that animals are better protected?' The importance of knowledgeable and caring animal husbandry is recognized as an essential prerequisite to maximizing animal welfare (Hemsworth et al, 1993). Fraser (1999, 2001a, 2001b) has emphasized the importance of the linkage between animal ethics and animal welfare and the vital relationship, in terms of public and societal opinion, between historical cultural attitudes to animals and their use in modern agricultural systems. He argues that there is an urgent need to create a new consensus regarding the use of animals in agriculture. The appearance of bovine spongiform encephalopathy (BSE) and recent outbreaks of classical swine fever (CSF) and foot and mouth disease (FMD) in Europe have led to the slaughter of millions of animals and intense political and professional debate on the ethics and scientific basis of certain production systems. The veterinary profession, at large, and the OIÉ, in particular, are well positioned to make an important contribution to these debates.

International trade considerations

The conclusion of the General Agreement on Tariffs and Trade (GATT) Uruguay Round, in 1994, and the establishment of the World Trade Organization (WTO), with its associated Sanitary and Phytosanitary (SPS) and Technical Barriers to Trade (TBT) agreements plus the Agreement on Agriculture, were seen to set the stage and create a framework for all member nations to reap the benefits of agricultural trade liberalization. There has, however, been a growing concern, particularly amongst some non-governmental organizations (NGOs) (RSPCA, 1998, 2000; RSPCA et al, 1998; RSPCA and Eurogroup for Animal Welfare, 1999; Bowles, 2000), that the WTO rules-based trading system does not adequately address consumer interests and that the credibility of, and public support for, the WTO is thus at risk. The NGOs involved believe that the outcome of the tuna/dolphin and shrimp/turtle disputes and the issue of leghold traps support their view that the WTO does not allow animal welfare considerations to be used to restrict trade (RSPCA, 1998). Bayvel (1993, 1996, 2000 and 2004) has reviewed the topic from both a New Zealand and international perspective.

There is no single international organization with a standard-setting role or a responsibility for the provision of expert advice on animal welfare, although a number of organizations and agencies have a significant interest in the area. The largest of these is the Council of Europe, which developed the Convention on Farm Animals in 1976 and now has three other conventions on animal welfare relating to welfare during transport, welfare at slaughter and welfare of companion animals. The Council of Europe has over 40 member countries and the standards developed relate to European farm systems.

By the late 1990s, there was growing support for the proposal that the OIÉ could be an appropriate, established, inter-governmental organization to address animal welfare issues and seek agreement on international standards.

Market trends

In parallel with the policy debate on animal welfare and international trade, important initiatives have been taken by some producers and retailers. A number of OIÉ member countries, including some European countries, Australia, New Zealand, the US and Canada have also gained valuable experience in the role of industry-led quality assurance programmes, in promoting animal welfare standards. This approach, underpinned by science-based national standards, provides an opportunity to define and monitor the animals' welfare. It is preferred to, and seen to be a much more cost-effective option than, a prescriptive regulatory approach. These schemes have, undoubtedly, had a positive impact on animal welfare and have helped to directly address consumer concerns.

Animal welfare standards

Defining and assessing animal welfare has become the subject of a significant body of literature over the last two decades. The most commonly accepted definition is that 'the welfare of an individual animal is its state as regard its attempt to cope with its environment, with attempts to cope including the functioning of body repair systems, immunological defences, the physiological stress response and a variety of behavioural responses'. (Broom, 1996).

The 1998 and 2001 European Directives on layer hens (hens used for egg production) 99/74/EC (Anonymous, 1999) and on pigs 2001/88/EC (Anonymous, 2001) are both based on extensive scientific reviews conducted by the European Commission Scientific Committee on Animal Health and Welfare. These Directives support the view that public perception does not necessarily equate to optimum animal welfare standards. The Directives continue to permit the use of (enriched and larger) cages for layer hens and confinement of sows in narrow crates for one week pre- and four weeks post-partum.

It is envisaged that standards developed by the OIÉ would follow the same science-based approach and draw on contemporary scientific consensus. To address the public perception issue, it is recommended, as advocated by Fraser (1999), that animal welfare policy and standards should also be complemented by robust ethical analysis. Blokhuis et al (2000) and MAFF (2001) further emphasize the important interaction between science and society.

Fraser (1999) emphasizes the importance of both scientific and ethical inputs by stating:

> As it has unfolded to date, the debate has been disappointing
> intellectually, ethically, and politically: intellectually, because the debate
> has not resulted in a genuine understanding of how animal agriculture
> affects animals, the environment, and the good of the public; ethically,
> because the polemical nature of many of the accounts of animal
> agriculture has tended to polarize the debate and to prevent real ethical
> analysis of important issues; and politically, because this polarized
> debate has failed to create a climate of dialogue and consensus
> building. As a first step towards rectifying these problems, there is an
> urgent need for scientists and ethicists to avoid simply aligning
> themselves with advocacy positions and instead to provide
> knowledgeable research and analysis of the issues.

These sentiments, and this strategic approach, are highly relevant to ensure that the OIÉ is to be both politically and publicly credible in the area of animal welfare.

Progress at the Office International des Épizooties

Since its establishment in 1924, the three principal aims of the OIÉ have been:

- the provision of information on infectious animal diseases worldwide;
- international promotion and coordination of studies on the surveillance and control of infectious diseases of animals;
- the harmonization of international agreements and regulations for disease control including the facilitation of trade in animals and animal products.

The work of the organization assumed a new prominence in the 1990s through recognition of its role in providing standards, guidelines and recommendations for animal health and zoonoses through the SPS agreement of the WTO.

The OIÉ has historically made a major indirect contribution to animal welfare globally via the organization's involvement in epizootic disease control, and has included a chapter in the animal health code on minimum animal welfare standards for trade. It has also played a standard-setting role in respect of animal transportation and, in 1994, published 'Animal welfare and veterinary services' in the *Scientific and Technical Review* series (Moss, 1994). This publication provides a valuable overview of the animal welfare role played by government veterinary departments in OIÉ member countries and includes review articles on specific international animal welfare issues.

In recognition of the increasing scientific, political and public attention being given to animal welfare, in general, and its role in international trade, in particular, animal welfare was identified as an important emerging issue during the preparation of the 2001–2005 OIÉ third strategic plan. At the 69th session of the OIÉ International Committee, approval was given to the Director General's work programme to implement the recommendations of the strategic plan. In this programme, it was agreed to establish a new department specifically responsible for international trade in animals and animal products, which would provide extra resources to address new topics, including food safety, zoonoses and animal welfare. It was agreed that initial scoping documents would be commissioned to assist in defining the degree and scope of OIÉ involvement with these new topics.

The 70th General Session of the OIÉ was held in Paris during May 2002. The Director-General, Dr Bernard Vallat, presented specific recommendations concerning the scope, priorities and modus operandi for the OIÉ's involvement in animal welfare (Anonymous, 2002) and these were fully endorsed by all 167 member countries. These recommendations were based on the work of an ad hoc group of international experts and included the following:

- The OIÉ should develop a detailed vision and strategy to recognize the complex nature of animal welfare issues.
- The OIÉ should then develop policies and guiding principles to provide a

sound foundation from which to elaborate specific recommendations and standards.

- The OIÉ should establish a working group on animal welfare to coordinate and manage animal welfare activities and the working group should advise on specific tasks to be carried out by ad hoc groups.
- In consultation with the OIÉ, the working group should develop a detailed operational plan for the initial 12 months, addressing the priority issues identified.
- The working group and its ad hoc groups should consult with non-government organizations (NGOs) having a broad international representation and make use of all available expertise and resources, including those from academia, the research community, industry and other relevant stakeholders.
- The scope of OIÉ involvement in animal welfare issues should be grouped into the following:
  - animals used in agriculture and aquaculture for production, breeding and/or working purposes;
  - companion animals including exotic (wild-caught and non-traditional) species;
  - animals used for research, testing and/or teaching purposes;
  - free-living wildlife, including the issues of their slaughter and trapping;
  - animals used for sport, recreation and entertainment, including in circuses and zoos, and that, for each group, in addition to essential animal health considerations, the topics of housing, management, transportation and killing (including humane slaughter, euthanasia and killing for disease control) be addressed.
- The OIÉ should give priority to animal welfare issues regarding animals used in agriculture and aquaculture and, regarding the other groups identified, the OIÉ should establish relative priorities to be dealt with as resources permit.
- Within the agriculture and aquaculture group, the OIÉ should firstly address transportation, humane slaughter, and killing for disease control, and, later, housing and management. The OIÉ should also consider animal welfare aspects, as issues arise, in the areas of genetic modification and cloning, genetic selection for production and fashion, and veterinary practices.
- When addressing zoonoses, the OIÉ should give priority to addressing the animal welfare aspects of animal population reduction and control policies (including stray dogs and cats).
- The OIÉ should incorporate within its communication strategy key animal welfare stakeholders, including industry and NGOs.
- The OIÉ should incorporate animal welfare considerations within its major functions and assume the following specific roles and functions:
  - development of standards and guidelines leading to good animal welfare practice;

- provision of expert advice on specific animal welfare issues to OIÉ stakeholder groups, including member countries, other international organizations and industry/consumers;
- maintenance of international databases on animal welfare information, including different national legislation and policies, internationally recognized animal welfare experts, and relevant examples of good animal welfare practice;
- identification of the essential elements of an effective national infrastructure for animal welfare including legislation/legal tools and the development of a self-assessment checklist;
- preparation and circulation of educational material to enhance awareness among OIÉ stakeholders;
- promotion of the inclusion of animal welfare in undergraduate and postgraduate university curricula;
- identification of animal welfare research needs and encouragement of collaboration among centres of research.

The working group

A working group, established after the May General Assembly, met for the first time in Paris from 16–18 October 2002.

The working group developed a work programme for 2003, which addressed the following issues:

- statements of mission, guiding principles and policies for adoption by the International Committee in 2003;
- development of expertise and stakeholder databases;
- animal welfare conference scheduled for late February 2004;
- terms of reference, scope and membership of ad hoc groups, with possible meetings of two ad hoc groups in the first half of 2003;
- increasing awareness of animal welfare in undergraduate training;
- increasing awareness of animal welfare research needs and funding requirements;
- promoting collaboration among academic and research institutions;
- communications plan addressing both internal and external audiences;
- identification of future activities and emerging issues (e.g. animal biotechnology and aquaculture).

The working group reviewed the scope, drafted terms of reference and identified potential members for four separate groups covering land transport, sea transport, humane slaughter (including a subgroup for religious slaughter) and killing for disease control. The working group also recommended that OIÉ continue to work with the International Air Transport Association (IATA) and the Animal Transport Association (AATA) on transport issues.

The OIÉ's mission

The following draft mission statement, guiding principles and policies have been prepared:

The draft mission is:

To provide international leadership in animal welfare through the development of science-based standards and guidelines, the provision of expert advice and the promotion of relevant education and research.

The OIÉ will achieve this mission through:

- promotion of science-based understanding of animal welfare;
- utilization of appropriate expertise;
- consultation with all relevant stakeholders;
- recognition of regional and cultural dimensions;
- liaison with academic and research institutions;
- use of communication tools appropriate to all relevant audiences.

The draft guiding principles are:

- that there is a critical relationship between animal health and animal welfare;
- that the internationally recognized 'Five Freedoms' provide valuable guidance in animal welfare;
- that the internationally recognized 'three Rs' (reduction in numbers of animals, refinement of experimental methods and replacement of animals with non-animal techniques) provide valuable guidance for the use of animals in science;
- that the scientific assessment of animal welfare involves diverse elements which need to be considered together, and that selecting and weighing these elements often involves value-based assumptions which should be made as explicit as possible;
- that the use of animals in agriculture and science, and for companionship, recreation and entertainment, makes a major contribution to the well-being of people;
- that the use of animals carries with it a duty to ensure the welfare of such animals to the greatest extent practicable;
- that improvements in farm animal welfare can often improve productivity and hence lead to economic benefits;
- that equivalent outcomes (performance criteria), rather than identical systems (design criteria), be the basis for comparison of animal welfare standards and guidelines.

Policies and initiatives

In undertaking its animal welfare role, the OIÉ seeks to adhere to the following draft policies:

- that it will make appropriate use of international scientific expertise in the development of animal welfare guidelines and standards;
- that, in addition to the use of established consultation processes, the OIÉ will consult with NGO and industry stakeholder interests, which can demonstrate a broad-based international approach to issues;
- that it will encourage the teaching of animal welfare and animal ethics in veterinary and other undergraduate curricula around the world;
- that it will encourage the identification of animal welfare research needs and the provision of public and private sector funds to address these needs;
- that it will encourage science-based methods to assess animal welfare outcomes;
- that OIÉ's initial priorities for animal welfare will be animals in agriculture and aquaculture particularly relating to transport, humane slaughter and humane killing for disease control purposes;
- that it will take into account regional and cultural dimensions;
- that it will use communication tools appropriate to audiences.

In pursuing this important initiative, particular attention is being given to the following specific points:

- the important OIÉ international leadership role;
- that the OIÉ is aware of the importance of involvement of a broad range of stakeholders;
- that the OIÉ recognizes the need to ensure standards are relevant to all Member Countries;
- the widespread support from international industry groups, NGOs and international science organizations;
- the major scientific and communications challenge which this initiative presents;
- that adequate resourcing is essential to maintain initial momentum and ensure early achievements;
- that the OIÉ sees future standards contributing to improved animal welfare internationally and valuable for bilateral agreements.

The four ad hoc groups met on two occasions, once in 2003 and once in 2004, and their reports were considered by the Permanent Animal Welfare Working Group and the OIÉ Terrestrial Animal Health Code Commission before being made available for external consultation prior to the 2005 OIÉ general session meeting. Membership of the ad hoc groups was drawn from all five OIÉ regions and included individuals with both internationally recognized scientific expertise and detailed practical familiarity with the topic under review.

Other key activities addressed by the OIÉ since the establishment of the Permanent Animal Welfare Working Group include:

- hosting a highly successful Global Conference on Animal Welfare in Paris in February 2004;
- coordinating the production of 'Animal welfare: Global issues, trends and challenges' in the OIÉ Scientific and Technical Review Series;
- inclusion of animal welfare information on the OIÉ website.

International perspectives

Animal welfare is a complex, multifaceted public policy issue that includes important ethical, economic and political dimensions. There is a real concern, in some quarters, that its recognition as an international trade policy issue is sought for 'trade protectionism', rather than 'animal protection' reasons. A strategic approach underpinned by science-based policy and standards and an incremental approach to animal welfare change management (Mellor and Stafford, 2001) helps, however, to directly address such concerns.

The need for international leadership in respect of animal welfare policy and standards has been evident for some time and is likely to be an expanding core role for the OIÉ in the decades ahead. International scientific and professional organizations such as the International Society for Applied Ethology (ISAE) and World Veterinary Association (WVA) have confirmed their interest in working closely with the OIÉ, as have international industry and animal welfare advocacy organizations. Other organizations such as the FAO and World Bank are also taking an interest in animal welfare and in March 2003 the Government of the Philippines hosted an inter-governmental meeting attended by 25 countries to discuss the possible development of a United Nations Declaration on Animal Welfare.

There is also, of course, a significant increase in interest in animal welfare at university undergraduate and postgraduate level, and the establishment of Animal Welfare Chairs in Universities in Canada, the US, the EU, New Zealand and Australia over the last few decades has provided academic and research direction to this interest. Progress in the area of animal welfare will, of course, be a case of 'evolution not revolution' based on the principle of incremental change management. It is vitally important that all such changes be science-based and validated, be implemented over realistic time frames and take account of economic and cultural factors.

Implementation of the agreed OIÉ strategic initiative on animal welfare presents significant challenges to ensure identification of priorities, an appropriate focus and effective use of resources. The approach adopted must recognize the intense interest of non-governmental organizations, the public and politicians and the significant scientific contribution that can be made by non-veterinarians. In its third strategic plan, the OIÉ has given increased priority, and allocated additional resources, to increasing its public profile and communication effectiveness. This initiative is particularly relevant to any future enhanced animal welfare role, as all forms of media take an active, ongoing interest in animal welfare issues.

In addition to full ownership of, and 'buy-in' to, OIÉ's animal welfare role by its 167 member countries, it is considered strategically and politically important that other stakeholder groups, including industry groups, NGOs and the WTO, are also fully supportive of this role. The major international conference held in February 2004 thus included all stakeholder groups.

The progress made by the OIÉ to date in relation to international animal welfare leadership is, by any standards, impressive. The future OIÉ modus operandi will be characterized by a commitment to communication, consultation, continuous improvement and incremental change, as part of a long-term 'journey', rather than any expectation of reaching a short- to medium-term 'destination'.

The notion of approaching animal welfare change management on a truly global, rather than a regional, basis represents a significant paradigm shift. The support, goodwill and esprit de corps so evident during the 2004 conference bode well for the future.

References

Adams, D. (2001) 'Animal welfare column', *Australian Veterinary Journal*, vol 79, no 7, p448

Anonymous (1999) 'Laying down minimum standards for the protection of laying hens', *Council Directive 99/74/EC, OJ 1999 L203*, p53

Anonymous (2001) 'Laying down minimum standards for the protection of pigs', *Council Directive 2001/88/EC, OJ 2001 L316*, p1

Anonymous (2002) OIÉ General Assembly Meeting Resolution No. XIV, OIÉ, Paris

Appleby, M. C. and Hughes, B. O. (1997) (eds) *Animal Welfare*, CAB International, Wallingford, UK

Bayvel, A. C. D. (1993) 'Animal welfare – a threat or an opportunity for research, farming and trade', *Proceedings of the NZ Society of Animal Production*, vol 53, pp223–225

Bayvel, A. C. D. (1996) 'Animal welfare and international trade', *Second Pan Pacific Veterinary Conference*, Christchurch, New Zealand, May 1996

Bayvel, A. C. D. (2000) 'Animal welfare and the international trade environment', *Workshop on Safeguarding Animal Health in Global Trade*, Hannover, Germany, September 2000

Bayvel, A. C. D. (2004) 'Science-based animal-welfare standards:The international role of the Office International des Epizootes', *Animal Welfare*, vol 13, supplement, pp163–169

Blokhuis, H., Ekkel, E., Korte, S., Hopster, H. and van Reenen, C. (2000) 'Farm animal welfare research in interaction with society', *The Veterinary Quarterly*, vol 22, no 4, pp217–222

Bowles, D. (2000) 'Is the World Trade Organization a friend or foe to high animal welfare standards?' *AWSELVA Newsletter*, vol 4, summer 2000, p1

Broom, D. M. (1996) 'Animal welfare defined in terms of attempt to cope with the environment', *Acta Agriculturae Scandinavica, Section A, Animal Science*, supplement 27, pp22–28

Delgado, C. (1999) *Livestock to 2020 – The Next Food Revolution*, The International Food Policy Research Institute, Washington, DC

Farm Animal Welfare Council (2001) *Interim Report on the Animal Welfare Implications of Farm Assurance Schemes*, Farm Animal Welfare Council, UK

Fraser, D. (1999) 'Animal ethics and animal welfare science: Bridging the two cultures', *Applied Animal Behaviour Science*, vol 65, pp171–189

Fraser, D. (2001a) 'The culture and agriculture of animal production', *The Australian and New Zealand Council for the Care of Animals in Research and Teaching (ANZCCART) News*, March 2001, no 1, pp1–2

Fraser, D. (2001b) 'The "new perception" of animal agriculture and a need for genuine analysis', *Journal of Animal Science*, vol 79, pp634–641

Harper, G. (1998) *Consumer Concerns about Animal Welfare and the Impact on Food Choice*, Comparative Literature Review, University of Reading, November 1998

Hemsworth, P. H., Barnett, J. L. and Coleman, G. J. (1993) 'The human–animal relationship in agriculture and its consequences for the animal', *Animal Welfare*, vol 2, pp33–51

Jago, J., Fisher, A. and Le Neindre, P. (2000) 'Animal welfare and product quality', in Balázs, E. (ed) *Biological Resource Management. Connecting Science and Policy*, Springer, New York, pp163–171

Kellert, S. R. (1988) 'Human–animal interaction: A review of American attitudes to wild and domestic animals in the twentieth century', in Rowan, A. N. (ed) *Animals and People Sharing the World*, Tufts University, Medford, MA, pp137–175

MAFF (Ministry of Agriculture, Food and Fisheries) (2001) 'Ethics and animal welfare: relationships between humans and animals' [Etik og dyrevelfaerd: forholdet mellem mennesker og dyr], *Dansk Veterinaertidsskrift*, vol 84, no 16, pp22–24

McInerney, J. P. (1998) 'The economics of welfare', in *Ethics, Welfare, Law and Market Forces: The Veterinary Interface*, Proceedings of a RCVS/UFAW Symposium, Royal Society of Veterinary Surgeons, London, pp115–134

Mellor, D. J. (2003) personal communication

Mellor, D. J. and Stafford, K. J. (2001) 'Integrating practical, regulatory and ethical strategies for enhancing farm animal welfare', *Australian Veterinary Journal*, vol 79, pp762–768

Moss, R. (1994) 'Animal welfare and veterinary services', *OIÉ Scientific and Technical Review*, vol 13, no 1

RSPCA (2000) *Impact of World Trade Organization on Farm Animal Welfare*, Royal Society for the Prevention of Cruelty to Animals, Horsham

RSPCA (1998) *Agenda 2000: The Future for Farm Animal Welfare in the European Union?* Royal Society for the Prevention of Cruelty to Animals, Horsham

RSPCA, Eurogroup for Animal Welfare and The Humane Society of the United States (1998) *Conflict or Concord: Animal Welfare and the World Trade Organization*, Royal Society for the Prevention of Cruelty to Animals, Horsham

RSPCA and Eurogroup for Animal Welfare (1999) *Food for Thought: Farm Animal Welfare and the WTO*, Royal Society for the Prevention of Cruelty to Animals, Horsham

24
Achieving Access to Ethical Food: Animal and Human Health Come Together

Tim Lang

City University, UK

This chapter is a short overview of just some of the complexities currently facing consumers of products from the food supply chain. As people buy food, they face competing demands for their 'morality'; these come from the viewpoint of animal welfare, environment, health, international justice and others. How can consumers make sense of these competing discourses? The conventional argument from policy-makers is that labelling is essential, together with education. This 'informed consumer' approach puts the responsibility for choice on the consumer; and conversely, if consumers do *not* consume ethically, this absolves the policy-maker. Policy can thereby compound the difficulties and complexities facing consumers. In fact, too often, policy is conducted in separate 'boxes'. The consumer, not society, has to do the joining up.

The problem that animal welfare proponents highlight – lack of integration – is structural, rather than peculiar to that one area. It might help to look at another huge policy area – public health – which has many linkages with animal welfare. A new approach to public health, known as ecological public health, is emerging (Lang and Heasman, 2004). This proposes that solutions to major health challenges require shifts in the environmental and societal infrastructure that determines who eats, what, when, where and how.

There are parallels and important overlaps for the animal welfare movement and scientists, as well as for their colleagues in modern public health. Organizations that currently work 'in silos' need to collaborate more, share campaigns and put pressure on politicians and the food supply chain to change, not just for the sakes of both their constituencies, but for the wider public and planetary good.

Today, many of us observing and analysing current food systems know that the existing policy paradigm, in place for most of the 20th century, is in disarray. It is under threat environmentally (think of climate change, water shortage and reliance on oil), societally (huge inequalities of access, affordability and choice) as well as for reasons of health (the toll of heart disease, diabetes and some cancers) and culturally (the spread of 'western' diets with their consequences to areas that cannot afford the hidden costs to healthcare or transport infrastructure).

This need for a new policy framework coincides with the increasing serious-ness with which arguments for dramatically curtailing exploitation of animals and reducing consumption of their products are being taken in policy-making circles. To take just one debating point, in a world of 9 billion people by the mid-21st century, can we afford to use prime land to grow crops for animals? Or will this be the preserve and right of the rich only? By what moral right is land used to grow feed for animals that might perhaps be better used to feed people directly?

Obviously, one cannot grow mangoes on the wet, northern hillsides of Lancashire (northwest England) where I used to farm. Maybe the marginal lands are where animals are best suited to be 'harvested', but even here, there are good grounds for cultivating other crops such as trees or just leaving an open space as an amenity, even though for hundreds of years they have been used for and by sheep. Certainly, we need to consider whether fertile, flat lands in good growing climates ought to be tied up servicing animals, whose welfare is often squeezed economically and physiologically, as others in this book testify. The land would be better utilized growing crops urgently needed for health. Simply put, does policy need to shift from intensifying animal prod-uction to producing fruit and vegetables? If so, there are considerable impli-cations for labour, skills, planning, infrastructure and food culture. Whether this kind of radical vision is adopted or not, huge problems already face the food supply chain. It has to change. The question is: into what?

The 20th century productionist paradigm

The 'old' approach to intensive production, which is now on trial from an animal welfare point of view, was forged with good intentions from a health point of view. From early in the 20th century, rising to a crescendo in the 1930s, there was sound evidence that with judicious application of science and capital, the land's productive capacity could be dramatically raised (Stapleton, 1935; Boyd Orr, 1966). A 'productionist' approach came to dominate food policy and was enshrined in the post World War II ministries around the world, and in world bodies such as the UN's Food and Agriculture Organization. The new consensus proposed better harnessing of modern technologies, used oil/tractors to replace animal power, applied science to plant and animal breeding and, in short, changed how food was produced dramatically. The assumption in this policy package was that lack of food was the problem; therefore anything that raised production would resolve it.

Today, just as in the 1930s (and throughout history), hunger is indeed a huge problem. In total, 800 million people are chronically malnourished (FAO, 2004). After dropping, that figure is once again rising. Sober as that fact alone is, today the health toll is both more complex and extensive. The burden of diet-related ill health is not just due to underproduction and underconsumption, but also mal- and overconsumption (WHO, 2002). A huge effort has been expended on making meat, fats and sugar cheaper, for example. Coupled with vast investment (to which I return below) in marketing these sweet, fatty, processed foods, food cultures and patterns of eating have been shifting. Partly, this is due to people voting with their money, but partly not. The supply chain 'tail' is wagging the societal 'dog'. Shops are full of cheap 'empty' calories rather than health-desirable nutrient-dense foods such as fruit and vegetables. As a result, there are good grounds for suggesting that more people are now overweight and obese, syndromes leading to the modern killers such as diabetes and heart disease, than suffer hunger (see Table 24.1) (Gardner and Halweil, 2000).

Table 24.1 *Global types and effects of malnutrition*

Type of malnutrition	Effects	No. of people affected
Hunger	Deficiency of calories and protein	At least 1.2 billion
Micro-nutrient deficiency	Deficiency of vitamins and minerals	2.0–3.5 billion
Overconsumption	Excess of calories, often accompanied by deficiency of vitamins and minerals	1.2–1.7 billion

Source: Gardner and Halweil, 2000, based on data from World Health Organization, International Food Policy Research Institute and UN Administrative Committee on Co-ordination/Sub-Committee on Nutrition (now Standing Committee on Nutrition)

The productionist paradigm did not appear from thin air. It drew on previous revolutions in chemistry, transport, land ownership, plant and animal breeding, and learning. The importance of productionism, however, was that this was offered as a universal policy package, promoted by national and international bodies such as the UN's Food and Agricultural Organization, founded at the end of World War II.

Productionism has been astonishingly effective. Outputs soared; more people have been fed (FAO, 2003). By promoting and institutionalizing a drive for efficiency, outputs were raised dramatically. Improved yields and breeds followed, as did changed use of labour. People left the land. Herds and landholdings have tended to grow in size. There was an expansion of infrastructural services such as fertilizers, pesticides and veterinary medicines (vaccines, antibiotics). Intensification has been the core idea – the systematic attempt to achieve more output from capital, land, equipment, animals and crops. Productionism was and still is given state support, with the objective of lowering the cost and increasing the availability of food for urban consumers. It has involved a close relationship between governments and the food industry, particularly food manufacturers, enshrined in subsidies in the developed world and a package of extension, aid and technology transfer from the developed to the developing world. Often the distinction was blurred between national and agricultural interests.

The productionist paradigm has also changed the role of animals (Table 24.2). One of the main effects of the rise of productionism was a reduction in the use of animals for draught (motive) power. Those who know about the exploitation of animals for draught power may well see the arrival of the tractor as undoubtedly a good thing. Ecologically, however, it is problematic; oil is running out, it is a pollutant and it is political dynamite (International Energy Agency, 2003). And there have been implications for health as well as for animal husbandry. As animals are used less for draught power and used more for meat and milk production, consumption of meat and dairy products has greatly increased, contributing to what is known as the nutrition transition (Popkin, 2002).

Table 24.2 *The productionist paradigm and its implications for animals*

Productionism – the package	Productionism – the animal impact
Efficiency	Less use for draught power
Scientific farming	More use for meat
Focus on quantity	Rise in meat trade
Intensification	Rise in dairy production
Appeal to consumers	Meat/dairy in diet as indicator of progress
Cheaper prices	Squeeze on animal welfare
Decline of labour	Animals as vectors for disease
State support and subsidies	Cheap meat = meat every day, not just 'feast days'
Reduction of waste	

The nutrition transition and its effects on health

The nutrition transition is the term used to describe the remarkable shift in diet that seems to occur when societies get richer. They change what and how they eat (Table 24.3). Consumers might enjoy the new variety of foods that greater wealth offers, but are often unaware of the risks of disease that can follow.

Table 23.3 *The nutrition transition: Changes in consumption*

As people get richer, they consume more...	...And less or not enough...
Meat	Staples/grains/cereals
Fats	Fruit and vegetables
Sugar	Fibre
Soft drinks	Water
Energy-dense foods	

The dietary transition is associated with a shift from rural to urban and industrial lifestyles; it also troubles health policy specialists. Low- and middle-income countries cannot afford the healthcare costs that follow. Nor, often, do they have the healthcare infrastructure needed to cope. As the World Health Organization (WHO) has shown, the anticipated growth of health burdens in the developing world is precisely in these non-communicable diseases (NCDs) such as heart disease, diabetes and some food-related cancers. Figure 24.1 shows the growth of NCDs that the WHO anticipates from 1990 to 2020. By 2020 they are expected to be the largest cause of death in developing countries, significantly changing the future global burden of disease.

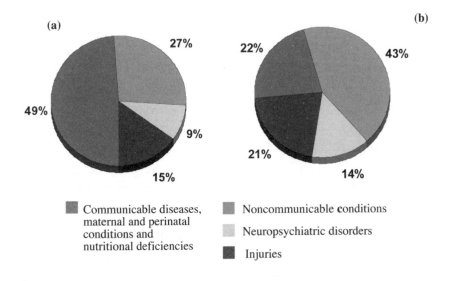

Figure 24.1 *Global burden of disease 1990–2020 by disease group in developing countries: (a) 1990 (b) 2020 (baseline scenario)*

Source: WHO

Figure 24.2 gives an estimate of the global deaths in 2000 that could be attributed to selected risk factors, taken from a vast study by the WHO on the burden of disease. The role of nutrition is clear; either eating inappropriately or lack of exercise (to burn off the calories and keep the body working optimally) accounts for a high proportion of the leading risk factors determining health. Tobacco and unsafe sex, of course, are hugely important too, but they are not the subject of this chapter. To put it another way, there is strong evidence that if societies wanted to improve their health and reduce the likelihood of ill health due to diet, they ought to eat differently and ensure that their supply chains deliver appropriately.

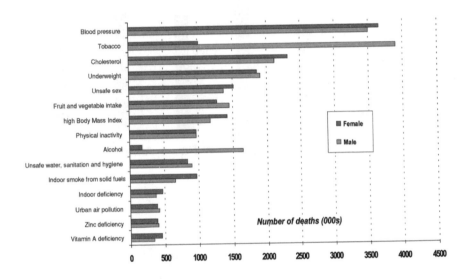

Figure 24.2 *World mortality in 2000 attributable to selected leading risk factors, by sex*

Source: WHO

This is why obesity is now such a hot policy issue. Even the US has declared war on obesity; its private healthcare insurance companies cannot afford the consequences. But what about the developing countries (and the 45 million US citizens without insurance)? Whereas poverty used to be measured in short stature – the issue of stunting – it is now also being measured in girth – how fat we are around the middle. This is unprecedented in human history. Figures from the second half of the 1990s, for instance, show that a body mass index (BMI) of 25 or above can be found in 24.4 per cent of males in Mexico, 6.4 per cent of males and 12.4 per cent of females in Brazil, 16 per cent of males in Morocco, 12.4 per cent of males and 32.1 per cent of females in Egypt and 31.8

per cent of females in South Africa. Thailand had 25 per cent of females and 13.2 per cent of males with a BMI of over 30 (Popkin, 2002). This has been accompanied by a dramatic spread of diabetes (International Diabetes Federation and World Diabetes Foundation, 2003), with the largest percentage increases among adults between 2000 and 2025 predicted by the WHO to take place in the Southeast Asian and Eastern Mediterranean regions (Figure 24.3).

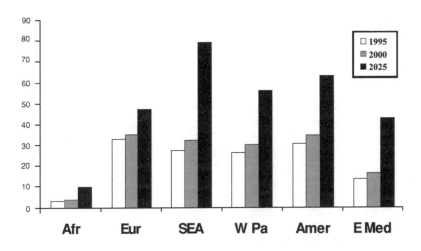

Figure 24.3 *The anticipated prevalence of diabetes in adults (millions), by WHO region*

Source: WHO

Food policy, supply and culture out of synch?

For policy-makers, the concern is whether this pattern of disease can be addressed and, if so, by what mechanisms. Is there a technological fix as effective as antibiotics have been for infections? Many analysts are doubtful, simply because this new pattern of diet-related ill health is societally determined, and therefore requires societal rather than technological resolution (Marmot and Wilkinson, 1999). Just as malnutrition and episodic famine are societal diseases due to inequalities in wealth, access and what Amartya Sen called 'entitlement' (a belief that one has the right to food), so the nutrition transition's pattern of disease requires a different way of eating and living. This requires a different food supply chain and food culture.

Such a transformation is not happening at present, or not radically and rapidly enough. Without demonizing advertising in framing what we aspire to and consume, its role does illustrate the point. Figure 24.4 was produced by the Food Commission, a UK NGO working on food and health matters. It illustrates, on the left, a typical health guidelines 'pyramid' of what is desirable to eat; we should eat lots of what is at the bottom of the pyramid, much less of what is at the top. On the right, in the second pyramid, is what actually gets advertised in the UK. Advertising is either warping or symbolizing the inappropriateness of key food cultural messages. The rules for eating stress instant pleasure, rather than longer-term implications. Thus health messages become killjoys rather than givers of joy. This dichotomy is familiar to proponents of animal welfare; so often they are presented as stopping people from eating what is their right or prioritizing animals over humans. In fact, the new ecological public health thinking suggests equal accord to both humans and animals.

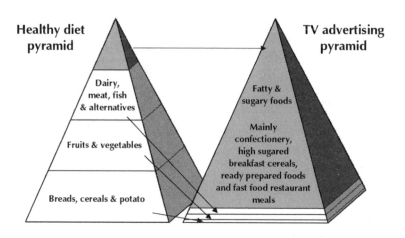

Figure 24.4 *The gap between health and advertising reality*
Source: Food Commission UK/Food Magazine

The diet-related health picture poses a challenge to us to rethink our demands for food and agricultural policy. Sufficiency is no longer an adequate goal: quality and lifespan are now just as important. Health must be at the heart of a new policy paradigm. This will require enormous change. It has been calculated that, to meet WHO and FAO health guidelines (WHO/FAO, 2003), current production levels of pig meat, butter, cream, animal fat, soybean oil and rapeseed oil need to be reduced by up to about a third (Irz et al, 2003). The other side of the coin is that production of fruit, vegetables, cereals, nuts and fish will have to increase. Table 24.4 gives some estimates; the data in the left column was from research funded by farmers worried about the health message's impact on their sectors; no one has funded the positive news in the right column, which speaks volumes! The issue of fish is problematic. Nutritionists are united on the need for people to eat fish for their omega-3 essential fatty acids, but conservationist evidence is equally strong on the case for dramatically curtailing consumption to protect stocks (Royal Commission on Environmental Pollution, 2004). Fish farming cannot resolve the conundrum because the fish are themselves mostly fed on 'waste fish' from the sea. In practice, the omega-3s will have to come from sources such as nuts and other crops: the 'not animals, but crops' story again.

Table 24.4 *Changes in farm production required to meet WHO/FAO guidelines*

Product	Lower production*	Higher production**
Pig meat	5 per cent decrease	
Butter	13 per cent decrease	
Cream	18 per cent decrease	
Animal fat	31 per cent decrease	
Soybean oil	14 per cent decrease	
Rapeseed oil	30–35 per cent decrease	
Fruit		100 per cent increase?
Vegetables		100 per cent increase?
Cereals		increase (undetermined)
Nuts		increase (undetermined)
Fish		increase (undetermined)

* Irz et al, 2003
** to meet five-a-day/400g/day goals requires huge increases; to meet nine-a-day requires even more

Engaging with the powerful?

The task ahead is awesome. Knowing where power lies in the supply chain is thus important; and whether to confront or negotiate with the powerful is a key question. Some argue that consumers have the power; therefore, the key is to help the public change, to use their consumer 'votes' at the checkout. The goal is to encourage value-for-money consumers to become ethical consumers, a strategy that has certainly helped grow the fair-trade movement (Harrison et al, 2005).

Another line of policy thinking focuses on existing power. Although there are hot debates among academics about which has greatest relative power over food – manufacturers, retailers, food service industries or cultural industries (advertising and marketing) – most agree that today, retailers and distributors are central powerbrokers. They mediate between producers and consumers. If small shops are wiped out, even big manufacturers need to get onto the shelves of supermarkets giants like Walmart, Carrefour, Ahold, Metro and Tesco who have spread rapidly in the last 20 years (Figure 24.5) (Vorley, 2003). In 2003 Cap Gemini, a large consultancy company in Europe, studied the concentration of power in the food supply chain of the then 15 member states of the EU. The 600 supermarket chains, and their 110 combined buying desks, dominated the flows between not just the farmers but also manufacturers and the 250 million consumers/shoppers (Grievink, 2003). Power lies at the narrowest point in the supply chain funnel (Table 24.5).

Number of countries where operating

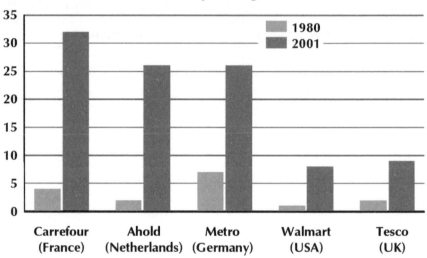

Figure 24.5 *Global expansion of transnational supermarkets, 1980–2001*

Source: Vorley/UK Food Group (2003)

Table 24.5 *Cap Gemini study of food supply chain funnel in the EU15*

Unit	Numbers in unit (EU15)
Consumers (eaters)	160,000,000
Customers (purchasers, also eaters)	89,000,000
Outlets	170,000
Supermarkets	600
Buying desks	110
Manufacturers	8,600
Semi-manufacturers	80,000
Suppliers	160,000
Farmers/producers	3,200,000

Note: The European Union in 2002 had a population of about 250 million
Source: Grievink/Cap Gemini, 2003

Conclusion

New, disturbing and challenging demands are emerging from evidence from different academic and policy sources. Policy is not catching up. Yet we know that the world will need to change if we are serious about protecting the environment, helping societies achieve their potential, delivering just economies and supporting morally sound cultures. We might be forgiven for burying our heads under the blanket! Ignore it all; enjoy the present. One can sympathize with, but not condone, this position. In fact, hard policy choices are emerging. Figure 24.6 summarizes just some of these issues (Lang, 2005). I am optimistic. If we see these awesome challenges, we can try to do something about them. As many recognize, multi-sectoral and multi-level solutions are needed. Where better to begin than for animal welfare proponents and public health specialists to engage and to forge alliances so as to encourage political structures that can deliver real public benefit. A lot hangs on this.

Sector	'Old' policy demands	'New' policy demands
Policy goals	Intensification	Extensification
	Quantity	Quality
	Food control	Food democracy
Farm	Animal-focused	Plant-focused
	Large farms	Small farms
	Labour replacement	Labour retention
	Monoculture	Biodiversity
	Long-distance food	Local food
Processing	Assembly	Cooking
	Factory cooking	Home cooking
	De-skilled / machine-minder	Skilled/artisanal
Culture	Hypermarket	Street market
	Global food	Regional food
	Fast food	Slow food
	Consumerist	Citizen
	Advertising / marketing	Education
Nutrition	Nutrient-lite	Nutrient-rich
	Domination by cheap commodities such as sugar and fat	Nutrient diverse
	Individualized approach to health	Population approach to health
	Nutrigenomics	Social nutrition
Economy	Food prices do not include externalized costs (eg health, environment, justice)	Full-cost accounting (attempts to internalize those costs)
	Cheap / low prices	Expensive / high prices
	Industrial / post-industrial	Craft / industrial
	Traceability-based confidence	Trust-based relationship

Figure 24.6 *'Old' versus 'new' policy demands*

Source: Lang, 2005

References

Boyd Orr, J. (1966) *As I Recall: The 1880s to the 1960s*, MacGibbon and Kee, London

FAO (2003) *World Agriculture: Towards 2015/2030: An FAO Perspective*, Food and Agriculture Organization, Rome, Earthscan, London

FAO (2004) *The State of Food Insecurity in the World 2004: Monitoring Progress Towards the World Food Summit and Millennium Development Goals*, Food and Agriculture Organization, Rome

Gardner, G. and Halweil, B. (2000) 'Underfed and overfed: The global epidemic of malnutrition', *Worldwatch paper 15*, Worldwatch Institute, Washington, DC

Grievink, J. W. (2003) *The Changing Face of the Global Food Supply Chain*, paper presented at the Changing Dimensions of the Food Economy, The Hague, 6–7 February, Organisation for Economic Co-operation and Development, www.oecd.org/document/47/0,2340,en_2649_33781_20175727_1_1_1_1,00.html

Harrison, R., Newholm, T. and Shaw, D. (2005) *The Ethical Consumer*, SAGE, London

International Diabetes Federation and World Diabetes Foundation (2003) *Diabetes Atlas 2003*, 2nd edn, IDF Executive Office, Brussels

International Energy Agency (2003) *World Energy Outlook*, IEA, Paris

Irz, X., Shankar, B. and Srinivasan, C. (2003) *Dietary Recommendations in the Report of a Joint WHO/FAO Expert Consultation on Diet, Nutrition and the Prevention of Chronic Diseases (WHO Technical Report Series 916, 2003): Potential Impact on Consumption, Production and Trade of Selected Food Products*, report for the International Federation of Agricultural Producers and Institute for European Food Studies: 59, University of Reading, Dept Agricultural and Food Economics, Reading

Lang, T. (2005) 'Food control or food democracy: Re-engaging nutrition to civil society, the state and the food supply chain', *Public Health Nutrition*, vol 8, no 6A, pp730–737

Lang, T. and Heasman, M. (2004) *Food Wars: The Global Battle for Mouths, Minds and Markets*, Earthscan, London

Marmot, M. G. and Wilkinson, R. G. (eds) (1999) *Social Determinants of Health*, Oxford University Press, Oxford

Popkin, B. M. (2002) 'An overview on the nutrition transition and its health implications: The Bellagio meeting', *Public Health Nutrition*, vol 5, no 1A, pp93–103

Royal Commission on Environmental Pollution (2004) *Turning the Tide: Addressing the Impact of Fishing on the Marine Environment*, 25th report, Royal Commission on Environmental Pollution, London

Stapledon, S. G. (1935) *The Land: Now and Tomorrow*, Faber and Faber, London

Vorley, B. (2003) *Food Inc.: Corporate Concentration from Farm to Consumer*, UK Food Group, London

WHO (2002) *World Health Report 2002: Reducing Risks, Promoting Healthy Life*, World Health Organization, Geneva

WHO/FAO (2003) 'Diet, nutrition and the prevention of chronic diseases', report of the joint WHO/FAO expert consultation *WHO Technical Report Series*, no 916 (TRS 916), World Health Organization and Food and Agriculture Organization, Geneva

25
Conclusion

Joyce D'Silva

Compassion In World Farming Trust, UK

Many of this book's authors have, in essence, thrown down a challenge to tradition, to culture and to the status quo. They have challenged the accepted paradigm of human–animal relationships. But what *is* that paradigm?

Beyond the millions of companion animals of various species popular across the globe, each year 53 billion farm animals are slaughtered for meat, millions more for their fur, many are hunted with everything from spears to sophisticated high-tech weaponry, others are used for sport or entertainment, millions are traded across the globe to supply a local demand for a particular kind of meat or for laboratory use and up to 100 million are used in laboratory experiments.[1]

If each of those billions of animals is a sentient being, then some obvious questions arise: How are our activities affecting their welfare? For example, how much does it matter to a pregnant pig that she cannot turn round throughout her long pregnancy? How does a dairy cow *feel* when her calf is taken from her? What effect does a two-to-three week voyage at sea have on the millions of sheep exported from Australia to the Middle East every year? How does an Arctic fox feel when caged for life or dying slowly in a trap in her own habitat? How does a circus lion feel in such an alien environment? How does a young elephant feel when his mother is gunned down in front of him for her ivory? How painful is it for a young piglet to be castrated without anaesthesia?

These are just some of the daily log of situations in which sentient animals find themselves because of *us*. If you take the traditional, anthropocentric view, then, although some of these situations might be regrettable in terms of animal suffering, they are necessary in order to supply our own species with food, fun, adornment, medicine, a livelihood or just plain profit.

Not one of the authors who have contributed to this book is suggesting we take this view. All are courageously seeking a way forward, though to different degrees and in different situations. They do not take the view that the status quo is acceptable.

Realistically we know that institutions – be they religious, academic, political or business – do not change overnight. But we also know that they are capable of change. If we look at the history of major social movements, such as labour movements or the women's movement, we know that culture and belief are open to growth and development, that business can develop values other than profit, that Governments and global institutions can react positively to pressure for fundamental policy change.

Right now, many inherited belief systems are facing challenges. A logged-on world is sceptical of secrecy and is finding new ways to spread the message of change.

Climate change, human poverty, terrorism and its legal twin, warfare, are huge issues affecting our national and international institutions and our personal lives. I believe that the implications of international recognition of the sentience of animals will have equally far-reaching implications for us all as individuals and for global policy-makers and institutions.

At the end of the Compassion in World Farming Trust conference on which this book is based, a conference statement was proposed by Professor John Webster and was adopted by an overwhelming majority of the conference delegates, who themselves – all 600 of them – came from 50 different countries and a huge variety of professional backgrounds. The statement read 'This conference calls on the UN, the WTO, the World Animal Health Organisation (OIÉ) and their member governments to join us in recognizing that sentient animals are capable of suffering, and that we all have a duty to preserve the habitat of wild animals and to end cruel farming systems and other trades and practices which inflict suffering on animals.'

Popular wisdom says it takes 30 years for a campaign to achieve some kind of political and legislative change. The movement to protect animals from the worst human excesses has had its advocates in various locations at different times in our history – from the Indian Emperor Ashoka to St Francis of Assisi, from the Qur'an to Leonardo da Vinci. More recently, we see global spokespeople like Jane Goodall and influential academics like Tom Regan and Marc Bekoff constantly engaged in challenging our conditioned human-centredness and our animal-exploiting habits. They are making a difference. Our human consciousness is being affected.

Organizations too are making a difference. CIWF is rightly proud of leading the campaign to have animals recognized as sentient beings in the European Treaty. It is the hope of CIWF Trust and of many concerned citizens globally that more and more individuals, governments and relevant institutions will accept that animals are indeed sentient beings and will amend their lifestyles, policy or practices accordingly.

In CIWF's own field – farm animal welfare – we seek an end to rearing systems that confine, crowd or isolate animals and to practices of selective breeding for productivity at the expense of fitness. Alternatives to painful mutilations and long-distance transport are already available and should be utilized. The long-term viability of animal farming must place animal sentience at the very top of its strategic planning agenda. No farming system can be truly sustainable if it is unsustainable for the animals themselves.

It was Albert Schweitzer (1949) who said 'Until he extends his circle of compassion to all living things, man will not himself find peace'.

Those of us who agree with the Goodalls and Bekoffs, the Singers and Regans of this world, feel a deep frustration at the slowness with which the establishment responds to our calls for change. Yet the truth is that we must understand how hard it may be for the Bayvels, Ryans and Kennys to achieve change within their own institutions or for Islamic teaching to be translated into daily reality in animals' lives. All the institutions they represent are currently engaged in dialogue with animal welfare organizations, such as Compassion in World Farming and other stakeholders. Their efforts deserve encouragement rather than critique.

We can, of course, be critical of ourselves. We can audit our own responses to the animals whom we affect through our own lives. Do we always extend our own circle of compassion to wild creatures near our homes and to the unseen but equally real animals whose lives are used for our clothing, furniture, medicine, entertainment and food?

So this book carries a challenge for all of us, be it in our private or professional lives. As Jane Goodall so earnestly suggested in her keynote speech, perhaps the very best guide as to how we should behave towards other animals is to listen to what we feel in our own hearts.

Note

1   The CIWF Trust conference out of which this book arose did not address the issues surrounding animal experimentation, believing that this topic deserved its own separate conference.

References

Schweitzer, A. (1949) *The Philosophy of Civilization*, The Macmillan Company, New York

Annex: Further contributions to the conference 'Darwin to Dawkins: The Science and Implications of Animal Sentience'

It was not possible to include in this book all the contributions presented at the conference out of which the book arose. The following is a list of the remaining invited papers, focusing on the scientific study of animal sentience and its applications in a number of areas of human use of animals. The majority of these are published by Elsevier in a special issue of the journal *Applied Animal Behaviour Science* (AABS), 2006, edited by John Webster. AABS is the official journal of The International Society for Applied Ethology (ISAE).

Science and animal sentience

Through animal eyes: What behaviour tells us

Marian Stamp Dawkins, Department of Zoology, University of Oxford, Oxford OX1 3PS, UK

The changing concept of animal sentience

Ian J. H. Duncan, Department of Animal and Poultry Science, University of Guelph, Guelph, Ontario, Canada N1G 2W1

The evolution of morality

Donald M. Broom, Department of Veterinary Medicine, University of Cambridge, Cambridge, CB3 0ES, UK

The study of animals' consciousness, cognition and emotions

Cognitive and communicative abilities of grey parrots

Irene M. Pepperberg, Department of Psychology, Brandeis University, Waltham, MA 02454, US

Behavioural reactions of elephants towards a dying and deceased matriarch

Iain Douglas-Hamilton, Shivani Bhalla, George Wittemyer and Fritz Vollrath Save the Elephants, PO Box 54667, Nairobi 00200, Kenya Email: iain@africaonline.co.ke; shivanibhalla@africaonline.co.ke

The life of a bear

Victor Watkins, World Society for the Protection of Animals, 14th Floor, 89 Albert Embankment, London SE1 7TP, UK

Into the brains of whales

Mark P. Simmonds, Whale and Dolphin Conservation Society, Brookfield House, St. Paul's Street, Chippenham, Wiltshire, SN15 1LJ, UK

Onset of sentience: The potential for suffering in foetal and newborn farm animals

David J. Mellor and Tamara J. Diesch, Animal Welfare Science and Bioethics Centre, Massey University, Palmerston North, New Zealand

How animals learn from each other

Christine Nicol, Division of Farm Animal Science, Department of Clinical Veterinary Science, University of Bristol, Langford, BS40 5DU, UK

The natural (and not so natural) history of chickens

Joy A. Mench, Department of Animal Science, University of California, Davis CA 95616, US

Practical applications of studies of animal behaviour and animal sentience: Farmed and working animals

Domestication and animal behaviour

Per Jensen, Department of Biology, Linköping University, Linköping, Sweden

Making the opportunity for natural behaviour in animal farming systems

Marek Špinka, Ethology Group, Research Institute of Animal Production, CZ-104 01 Prague – Uhříněves, Czech Republic

Progress and challenges in animal handling and slaughter in the US

Temple Grandin, Department of Animal Science, Colorado State University, Fort Collins CO 80523, US

Using preference and aversion tests to ask scientific questions about farm animals' feelings

Richard D. Kirkden, Animal Welfare Program, Faculty of Land and Food Systems, University of British Columbia, 2357 Main Mall, Vancouver, BC, V6T 1Z4, Canada

Edmond A. Pajor, Department of Animal Sciences, Center for Food Animal Well-Being, Purdue University, Poultry Science Building, 125 South Russell Street, West Lafayette, IN 47907-2042, US

Identifying and preventing pain in animals

Daniel M. Weary, Lee Niel, Frances C. Flower and David Fraser, Animal Welfare Program, Faculty of Food and Land Systems, University of British Columbia, 2357 Main Mall, Vancouver, BC, V6T 1Z4, Canada

The relationship between working equine animals and their owners

William J. Swann, Brooke Hospital for Animals, 21 Panton Street, London SW1Y 4DR, UK

Welfare at work

Roland James Bonney, Food Animal Initiative, The Field Station, Wytham, Oxford OX2 8QJ, UK

Learning to assess the animal's point of view

Françoise Wemelsfelder, Sustainable Livestock Systems Group, Research and Development Division, Scottish Agricultural College, Midlothian, EH26 0PH, UK

Poster presentations

Poster presentations at the conference covered a wide range of subjects related to animal sentience and animal welfare. The poster abstracts are available from Compassion in World Farming Trust, email: ciwftrust@ciwf.co.uk

An additional, optional presentation on Bear Farming in China was given at CIWF Trusts' Conference by Jill Robinson, Director of the Animals Asia Foundation, www.animalsaisa.org.

Film of the conference

A film (110 min) has been made of highlights of the conference presentations, including the authors featured in this book. It is obtainable free on DVD or video (VHS or NTSC) from Compassion in World Farming Trust, www.ciwf.org.uk/darwintodawkins Email: ciwftrust@ciwf.co.uk

Index